American Project

American PROJECT

The Rise and Fall of a Modern Ghetto

SUDHIR ALLADI VENKATESH

HARVARD UNIVERSITY PRESS   CAMBRIDGE, MASSACHUSETTS   LONDON, ENGLAND

2 0 0 0

Library of Congress Cataloging-in-Publication Data

Venkatesh, Sudhir Alladi.
    American project : the rise and fall of a modern ghetto / Sudhir
Alladi Venkatesh.
        p. cm.
    Includes bibliographical references and index.
    ISBN 0-674-00321-7 (alk. paper)
        1. Robert Taylor Homes. 2. Public housing—Illinois—Chicago.
3. Afro-Americans—Housing—Illinois—Chicago. 4. Poor—Housing—
Illinois—Chicago. 5. Crime in public housing—Illinois—Chicago.
6. Inner cities—Illinois—Chicago. I. Title.

HD7288.78.U52 C476 2000
363.5'85'0977311—dc21   00—039621

To my mother, my father, and Urmila

Contents

Foreword

In the United States, the rights of citizens to basic economic welfare and security, according to the prevailing standards in the society, have been experienced at levels significantly below those enjoyed by the citizens of Canada and Western Europe.[1] The discrepancy is particularly evident in the area of public housing. Whereas it is common in European welfare states to provide direct financial housing subsidies for low-income families, this practice is rare to nonexistent in the United States.[2] The state support of housing for poor American citizens tends to be confined to a limited number of public projects largely concentrated in inner-city neighborhoods, neighborhoods that feature weak, informal job-information networks and that tend to be removed from areas of employment opportunities.

Indeed, the location of public housing projects in neighborhoods of highest poverty concentration is the result of federal toleration of extensive segregation against African Americans in urban housing markets, as well as acquiescence to organized neighborhood groups' opposition to public housing construction in their communities. However, this has not always been the case. The federal public housing program in the United States has featured two stages representing two distinct approaches. Initially, the program mainly helped two-parent families displaced temporarily by the Depression or in need of housing following the end of World War II. Public housing for many of these families was the first step on the road toward economic recovery, and their stay in the projects tended to be brief. Their economic mobility "contributed to the sociological stability of the first

public housing communities, and explains the program's initial success."[3]

The passage of the Housing Act of 1949 ushered in the second policy stage. It instituted and funded the urban-renewal program to abol-
ish urban slums: "Public housing was now meant to collect the ghetto
residents left homeless by the urban renewal bulldozers."[4] The Federal Public Housing Authority lowered the income ceiling for public
housing residency and evicted families with incomes above that ceiling. Access to public housing was thereby restricted to the most economically disadvantaged segments of the population.

The mass migration of African Americans from the rural South to
the cities of the Northeast and Midwest coincided with the change in
federal housing policy. Since white urban and suburban communities
prevented the construction of public housing in their neighborhoods,
the units were overwhelmingly concentrated in the overcrowded inner-city areas; indeed, "this growing population of politically weak
urban poor was unable to counteract the desires of vocal middle- and
working-class whites for segregated housing."[5] In short, public housing in the United States, as a federally funded institution, has
significantly contributed to the isolation of families by race and class.

No scholar better captures the consequences of the second stage of
federal housing policy in the United States than Sudhir Alladi
Venkatesh in this insightful book. As Venkatesh points out, the Robert Taylor Homes housing project in Chicago was a mammoth social-engineering experiment built in the early 1960s to provide the
overcrowded African-American population in Chicago with affordable, decent housing. But its construction in the heart of the inner
city reinforced the concentration of poverty in the city's segregated
black neighborhood.

Venkatesh carefully demonstrates, however, that the decision to
build Robert Taylor Homes in the heart of the black ghetto drew the
support not only of city officials concerned about keeping the black
poor out of white neighborhoods, but also of those with good intentions. Among the latter were those concerned about the severe short-

age of housing for low-income residents in the ghetto, including black politicians who confronted the difficult choice of either ghetto public housing or no low-income housing for blacks at all.

Venkatesh provides a comprehensive framework that enables the reader to understand how the fate of the Robert Taylor Homes and prospects for life in the projects were inextricably linked to the economic and social transformations of the larger society. The steps that Chicago Housing Authority (CHA) officials, urban designers, service providers, and politicians could take to improve conditions at Robert Taylor Homes were thwarted by forces that were both local and national in scope. The local forces that stymied their efforts included, most notably, the law enforcement agencies' explicit failure to police and secure the housing project. The national forces included those that were ostensibly related to public housing, such as the dramatic federal cuts in the nation's public housing program since the mid-1960s; and those that were indirectly or subtly related, such as the disappearance of job opportunities for black workers owing to the decreased relative demand for low-skilled labor.

Venkatesh brilliantly describes how, in the face of these negative forces, the tenants of Robert Taylor Homes made impressive efforts—through various innovative strategies, ranging from tenants' networks and associations to tactics that involved working outside the law—to enhance the social organization of the projects and ensure their welfare and safety. They displayed considerable resilience, but their efforts amounted to short-term solutions that proved to be inadequate given the continuing hardships of life in this enormous housing development and the declining support from the broader society.

After reading this important book, readers will come to realize the extent to which the tenants of public housing developments like Robert Taylor Homes lack the basic entitlements that the rest of society takes for granted. As the twenty-first century dawns, we can hope that *American Project* will trigger a discussion on the need to restructure in major ways the institutions that serve these truly disadvantaged

communities. In the process our nation might become more apprecia-
tive of the need to confront seriously the institutionalized racism—rooted in our economic, political, and social structures—that
shapes the larger society's response to impoverished public housing
projects.

William Julius Wilson
Harvard University

Preface

The idea for this book began taking shape in 1990, when I was conducting interviews for a research project on African Americans in Chicago. I came to the University of Chicago to begin graduate studies in the Department of Sociology. Until then, my exposure to cities had been minimal. Although I was born in the bustling city of Madras, on the southeastern Indian coast, I left the subcontinent as a child and lived in various mid-size suburban communities in upstate New York and Southern California. My college years at the University of California, San Diego (UCSD), were spent mostly in the all-white beach towns neighboring La Jolla, far away from the vibrant, multiethnic downtown area. Cities struck me as inhospitable, unnatural environments.

I had completed a bachelor's degree in mathematics, but toward the end of my undergraduate education, I met Aaron Cicourel and Hugh Mehan, two sociologists at UCSD who introduced me to social science, where even the assumptions about reality were up for debate. Nothing seemed quite so certain anymore, not only in scholarship but also in my personal life, as issues relating to my own identity and place in the social world became more salient. The halcyon pace of suburban San Diego belied my own uneasiness as a young South Asian–American, and I made a decision that is hardly uncommon for immigrant youth: I thought a radical change in physical setting would lead to emotional and psychic betterment, and with the encouragement of my advisors and my family, I left for urbane Chicago.

Soon after my arrival, I collected data for an urban poverty research project, which required me to travel into the poor, predominantly African-American neighborhoods surrounding the University of Chicago. I met with many young people, some of whom belonged to a street gang. My repeated visits sparked brief conversations regarding the nature of my interviews and the focus of the research. I explained that the project compared poor African-American households with their middle-class counterparts in an effort to document the different effects that neighborhood structure has on social-mobility opportunities among the young. They read my survey instrument, informed me that I was "not going to learn shit by asking these questions," and said I would need to "hang out with them" if I really wanted to understand the experiences of African-American youth in the city. Over the next few months, I met with many of them informally to play racquetball, drink beer on the shores of Lake Michigan, attend their parties, and eat dinner with their families. A relationship was emerging, largely out of my curiosity and theirs. Most students at the university do not have occasion to venture into the disenfranchised communities surrounding their own enclave, so I was an obvious source of interest to them. In turn, their views on life, getting ahead in America, the status of blacks, and "gangland" challenged some of my preconceived notions about these topics.

Some of the youth lived in the Robert Taylor Homes housing development. Over an eighteen-month period, I logged notes on the activities of their gang, called the Black Kings. But it was the gang's relationship with other people in the housing development that piqued my interest. Gang members were also schoolchildren, nephews, churchgoers, fathers, husbands, and so on. They were "gang members" at certain times and in certain contexts, such as narcotics trafficking and meetings in open park space, but most of the time their lives were characterized by involvement with work, family, school, and peers. Their identity as "gang members" sometimes conflicted with other identities they held. For example, family dinners were occasions not only to discuss their school performance or work history, but also to see parents and relatives challenge their involvement in the Black Kings. The young people I met were deeply concerned about their future in America and the role that gang membership played in their life course. So, too, was there a deep-seated compassion in the broader Robert Taylor community for wayward youth, which manifested itself in a range of emotions, from sadness to anger to disbelief.

Graduate student apprenticeship is invaluable because it affords an unprecedented opportunity to devote years of continuous time to participant-observation in a fieldwork setting. I took advantage of the situation to learn about different segments of the housing development population and how each perceived and related to the street gang. My travels around the community were motivated by the basic need to understand the range of social relations through which the gang was woven into the fabric of the housing development. Men on the street corner and underground entrepreneurs exhibited views on, and interactions with, gangs that differed from those of non-gang-affiliated youth, both of which differed from the views of young women, and all of which were somewhat askew from the relations of gang members with older residents who had arrived in Robert Taylor during the 1960s and 1970s. As the fieldwork progressed, I formed loose impressions of different social roles, all the while realizing that they were not mutually exclusive and that the same individuals could often take on various roles, depending on the context. Just as the gang member was also a nephew, a student, and so on, depending on the circumstances, so too were the men who spent time outside the local liquor store invested in other roles, including that of parent, advocate, and part-time laborer.

As I met with all these people, it became apparent that their contemporary experience was inextricably linked to their past and to their history of residence in Chicago public housing. They understood their present-day circumstances, including the role of the gang in the community, in light of earlier periods of tenure in Robert Taylor. "Gangs have always been around," people would often remark, and their recollections of the changes and continuities in gang activity formed part of their overall memory of the shifting contours of

"project living." This appeared as a rich and colorful set of recollections, which they revisited and rewrote as they acted in the present to
make their homes and their community a habitable place to live.

In the pages that follow, I present this collective memory of Chicago's Robert Taylor Homes. Field researchers are dependent on the
kindness and cooperation of people who may never gain anything
practical from the published studies and who may disagree with the
story that is eventually told. Members of the Robert Taylor community tolerated my presence, which was often intrusive, and answered
my questions and queries with patience. They allowed me to see at an
intimate level their struggle to build a community amid poverty and
minimal resources. But with equal resolve they imparted to me the
lesson that their lives cannot be reduced to victimhood or equated
with hardship alone. Only to the degree that observers of the social
world faithfully reproduce the multilayered aspect of experience will
our task merit the generosity of those who tolerate our presence.

American Project

Introduction

On a hot afternoon in the middle of June 1992, four people met in the Robert Taylor Homes public housing development to address the recent escalation in gang-related violence. On one side of a large metal table sat Will Jackson, the director of the Grace Center, where the meeting was being held, and Edith Huddle, an officer of the Local Advisory Council (LAC), the elected tenant-management association representing the interests of Robert Taylor's twenty thousand residents.[1] They sat across from Prince Williams, a leader of the local Black Kings street gang, which was involved in recent shootings that had occurred at the Robert Taylor Homes, and Jeremy Coals, the founder and president of No More Wars, an agency specializing in dispute resolution between gangs in the city of Chicago. In the back of the room, several people, including myself, listened intently. The meeting at the Grace Center was arranged by Will Jackson and Jeremy Coals. Will had been working to establish lines of communication between street-gang leaders and tenant leaders; he brought Jeremy Coals to the meeting after learning of the influence that No More Wars had with the city's street gangs, among which the Sharks and Black Kings were two of the largest.

Several days before the meeting, the first gang war of the year had commenced in the Robert Taylor Homes. The Sharks had conducted drive-by shootings and injured two members of the enemy Black Kings gang. To retaliate, Prince declared "war" against the Sharks, and for the next thirty-six hours, there was an intermittent exchange of gunfire between the two gang families. After the injury of the two Black Kings members, a twelve-year-old girl was fatally shot, and her friend critically injured, while playing in an open concrete expanse that surrounded the housing development's high-rise buildings. A community already in shock from the injuries to the two youths now grieved for the family of the young girl and for her friend, who lay in critical condition at a local hospital. The exhaustion on residents' faces showed the toll that the violence had taken on their lives: their energies were spent navigating safe excursions to the grocery store. Some took leaves of absence from work or rearranged their schedules to help other families, and they were all faced with restless children they had confined to apartments and areas inside the buildings.

The initial gathering at the Grace Center proved to be a catalyst for a novel forum that allowed tenants to address not only conflicts between street gangs but also a range of practices that involved gang members. Edith Huddle and Jeremy Coals formed a jury of peers that included themselves, staff members of the Grace Center, and a few ex-street-gang leaders. Several times each month, tenants would relay to this mediating body incidents in which gang members had harassed residents or been involved in domestic abuse or other criminal acts. Instead of immediately resorting to physical or armed conflict, the gang leaders from warring families would attempt to resolve their own disputes in front of this body. In public, the gang leaders justified their participation altruistically, with claims that they were "helping the community," but when pressed they did not deny more selfish motives: namely, reduced conflict also helped to stabilize their underground economic ventures—most notably their drug trade and extortion of local businesses and entrepreneurs. Edith Huddle and the other jurors adjudicated the reported infractions and then meted out punishments. They assigned monetary redress or commanded apologies from gang members, and, in their separate closed-door meetings, the gang leaders inflicted physical punishment and imposed their own monetary fines on their members.

In public and private forums, tenants passionately debated the value of this kind of local control. Their opinions regarding the community court were diverse. Some expressed outright disgust that gang members were being used for policing and enforcement; others shared this opinion but added that tenants should organize protests against law enforcement agencies that should have been performing

such functions. Dissenting voices argued that the housing development was in a state of emergency and should use any resource available to address its needs. Some extended this line of argument by
stating that since gangs were deeply entrenched in local affairs, any
realistic attempt at mediation would have to include them. In public
"townhall" meetings with representatives of several government
agencies, tenants used the success of the community court to critique
existing law enforcement tactics; local police officers responded by
urging caution when cooperating with street gangs.

Throughout the discussions and debates, the word "community"
anchored the expressed sentiments of the parties involved. In formal
meetings with tenants, gang members asked to be recognized as legitimate "members of the community." In the townhall meetings,
Housing Authority representatives warned that gangs were "taking
over the community," to which tenants would often reply, "It's our
community, not yours." Tenants criticized their own elected leaders
for "not fighting for the community," and the leaders responded to
these allegations by saying that the highly critical tenants "only complain and don't get involved in the community."

In many of their invocations of "community," tenants repeatedly
made reference to the past. One tenant said, "It used to be our community, but it's theirs now. [The gangs] have taken over." Edith Huddle stated another common opinion: "Gangs have always been part of
the community, they always will be. It's just that now, they control
us." Along with general assessments of how gangs had changed, tenants referred to specific times when gang activity was not so threatening. For each of those periods, they could list individuals who had
control over gang members, as well as gang leaders who minimized
conflict and lent assistance to residents. There appeared to be a
strong, established history of innovative attempts by tenants to supplant or supplement the work of law enforcement, with respect not
only to street-gang violence but also to domestic abuse, theft and burglary, and enforcement of contracts in the underground economy.

The street gang did not necessarily appear as an "enemy within" that preyed on the housing development but rather as one of several threats to household security. Controlling the behavior of young people was the most recent and highly visible challenge, and it made extraordinary demands on personal and collective energies. However, tenants also had to work diligently to ensure adequate building maintenance, apartment repair, and usable public space, all of which affected personal safety and ease of intercourse in the housing development. In fact, tenants did not draw sharp distinctions between security- and maintenance-related issues, and when discussing the challenges posed by gangs, they referred to such issues as stairwell lighting, accessible lobbies, and vacant apartments. Attending to gang-related activity, then, was part of a larger, ongoing struggle to reproduce a safe living environment—however tenuous and fragile that equilibrium might be.

The struggle by tenants of Chicago's Robert Taylor Homes to create a safe, habitable "community" is one that has engaged public housing tenants nationwide. Coping with crime and socioeconomic hardship, battling local government agencies over inadequate service provision, and searching for external resources to meet local needs have become commonplace for those who live in public housing. The weight of their hardship has led to heated public debate in America over the question, Can people living in large public housing complexes such as the Robert Taylor Homes sustain a viable, healthy community? The future of public housing depends on how this question is answered. At the time of this writing, in response to pressures from the federal government, the Chicago Housing Authority (CHA) has demolished nearly half of the twenty-eight buildings in the Robert Taylor complex, declaring that they are no longer habitable, and others are expected to follow. Federally mandated "viability" studies have also led to the complete demolition of some other housing developments in Chicago and other cities as well; the tenants once living there are now "scattered" across their respective metropolises.

Creating and sustaining local spaces for the healthy development of individuals and families is a core concern of Americans. It is a challenge that is ingrained in the American way of life, whether in a rural farm town, a suburban tract, or a public housing development. It is at the heart of the American dream, deeply intertwined with other national principles such as unrestricted mobility and the freedom of individual expression. The capacity of Americans to live in decent homes and neighborhoods has become such a matter of national interest that examples of troubled or successful communities rise quickly in the popular discourse to reflect on the state of the nation overall. Indeed, the high-rise public housing complex has become a contemporary mirror for American self-examination; the ardent conservative, the mawkish liberal, and the hopeful progressive are all equally bothered by the persistence of these pockets of social and economic deprivation in a country experiencing great prosperity.

The history of the struggle to create "community" in the Robert Taylor Homes is part of the ongoing saga of African Americans' attempt to root themselves in the national citizenry. Around the turn of the century, blacks looked increasingly to the American North to reap the fruits of liberty. The urban community would become their primary space of settlement, serving as a refuge from the burdens of Southern sharecropping and holding the promise of better days to come.[2] The history of Robert Taylor presents another account of this diasporic movement, one of hardship, resolve, and courage but also of joy and triumph. It is a paradigmatically American story. It is a tale of citizens who are committed to making the American dream of safe, prosperous communities come true.

———

The urban community has been a great interest of social observers for more than a century. In the early twentieth century, there was tremendous popular concern with the emerging American metropolis. The city was a hodgepodge of diverse social groups including ethnic immigrants, Southern black and Appalachian migrants, and the wealthy and the downtrodden, all of whom lived in close proximity to one another. Social reformers paid attention to expansive slums, the difficulties of immigrants and migrants who were unfamiliar with the urban lifestyle, and overcrowded housing. Industrialists stared out at a pool of eager laborers, ready to work in their stockyards, mills, and factories. City officials were kept busy coordinating traffic, providing sanitation services, ensuring adequate distribution of firehouses and police stations, and addressing the myriad issues of municipal governance. Policy makers and their advisors in the academy saw all this and assisted the parties in their respective efforts to service, reform, employ, and manage the city's inhabitants.

In their drive to understand basic processes of urban integration, observers found that people segregated themselves in various ways: there were enclaves of Poles, Germans, blacks, Irish, and other ethnic groups where people shared different languages, customs, traditions, and associations. The rich lived in certain areas, the poor lived in others, purveyors of vice and illicit activities were cordoned off, and so on. The city was described as a mosaic of "little worlds," each a distinct settlement but all interrelated into the larger metropolis. In this view, each of the settlements was understood to be a physically, socially, and culturally coherent entity, what would later be called by a simpler term, a "community."[3] A community had territorial integrity, that is, it had identifiable borders and was separated from its neighbors by natural or manmade boundaries. A community had a cultural unity: people shared outlooks, customs, languages, and perhaps some physical features. A community also varied in terms of the types of social institutions that helped residents to meet their basic needs, provide assistance to one another, and pass on values and norms to children and youth. Observers differentiated communities in terms of their ability to maintain order and integrate their members into city life. The capacity to control local problems quickly became a defining attribute.

Postwar social and economic transformations dramatically redefined the metropolitan landscape, and the perspective on the urban community changed accordingly.[4] On the one hand, entirely new communities formed as suburbanization drew millions of city dwellers to outlying and unincorporated areas of the central city. The suburban tract development, with its single-family homes, manicured lawns, new schools, and the apparent absence of pollution and congestion, seemed to provide ideal conditions for the American family. By 1960, many early criticisms, such as the sense of isolation or homogeneity of suburbia, were no longer as conspicuous.[5] Within the central city, "urban renewal" had created new spaces of commerce and settlement, but the reviews were mixed. Middle- and upper-class whites moved into redeveloped slum areas, and their aspiring black counterparts created vibrant new settlements in places that had been abandoned by fleeing whites. On the other hand, expansive ghetto tracts remained. In the popular eye, they stood in marked opposition to the suburban community, and some observers suggested that the ghetto was moving away from the rhythms of mainstream American community life.[6]

These social forces had realigned metropolitan landscapes to such a degree that it no longer appeared that people were intimately connected to their immediate community.[7] They were using cars, expressways, and public transportation to traverse and inhabit a much broader metropolitan area. Observers spoke of urban communities less as distinctive "natural areas" of homogeneous settlement than as Janus-faced regions, with some communities participating in the prosperity and others left behind. The nation's larger metropolises were chocolate cities and vanilla suburbs; they were gentrified and renewed on the one hand, slum-ridden and blighted on the other. Moreover, the suburb had become the exemplar of the normative or "mainstream" American community, built on a culture of progress, while the ghetto was the breeder of a "culture of poverty."

The large high-rise public housing complex sat tenuously at the crossroads. Built in the 1950s and early 1960s and located in the heart of the black ghetto, large public housing developments were an offshoot of postwar reformation, and they held the hopes of an urban citizenry seeking to revitalize its neighborhoods.[8] However, these mammoth steel and concrete developments, many of which were as visibly jarring as the sprawling symmetry of the suburban tract, were surrounded by fields of extreme poverty and so conjured up images of isolation and helplessness. In the discourse on American urban community, this uneasiness manifested itself in equivocal assessments of the viability of public housing. Some spoke of it as an island in a sea of despair and the promise of a better life for the predominantly African-American population that lived there. In their view, public housing represented a demonstrable advance for ghetto dwellers in desperate need of habitable communities. But others referred to public housing as a colossal failure waiting to happen, and they foresaw only decreased security and stability for households. To these skeptics, the newly furbished apartments and the modest increase in city services that accompanied public housing would never meet local demand; inevitably, the criminality and hardship of the surrounding ghetto would overtake the community, thereby reproducing an alienated urban poor.

In these polemics, which recurred throughout the 1960s, both proponents and critics of public housing drew on a widely held perspective of the African-American ghetto community that may be called "city within a city."[9] In this view, the ghetto was a separate place—that is, a quasi-independent "city"—where residents were at once removed from the rest of society, actively evading that society, and creating lifestyles at odds with that society. The large public housing development was the extreme example of this self-governing but ultimately dysfunctional urban community, unwilling and unable to follow the ideals of mainstream society. Not surprisingly, the two most common remedies that were offered to alleviate the ills of public housing both were premised on the notion of a chasm between the ghetto poor and the rest of America: outright demolition of housing developments would enable the integration of tenants into the larger (mainstream) city; or, according to a more liberal voice, mass infusion of education and other public resources into high-rise complexes would cultivate a more mainstream lifestyle among the inhabitants.

The city-within-a-city view continues to define contemporary evaluations of public housing viability. Although this has been a useful rhetorical device to draw attention to tenants' marginality, it can also be a limiting heuristic for understanding their lives. Certainly, in the Robert Taylor Homes and other Chicago high-rise public housing developments, where more than 90 percent of the populace is unemployed and must be quite creative to make ends meet, it is almost assured that aspects of daily life will be somewhat unique and possibly at odds with institutions in the wider world. It would be naive to equate the tenor of public housing residence with life in the American suburb, for example. Moreover, given the stark impoverishment in our nation's "projects," the singular experience of living there is perhaps deserving of greater attention. But one can also find commonalties, one of the most basic being the ongoing challenge of building a habitable community by procuring adequate city services and controlling the behavior of local youth. This is not a task of tenants alone, but an ongoing effort that involves individuals and organizations in the larger city. Developments such as the Robert Taylor Homes, however isolated they may appear, are nevertheless managed, subsidized, and administered by a number of social actors, including government and philanthropic agencies that range from the Chicago Housing Authority to social workers to national foundations. As such, they should not be seen as completely different or separate from the rest of American society. The city-within-a-city perspective can be counterproductive if it does not shed light on the similarities and the relationships between public housing and other American communities.

Sadly, in the recent history of writing on the public housing community, the particularities of residents' hardships have commanded national attention, at the expense of an understanding of how tenants work with others, sometimes productively and at other times conflictually, to improve their living environment. The result has been a circumscribed discussion of public housing viability in which evaluations of the merits and drawbacks of large high-rises are based overwhelmingly on incidents of crime and poverty. Such indicators may reveal the scope of local problems, but they tell little about how these affect the community. More important, they leave open the question of the means by which these instabilities are addressed and resolved, if at all. As such, statistical measures of public housing hardships have not provided an adequate framework for evaluating the potential of such high-rise developments to be communities for the nation's urban poor.

In the pages that follow, I root the perspective on American public housing in the ongoing work of tenants in the Robert Taylor Homes to create a community. As much as I seek to explicate the novelty of the issues that the residents face, I am especially mindful of the processes through which problems are addressed, and how this collective activity to produce an ordered environment has changed over time. While those at the heart of the struggle will certainly be tenants and local organizations based in Robert Taylor, I also explore the activities of a diverse array of individuals, groups, and institutions that routinely come into contact with the populace. The guiding premise is that a more thorough understanding of the fabric of "project living" is necessary in order to evaluate the viability of the high-rise public housing development, and that this is best woven from the threads of hardship as well as victory, distinctiveness and commonality, inclusion as well as exclusion.

This caveat is not entirely novel; nor is it specific to the contemporary public housing community. It is a point made consistently and forcefully by observers of the African-American experience.[10] Nearly a century ago, W. E. B. Du Bois, the black scholar and activist, wrote extensively about the particular and peculiar status of the diasporic African population in American society. The uniqueness of the black American experience, Du Bois suggested, stemmed not from cultural or psychological traits but from a tension that inhabits African Americans and that shapes their actions. Theirs is an ongoing striving, "two warring ideals in one dark body." "[The Negro] simply wishes to make it possible for a man to be both a Negro and an American," Du

Bois wrote. That is, black Americans are American in their alignment with society's ideals and goals, but they evoke patterns of thought and practice that are inescapably shaped by the inability to pursue the ideals in the manner of their white counterparts. Until full freedom and citizenship are achieved, Du Bois argued, their history will produce a liminal identity, a "double consciousness," one defined in part by the victories and setbacks along the way, but perhaps more so by the "history of this strife." To see the contours of this struggle, Du Bois noted that it would be futile to remain behind ghetto walls. The builders of those walls shaped the life for those who lived inside, and so their own practices could never be left out of the picture.

Du Bois's commentary, written nearly a century ago, is an invaluable road map for understanding the experiences of black Americans who live in contemporary public housing communities. His words motivate this study not only by directing attention to the relations of Robert Taylor with the outside world, but also by calling into question the sources and voices that can inform the experience of those living in the housing development. Because the African-American experience has been structured by exclusion as well as resistance, Du Bois argued in his own study of a Philadelphia ghetto community, the observer must call upon an array of resources in order to form a portrait of any single person, process, or community.[11] Archives exist, but rarely do they capture the nuances of an American group whose life has been so selectively represented and so consistently expunged from full, meaningful participation in the national record. Indeed, any formally available source of information can never document a history defined by contest, resistance, and at times evasion of a public gaze. It is the human voice that must be carefully heard; it is personal and collective memory that must be tilled with rigor and then matched against the formal record.

Thus, in order to form a systematic portrait of the ebb and flow of community life in the Robert Taylor Homes, I let the voices of its tenants chart our course (as well as the testimonies of those who have had some direct engagement with the housing development, such as police officers and CHA managers).[12] Their recollections, remembrances, tales, and revelations are the primary documents, but to fill out the picture I make ample use of government files, journalistic reportage, census data, and other statistical sources.[13] By piecing together all such available records, in memory and on paper, it is possible to reveal some of the richness of the everyday struggle by individuals and households to make the Robert Taylor Homes a habitable community.

1 | A Place to Call Home

From its inception, the Robert Taylor Homes was more than a residential complex. For the nation's disenfranchised, the housing development would serve as a stop on the way to property ownership, Thomas Jefferson's cradle of American democracy, as well as to an awareness of the rights that entailed. It signaled the commitment of federal, state, and local governments to addressing the needs of all citizens, black and white, rich and poor. For Chicago, Robert Taylor signified the city's promise to remove its ghettos, and for the city's black community, the housing development promised immediate relief from overcrowding, blight, and inadequate living conditions in the black belt. For the new tenants, Robert Taylor provided an opportunity to become citizens in another, perhaps unexpected, sense: they would have to work together, at times in an organized political capacity, to ensure that the "$70 million ghetto" remained a viable place to live.

With 4,500 apartments that were three-, four-, and five-bedroom units, the Robert Taylor Homes anticipated large households with many children and extended families. Those in need of housing were not just the poor and downtrodden of Chicago's black community. Indeed, more than half of Robert Taylor's initial occupants were employed families who could not find decent, affordable housing elsewhere in the city owing to racial segregation or prohibitive housing prices. Ideally, residence in public housing would give them time to find a private-market domicile. Meanwhile, they would live next door to their poorer brethren who were struggling to find jobs and to make their first step toward personal independence.

When the Robert Taylor Homes opened in 1962 and Chicago Mayor Richard J. Daley welcomed the first tenant, James Weston, on March 5, faith in the power of public housing seemed justified. The construction of the housing development along South State St. had been a politically contentious process designed to invigorate an otherwise depressed slum neighborhood that was known only for its "junkyards and flophouses."[1] The battles of the city leaders, as well as of black and white residents, over the design and placement of Robert Taylor brought to the fore the racism and patronage that characterized city politics and that had long kept blacks in a subordinate position. For a moment, anyway, the trees, gardens, and decorative flower beds interspersed amid the startling high-rises helped Chicagoans forget about this recent history. External galleries on the buildings gave thousands a remarkable view of the city's South Side, a clear day revealing the downtown skyline. The gray and red concrete of the façades had not yet been beaten and dirtied by inclement weather or by pollution from the expressways and factories to the west. There were no haunting black oval burns around windows, the result of apartment fires. Indeed, there were only signs of life and vitality: throngs of children climbed on new playground equipment, men and women colonized parking lots and alleyways with music and festivities, and softball and basketball games filled the park areas.

The neighboring Greater Grand Boulevard ghetto was lined with abandoned and burned structures and garbage-strewn streets, but Robert Taylor's bright high-rises and well-maintained grounds did not bear the mark of municipal neglect. The Housing Authority inundated tenants with mailings and communiqués that promised construction of parks, playgrounds, schools, free dental clinics, and recreational centers. In one letter to the incoming tenants, CHA Executive Director Alvin E. Rose personally thanked them for "making our communities the most beautiful in the whole city. I hope you are as proud as I am of your fine lawns and flower beds and the cleanliness of the buildings in which you reside."[2]

Building a community in Robert Taylor did not end with the construction of the twenty-eight high-rises, the flower beds, and the laundry rooms. Having moved into the city's densest residential neighborhood, tenants had no choice but to work cooperatively with one another and to learn to live as neighbors in close proximity. They did so from the outset, creatively developing an array of personal networks, informal groups and clubs, and formal organizations that could address the needs of households. Theirs was not a solitary task. They would work closely with their landlord, the Chicago Housing Authority, for which the maintenance of the twenty-seven-thousand-person housing development was also a formidable challenge. If the tenants' responsibility, and that of the CHA, did not end with their move into apartments, then neither could Mayor Daley and the city simply hand over the keys and watch from afar. All of these parties found themselves at the start of a long journey to determine whether large high-rise public housing could be a viable project. If ever there was an American community that required the continuous and active involvement of its residential body, at the dawn of the 1960s it was Robert Taylor.

Building the Robert Taylor Homes

The Robert Taylor Homes were built in an effort to provide Chicago's overcrowded black population with decent, affordable housing. It was a social engineering experiment of sizable proportion. Planners and politicians hoped that it would be a first step in turning miles of blighted South Side ghettos into equal members of the "city of neighborhoods." The design of Robert Taylor bore witness to the reigning ideas of rational city planning in the mid-twentieth century that specified the optimal use of city landscape, one that promoted the health and welfare of all its citizens. However, the development's placement in the heart of the ghetto signaled the presence of an equally powerful set of forces, namely, the racial ideologies of Chicago's political leaders, which determined how (and to what degree) the city's black population would be integrated into the larger city. As the idealism of architects and planners encountered the strength of the Chicago political machine, Chicago watched its newest community take form.

The Robert Taylor Homes were a testament to a legacy of struggle on the part of social reformers to make American urban communities livable. In the 1930s, the working class and the poor had mobilized in large numbers to protest their slum conditions, and politicians were forced to respond by developing government housing initiatives, ranging from direct construction to financial inducements for private-market developers and contractors.[3] Progressive reformers also fought for improvements in housing design and neighborhood planning, crying for more expansive low-income settlements, free of pollution and filth and bathed in "air and light." They tied the health and welfare of low-income urbanites to the "openness" of their habitats, an attribute that typically referred to residential places freed from the chaos of transit.

Similar debates on city planning were occurring farther away in Europe. The need for "openness" and the isolation of lived spaces from thoroughfares were incorporated into the architectural and urban design visions of European modernist artists. The best known of these figures was Le Corbusier, whose plans for cities shared the progressive-era belief that the built environment had a direct impact on the lifestyles of its inhabitants.[4] Le Corbusier made vertical aggregation the centerpiece of his urban planning, its physical embodiment being the high-rise building. The high-rise was the solution to the twin prerogatives of urban planning, namely, adequate housing units and sufficient, bright open spaces for recreation and intercourse. Le Corbusier reduced the city to composites of steel and glass high-rises, vast isolated tracts of unused public spaces, and expressways that moved through the expanse to connect the physical structures with one another.

Architects and planners in Chicago imported reformist principles and European modernist aesthetics into their blueprints for public housing development. They did so through government agencies, most notably the Public Works Administration (PWA) and later the Federal Housing Authority, which devised regulations that standardized the design and construction process for public housing.[5] These guidelines steered architects toward planning techniques in which form was to follow the functional dictates of the mass-produced, "rational" city. Government had redefined aesthetic creativity in architecture as largely a problem-solving task in which the architect must devise an appropriate use of space that would support the "inner logic" regulating how cities functioned.[6] To offer only one example, PWA guidelines stated that housing designs should ensure sufficient "open areas" around buildings. Reminiscent of Le Corbusier's writings, residential areas were to be "naturally separated into two parts—namely, the space required for circulation and that for uses other than traffic"; in addition, some open areas could be used, but others should be blank, nonutilized spaces of "passive recreation" that supported viewing and gazing from the building itself.[7] Faced with such guidelines, public housing planners and architects used vertical aggregation, building up whenever possible, to leave sufficient open space. Thus was conceived the public housing "superblock," that is, a collection of large high-rise structures surrounded by vast unused areas.[8]

The blending of European modernism, state governance, and progressive ideals could be seen in the work of architects and designers employed by the Chicago Housing Authority. Although they experimented in the 1940s with public housing designs that deviated from the monotony of mass-produced housing and from high-rises,[9] from 1955 to 1963, CHA developments built to house African Americans were predominantly "dreary high rise blocks with their rows of uniform windows punched out of clifflike walls of brick."[10] "In fact, of the nearly 21,000 low-income family apartments built by the CHA from 1955 through 1968, all but about 2,000 were in high-rises."[11] The designs for Robert Taylor exemplified this change. The earliest proposed design made creative use of the assigned two-mile-by-two-block corridor for Robert Taylor by incorporating eight-story high-rises and two-story apartment buildings. The plan set aside acreage for public spaces such as park areas and playgrounds, waterways and ponds, and winding pathways that moved through the natural landscapes. Federal officials at the Public Housing Authority rejected this variegated design because it exceeded cost guidelines, and so the CHA submitted another plan, with twenty-eight sixteen-story high-rise residential structures in uniform groups of two and three, which was eventually accepted. Physical structures covered only 7 percent of the ninety-six acres, and apart from two park areas, the remainder was nonutilizable or "dead" space, mostly of concrete and asphalt for which no use was intended or specified.

Critics charged that the use of twenty-eight high-rises was a poor design choice. The historian Devereaux Bowley argued that the CHA could still have mixed high- and low-rise structures when building Robert Taylor.[12] Catherine Bauer, a leading proponent of public housing in the New Deal era, issued the most trenchant criticism of the preference for high-rise development by the CHA and other public housing authorities across the country:

> The public housing project therefore continues to be laid out as a "community unit" as large as possible and entirely divorced from its neighborhood surroundings, even though this only dramatizes the segregation of charity-case families. Standardization is emphasized rather than alleviated in project design, as a glorification of efficient production methods and an expression of the goal of decent, safe and sanitary housing for all. But the bleak symbols of productive efficiency and "minimum standards" are hardly an adequate or satisfactory expression of the values associated with American human life.[13]

The placement of Robert Taylor was an equally contentious process. The city had set aside an uninterrupted stretch of land in 1949–1950, and another in 1956 and 1957, for a large development, but it was also looking at vacant lands in predominantly white communities. Powerful white ethnic leaders on the City Council rejected the CHA's proposed sites for lands in white neighborhoods, refusing to tolerate a large black presence in their wards. Together with the black politicians who wished to retain a black constituency in the ghetto, the Council approved only the sites in the existing ghetto.[14] Addressing specifically the Robert Taylor site, the historian Brad

Hunt suggests that discrimination played an important role, but that CHA officials and black aldermen were also complicit in their intention to place more than seven thousand public housing units in the existing, overcrowded ghetto:

> CHA officials chose Robert Taylor's site and a black alderman expanded it, while federal officials, eager to produce more housing, readily approved . . . Most scholars have treated these battles as defeats for the CHA, with the city council forcing bad sites on a reluctant agency. But, significantly, the CHA under progressive Elizabeth Wood had proposed or accepted sites similar in nature to Taylor's. Even if Wood and the CHA had been allowed complete freedom to select sites, the agency would still have sought to rebuild the poor housing conditions of the black south side slums, including those along South State Street.[15]

Although the CHA was popularly thought to have been at the vanguard of the integration movement, its decision to erect continuous, predominantly high-rise public housing along State St. proved a clear example of the agency's role in perpetuating metropolitan residential segregation.

The designated tract along State St. that would host the Robert Taylor Homes had been called the "largest contiguous slum in the U.S."[16] Nearly all the housing units lacked adequate water and sanitation facilities, and most had been designated "dilapidated" from the 1930s onward. Curiously, although the CHA's plan for that corridor was inflected by the modernist belief in the transformative power of high-rise structures, its overall site usage did not obey other planning tenets. For example, it ignored precepts that large residential quarters be surrounded by lived spaces that promote interaction and daily commerce, social control, and neighborliness. Instead, Robert Taylor was situated along a truck route—with primarily industrial uses—that was set apart from civic life in the surrounding Black Metropolis. To make matters worse, Mayor Daley brazenly constructed a large expressway at taxpayer expense, effectively shielding the housing development from the predominantly white community of Bridgeport, where he lived. Thus, from the outset, Robert Taylor was on the periphery, separated from the resource-rich community of Bridgeport by an expressway, and removed from the single-family homes, commerce, and institutions of the ghetto that lay east of it.

The construction of the Robert Taylor Homes was an expedient operation. Having built the nearby McCormick Place convention center, the contractors, Newberg Construction Company, needed only to move their machinery and labor westward several blocks to the State St. corridor to begin construction. The bulk of the operation was completed in three years, eleven months ahead of schedule, at a cost of nearly $70 million. The housing development was an awesome sight. It towered over the surrounding residences, most of which were single-family homes and low-rise apartment buildings. Its concrete structures were either gray or brick red, and in the light, the steel windows shone brilliantly, while cloudy days cast a breathtaking gloom over the development. Neatly confined to a narrow stretch of land at the ghetto's western edge, Robert Taylor was unmistakable to pedestrians as well as motorists who drove past on the newly constructed Dan Ryan Expressway that ran alongside the length of the complex.

Robert Taylor's vastness and newness seemed to overshadow all of the earlier political debates regarding its design and site selection. Mayor Daley and the city's black leaders heralded its November 1962 opening as a step toward the eradication of slum housing throughout Chicago. At the ribbon-cutting ceremony, political leaders and CHA directors beamed with optimism, and at successive news conferences they confidently rebuffed critics who charged that the agency was relocating black slum evictees within the ghetto. The CHA argued that Robert Taylor's "mix" of working and poor families would help decrease the sense of social isolation of its poorer families because they would benefit from propinquity to their employed, two-parent neighbors. They spoke of plans to conduct watchful screening so that the development would always be a (class) heterogeneous place. They promised that tenants would be part of this process, with a voice in decisions that affected their buildings, and that they would eventually take the management reins in future years. In 1962, as apartments were filling up with new arrivals, the mood of the community reflected this optimism. There was little doubt that the Robert Taylor Homes would "be one of the most attractive and livable [communities] in Chicago."[17]

"A Giant Black Playground"

A variety of families moved into the new apartments of the Robert Taylor Homes. There were single women, but more common were two-parent households with children, and in some cases three and four generations of kin. What the CHA defined as a "normal" household—one consisting of two parents and at least one child—represented two-thirds of the 4,500 apartments in the early years.[18] Almost one-half of households received some form of public housing assistance, but nearly a third of these consisted of two parents (both unemployed). These families, however, were generally larger than their counterparts in Chicago: "The average family at Taylor Homes consists of 6.3 persons, including 4.3 minors. Compare this with the average of 1.2 minors for the city of Chicago."[19]

The newness of the housing development stood in marked contrast to the squalor of the surrounding Greater Grand Boulevard community in the city's South Side. Despite the flight of middle- and upper-class blacks,[20] the residential density in the larger South Side ghetto was twice as high as in the rest of the city, its overcrowding three times as great, and the housing conditions of the past four decades had not improved.[21] By comparison, each apartment in Robert Taylor was furnished with its own cooking and bathroom facilities, amenities residents did not take lightly given that "conversions" and "kitchenettes" that forced families to share cooking and washroom facilities were still common in the surrounding ghetto. Buildings contained laundry facilities in the basement, and many had small convenience stores operated by residents. CHA workers planted trees and laid down flower beds ninety feet in diameter.

On the grounds of the housing development, one saw a prevalence of children, adolescents, and young adults, many of whom were accompanied by women—baby-sitters, mothers, grandmothers, and so on—acting as caretakers. The large open swatches of asphalt and grass, filled with playful youth and their guardians close behind, made quite an impression. In 1965, only three years after Robert Taylor's construction, the media would direct much of their attention to this female-dominated public activity; one prominent journalist even proclaimed that Robert Taylor was, "in good part, a woman's world and a children's world without men."[22] The media tended not to examine the factors responsible for the overwhelmingly young population, such as the higher percentage of three- and four-bedroom apartments in Robert Taylor compared with other Chicago public housing developments. But they were partially correct to make note of the public activities of women, who, in meeting the needs of their families, were increasingly thrust into the local spotlight, their mundane chores and duties becoming collective, community concerns.

By 1965, an estimated twenty-seven thousand tenants lived in the housing development, twenty thousand of them "children."[23] For Ottie Davis and his friends who grew up in Robert Taylor during the mid-1960s (Bobby Dowell, Kenny Davenport, and the brothers Tom and Jake Adams), the housing development was paradise: "It was a giant black playground!" Davis exclaimed. "I had hundreds of kids to play with, and many of them—like Bobby [Dowell]—I still hang out with today." However, for their parents and guardians, the optimism of a new beginning in Robert Taylor was guarded and always relative to the conditions of the broader community. Davis's aunt, hearing his description, replied by saying,

> Playground? Yeah, well, you *made* it into playground, Ottie. For me, it was a chore trying to keep up with these kids. Empty lots, and those train tracks! Ooh! You had to watch everywhere 'cause there wasn't no parks or nothing like that, just a lot of open space that [kids] would mess around in. And it wasn't no better 'cross the street, 'cause there wasn't no parks there either. So all *those* kids would come over to us.

Several small malls with grocery stores, health clinics, social service agencies, and small businesses were scattered throughout Robert
Taylor, and in addition, the Housing Authority planned to construct
three shopping centers, all privately developed. Tenants valued the
stores' proximity since, as one resident stated, "all the businesses
were closing down around us, so if we didn't have these stores close
by, we would've had to walk miles to get food." Similarly, the
planned construction of social and educational services (most of
which were ultimately delayed or postponed) raised tenant hopes, for
the decline of the South Side's institutional sector had followed that
of its commercial base. In the surrounding neighborhoods, schools,
libraries, job training programs, park department facilities, and social
services were overcrowded and fiscally strapped. Public health facilities, including clinics, hospitals, and dentists' offices, were too few in
number, and private physicians, "sensitive to income changes in a
neighborhood," were quick to relocate out of the ghetto when middle-class flight left them with a primarily poor clientele.[24] Agencies
and youth centers, public and private, were claimed by a local youth
population or were filled to capacity and so were inaccessible to most
younger residents of Robert Taylor. Mayor Daley's successful construction of a freeway next to the housing development effectively
cut off tenants from the wealth of services in the neighboring white
working-class communities to the west. This physical barrier was an
obstacle second only to the racism and harassment of blacks by the
predominantly Irish population who lived there.

In these circumstances, despite tenant optimism, Robert Taylor
provided facilities and programs inadequate to meet the social and
recreational demands of its children and young adults. A large park
sat in the middle of the housing development, two smaller playlots
stood on either side, and several sets of swings and basketball courts
were interspersed throughout. Although grass and trees lined the borders, much of the open space that surrounded buildings was concrete
or asphalt. Planners who designed the larger CHA developments assumed that the presence of open areas would lead to usable public

space, a design error that they would remedy after building Robert Taylor. One resident laughed as she described the wait to use a swing set in the 1960s: "I'd have this ice cream cone in my hand, you know, that I'd bought from the ice cream man, and I wanted to wait till I got on the merry-go-round to eat it. But the line was around the block for one merry-go-round! Every day, all day and night. That ice cream would just melt down my hand before I could get on."

CHA staff were aware early on that the facilities in Robert Taylor were inadequate and that the high rate of usage had shortened the life-span of most physical structures and play equipment. An early CHA report supports the young woman's testimony: "Children lined up seven and eight deep just waiting to use a piece of play equipment . . . upwards of 2,000 children may be cramped into one or two relatively small play areas."[25] The Housing Authority's options to address the problems were few, however. Once the built environment was constructed and families had moved in, it was not easy to realign public spaces; moreover, existing Housing Authority budgets did not provide for additional construction of playground equipment and alterations of physical space.[26]

Lacking sufficient recreational areas, children reconstituted any available public and semiprivate space for their enjoyment—perhaps as they would in any American community. For Ottie Davis and his friend Kenny Davenport, the railroad track on top of the viaduct near Twenty-fifth St. was the favored locale. From there, the two would hurl rocks, snowballs, and epithets either at the trains that ran beside them or at the people and cars that passed below. Davenport liked to play in stairwells because "you could slide down those long metal railings, and you tried not to fall in between 'cause you'd die right quick." Elevators, stairwells, lobbies, hallways, parking lots and alleyways, garbage cans, and laundry rooms became veritable playgrounds. Each possessed a particular set of hazards, which could add to their enjoyment. Parking lots were strewn with broken glass and power lines lay dangerously low; train tracks were bordered by steep concrete embankments and cars sped quickly through alleys; hallways and stairwells were the domain of gamblers and drinkers, says Davis, "who used to chase us little kids and throw bottles at us, 'cause they'd be so pissed they lost their money they'd need to beat someone up."

The presence of young children was most noticeable during summers and after-school hours, but there was always a visible young adult presence in the housing development. The number of school dropouts in Robert Taylor was increasing during the 1960s. In Chicago as in other cities, decades of municipal neglect—manifesting itself in underfunding and insufficient service provision—had produced overcrowded and deteriorating schools in poor and working-class black neighborhoods, and as middle-class flight lowered city tax bases, political officials responded by favoring white constituents. Chicago's entrenched white-ethnic-led political machine was miserly in its allocation of resources, not only to ghetto schools, but also to other institutions that had educational objectives, such as community centers and libraries. It is not surprising, then, that youth alienation from the school system was persistent throughout Chicago's ghettos. Institutions of higher education could not move blacks into meaningful, well-paying employment.[27] In Chicago's ghettos by the end of the 1960s, the "morale of both teachers and students" had reached depressingly low levels.[28] The Chicago Urban League led a citywide effort to publicize the inadequate educational funding that black communities received because educational resource streams were tied to local tax generation. The Daley administration did not deny inequities in the city's South Side school system, issuing a report on that area that stated, "In 1965, 61 of the 67 schools [in South Side communities] have average classroom occupancies in excess of the Board's recommended goal of 30 pupils per room . . . Most of the schools lack adequate playground space, and many are more than 50 years old."[29] For several reasons, Mayor Daley was loath to change the status quo: city funds were limited, and Daley generally ensured that his own voting bloc (Chicago's white ethnics) was served adequately; in addition, the mayor relied on ghetto leaders to inform him of their communities' needs, but these brokers did not always press fully for parity in school funding.[30]

For parents and guardians, monitoring the behavior of a large youth population was a difficult proposition. The design of the built environment exacerbated their difficulties. Cars used the open spaces as thoroughfares and parking lots, the play of children in hallways and stairwells was not easily observable, and surveillance from a high floor of the ground below was nearly impossible. Parents tried to keep children away from train tracks, frowned upon the use of elevators and lobbies as play areas, and steered children away from alleys. Many were hesitant to venture into the hallways and stairwells of buildings in which they did not live because, as one resident said, "you never did know what kind of things people was doing in there."

Because of its high rate of usage and central location, the elevator quickly became the most dangerous physical feature of the housing development.[31] For approximately eight hundred children in each of the buildings, the elevator provided hours of enjoyment. As Bobby Dowell states, "We used to ride them like we was at Great America [theme park]. Popping them buttons, loading as many kids as we could, trying to climb out of them if we could." By 1965, the deterioration of the elevators reached crisis levels. Several children had been seriously injured when an elevator stopped between floors—one child fell down the elevator shaft when attempting to climb out—and, in a 1963 incident, fire department workers reported that because of a broken elevator, they were unable to prevent the death of three children on the fourteenth floor of a high-rise. Slow elevators repeatedly delayed paramedics, and law enforcement and social services suffered because police and social workers feared riding faulty elevators and had to take precautions when using the stairwells. Before the end of the 1960s, the Housing Authority would declare that 75 percent of the elevators in Robert Taylor were "non-functional."[32]

It was the elevator, with "the screaming tangle of kids crammed together at the bottom, and the ceaseless nerve-jarring clang of the emergency bell [that added] its own special balm to the panic," that became one of the first targets of parental criticism.[33] To express their concern, residents generally called the CHA management office or met formally in CHA-sponsored tenant meetings. However, institutionalized forums for expressing grievances fell far short of the demand. The housing development was still young, and there was an expected lag between the occurrence of social problems and the development of suitable procedures for complaint and redress. A 1964 letter to a tenant from CHA Acting Director of Management G. W. Master indicates that the agency was trying to develop procedures to monitor and respond to tenant concerns:

> The problems mentioned in your letter, as well as others that we know are of some concern to the residents of Taylor Homes, are to be openly discussed at a series of resident meetings which are to commence at a very early date. It is our hope that these meetings . . . will result in arriving at ways and means which will assist in resolving these problems. Please watch for an announcement of a meeting with the residents of your area.[34]

During this early period of settlement, the CHA typically redirected tenants' letters and phone calls to the office of the "project manager," that is, to a small staff who were the primary liaisons for thousands of residents, until adequate grievance venues could be established.

There were some resident organizations and informal associations with which the project manager and his or her staff could collaborate to address emergent concerns, but their relationship to the Housing Authority was not clearly articulated. Tenants were still learning how to acquire assistance for their basic needs, and CHA staff were themselves determining appropriate and effective protocols to communicate with the resident body. Moreover, many of the factors redirecting youth to less constructive amusements in and around the housing development were products of the city's failure—not necessarily that of the CHA—to provide and maintain educational, recreational, and employment opportunities for ghetto youth. The inability of residents of Robert Taylor to use the already distressed and overcrowded facilities in the wider ghetto neighborhoods made them rely on parks, social service centers, and playgrounds within the complex to a degree perhaps greater than that anticipated by CHA planners.

It would be inaccurate to conclude that the challenge of controlling the behavior of children and youth was causing frequent large-scale tenant protest or continuous antagonistic interactions between residents and administrative agencies. The early correspondence between parties reveals a relatively cooperative relationship in which tenants felt free to voice their concerns and the Housing Authority replied—with letters to individuals and with larger resident meetings—in a fairly timely, conscientious manner. The letters that tenants wrote reveal an extraordinary empathy with the CHA's plight as landlord of a large, densely populated community, and many offered optimistic commentary to indicate that they remained assured that the housing development would be a hospitable place for their families.

Robert Taylor was a significant improvement for households that lived in other ghetto communities, and in the early years, the CHA had sufficient resources to maintain the residence and work with tenants to screen and place families in a manner that maintained a stable mix of working and nonworking, large and small, young and old families. Indeed, by most indications, Robert Taylor had to be considered a relatively successful community. It was not free of social problems and challenges, but this would be a faulty barometer on which to gauge any community's status. Perhaps most important, as concerns emerged, so too did mechanisms to address them, albeit not always successfully. This portrait of a relatively well functioning community received little attention in the gaze of media, which was dominated by reports of crime, profligacy, and rampant familial instability.

It was in the coming years that tenants' patience and the strength of their relationship with the CHA would be tested. Residents were building relationships and friendships with one another for social and recreational support. However, as the basic infrastructure of their housing development surpassed CHA upkeep and as the resources in the surrounding areas decreased even further, these networks, alli-

ances, and informal collectives became imperative for their livelihood. Tenants were increasingly less willing to accept the state of
affairs, and they began to transform some of their casual relationships
into more targeted efforts to improve their well-being. Not surprisingly, their relationship with the Housing Authority and other local
agencies would change accordingly.

Parents Mobilize

In order to "fill the empty time," Ottie recalls, small groups of truant
youths living in Robert Taylor engaged in various types of mischief
and petty crime. Tom and Jake Adams, two brothers who grew up in
the housing development, fondly remember stealing cars, riding mo-
torbikes on the train tracks in defiance of local police, and attacking
their peers with zip guns and slingshots. Davis's schoolmate Bobby
Dowell watched gleefully as his older brother's friends scared social
workers who walked up the poorly lit stairwells, at times holding
them hostage, taking their money, and telling them never to return.
To reach his apartment safely at the end of a school day, Davis had to
evade truant officers and street gangs and then navigate the hazards
inside the building:

> When it got really worse, you know like it is today? I couldn't get on the
> elevator on the ground floor [back then]. I had to walk up to the stairs, get
> on the elevator and take it up to, I think the tenth floor. 'Cause the Pent-
> house Kings gang controlled those floors, and me and my friends didn't
> like them. Once I got to the tenth floor, I had to take one stairwell 'cause
> the other one was where everyone gambled and drank liquor and
> shit—the door to the stairwell was busted on that side so you could go
> from the stairwell to the hallway easily, and this woman who lived on the
> corner let everyone drink and screw in her place, so none of us kids used
> to hang out in there. Then I could get back on the elevator up to my
> momma's apartment.

As the Housing Authority struggled to create tenant-management
liaisons, residents turned to more informal forums to watch over chil-

dren and assist one another. Monitoring their youth was becoming more challenging and necessitated newer types of cooperation and surveillance. In addition to the overuse of extant facilities and the lack of resources for their children, parents had to confront the early signs of delinquency and organized gang activity, which many account for in terms of truancy and the general idleness of the youth populace.[35] These problems were intertwined, according to Kenny Davenport, who says that gang activity appealed to youth as a social outlet:[36]

> You got to realize that you had thousands of young niggers hanging out man, on streets, in front of stores. Ain't nothing for them. We was growing up watching 'em beat each other up just for something to do. [The Blackstone Rangers gang] had as many niggers as they wanted just 'cause people were so bored, you'd join a gang just to say you was involved in something.

The most prevalent informal tenant mechanism for facilitating social control was the "Mama's Mafia," a term that two residents of Robert Taylor used when they were growing up in the housing development in the 1960s and 1970s.[37] These "Mafias" were support networks of predominantly adult women formed out of propinquity—geographically and in terms of shared interests and experience. Louisa Lenard, Mabel Harris, and Cathy Blanchard were heads-of-households in the 1960s. They met as friends and immediately worked together in the 218 building to deter gang recruitment efforts; in later decades, tenants of other buildings would cite their work as an example both of courage and of successful tenant mobilization. Ottie Davis's mother and Bobby Dowell's mother lived near each other on Chicago's West Side. After moving into Robert Taylor, they too marshaled their respective peer groups to provide baby-sitting, counseling, and informal neighborhood watches over their children. Davis describes his mother's "Mafia" regime as follows:

> "What made [Robert Taylor] better back then?" said Ottie. "People was more together. If I saw your kid out, nine or ten o'clock at night, I'm taking his ass home! And I knew better to call my neighbors a liar. Nine or ten o'clock at night I better not be downstairs. I lived on the fourteenth

floor. My range was the thirteenth and fifteenth floor, and I better not get past it. And sometimes it was just the fourteenth floor. So I got the whole fourteenth floor to roam and I cross that fourteenth, go in the hallways or the elevator and my mother not with me, she gonna call my neighbor and that neighbor gonna kick my ass all the way back to the fourteenth, and I gonna get another ass-whupping 'cause my mother will be waiting at the fourteenth floor."

Some of the Mama's Mafias became formal tenant groups, such as "Mothers on the Move against Slums" (MOMS), that worked in conjunction with "suburban housewives" to create social programs, but many simply remained peer groups. In either case, cooperation with one another brought tenants into contact with numerous agencies, many of which were ostensibly responsible for providing the services that Mama's Mafias were providing. To secure safe, clean conditions in hallways, parents and guardians learned to navigate a complex CHA bureaucracy. They met with school officials, staff members of day care and youth centers, and police officers assigned to prevent truancy and petty crime. And in some cases, they directly confronted the leaders of street gangs that sought to occupy public spaces for purposes of recruitment and gang meetings. Cathy Blanchard makes a direct comparison between her peers in Robert Taylor and those in "better-off communities":

> I know it ain't no easier in the suburbs or Chatham [a predominantly black working-class community area in Chicago], you know, in those better-off communities. But out there, you didn't have to struggle to get people to clean up urine, you know? By us watching over our kids, we learned how to fight to get what we deserved, you understand me. We marched with our kids to the police station, we went to the alderman, we yelled at garbage truck drivers, we learned we couldn't just sit back 'cause they wouldn't give us nothing. That's what got us fighting for our rights and that's what got us involved in making sure people had a decent place to live.

Whether as peer groups or as slightly more formal associations, networks of women were anchored in everyday support functions such as watching over children, food sharing, emergency loans, and assistance during episodes of domestic violence.

Organized on the basis of neighboring floors and buildings, these support networks reflected the layout of the physical territory. That is, the cooperative practices fostered intimate association among those residing in a particular building or among a set of two or three buildings that bordered one another. Tenants recall that within a building, particular floors were more likely to help one another: "Where I was at," said the tenant Carol Sanders, "it was [floors] three through five, we really was tight, you know, we cooked for each other, watched to see who was walking around on the floors." In general, however, the social networks in Robert Taylor could be loosely differentiated in terms of the buildings themselves, which were numbered by their placement either on Main St. or on Elm St. and which were conventionally referred to solely by their number—for example, 218 South Main St. was simply "218." The distance separating the twenty-eight structures from one another was great. Those on the northern end of Robert Taylor were two miles away from the three southernmost buildings, and the structures themselves were clustered in sets of two and three with a courtyard that tied them together and partially hid them from other clusters. The height of the structures also ensured that the individual high-rise would be a focal point for gathering. This verticality, combined with the occupational density of one thousand people per building (and eventually the floor-to-ceiling mesh wire enclosures of external hallways), focused the interaction within and around the high-rise. Tenants of buildings some distance apart from one another shared similar circumstances, and their household members may have attended the same schools and churches, but day-to-day intercourse was limited by the geographic distance separating the high-rises.

The support networks soon began to assume more visible leadership roles as the scope of their activities expanded into ensuring cleanliness of stairwells and lobbies, elevator maintenance, adequate laundry facilities, and disputing fines and evictions for late rent payment.[38] On the individual level, some people participated actively in tenant discussion groups, and their move to advocacy and direct lobbying was a natural next step. Local activism was even less of a transition for those who participated in broader collective struggles such as voter-registration drives or Black Panther Party activities. Collectively, some groups turned into quasi-block clubs that lobbied the CHA for funds to sponsor social activities, while others addressed more heated issues such as the harassment of tenants by security officers.

In some cases, CHA staff—usually the office of the project manager—helped to promote tenant networks and loose-knit organizations, and these collectives were also grounded in activities relating to household support and the upkeep of buildings and grounds. In each building, CHA formed "elevator committees" consisting of "volunteer mothers" who would operate the elevators during periods of heavy use. They created an overarching Citizens Committee of tenants and leaders in business, education, religion, and law enforcement who would "welcome the new Taylor Homes residents and integrate them into the fabric of the larger community."[39] They helped to develop "floor clubs" for tenants and selected individuals to be "janitors" and "special guards" who monitored traffic in lobbies. For the most part, they either recruited from the adult female population or supported existing networks of female heads-of-households through sponsorship or a small allowance; much less often, they worked with the Cook County Department of Public Aid to hire unemployed men as elevator operators and as guards who patrolled galleries and grounds at night. (Their predilection for women was due in no small part to the growing number of female-led households and the restrictions on welfare eligibility that forced male income earners to hide from CHA staff.) One CHA project manager in Robert Taylor understood the recruitment of welfare recipients to be a noteworthy achievement and cited the practice in his public speeches to dispel the myth that Robert Taylor would "fail" because the "best people—the so-called leaders—" would move out when finances permitted. "As a matter of fact," he stated, "some of our most effective leadership has come from mothers receiving Aid to Dependent Children [an important government public assistance program]."[40]

As members of peer groups and associations, the majority of individuals had a fairly circumscribed involvement in formal advocacy and lobbying. Most divorced themselves from confrontational stances in local matters.[41] To acquire resources, they either worked closely with CHA staff (and social workers, police officers, and so on) or met by themselves and then issued formal requests to police, local churches, and other community-based organizations. During this initial settlement period (until the late 1960s), their labors were confined to facilitating building upkeep, helping residents meet basic needs, and putting together small social or recreational activities. In this regard, Ottie Davis's parents exemplified many residents for whom Robert Taylor far surpassed the living conditions of their previous residence and for whom declines in maintenance or exploitative landlord practices were familiar and intractable aspects of ghetto living. Although supportive of tenant dissension and collective protest, argues Davis, neither his mother nor most others in her peer group played an active role in local politics. His recollections are confirmed by other people who lived in the housing development in the 1960s, less than 10 percent of whom recall formal involvement in local affairs. (Most point to a small number of tenants who represented their interests in wider social and political circles.)

Over the course of the 1960s, formal organizations became as important as the informal networks and associations for determining quality of life in Robert Taylor. The most prominent organization was the "council" structure put into place by Housing Authority management. This was a governance body composed of both elected and appointed tenants, many of whom were elderly and female. In theory, each floor would elect a representative to sit on the "Building Council" in his or her respective high-rise; tenants of all sixteen floors would elect the Building Council's president. However, in practice, tenants recall that elections were not ubiquitous, and the process of determining membership was not systematic. Not all tenants participated or perceived the councils to be an important collective voice. In any building, a tenant might be self-appointed as a council president or appointed informally by other tenants or by a CHA staffer who had observed her leadership in other venues; residents typically volunteered to be floor representatives, but they may also have been chosen by the existing council president.

Councils existed in thirty-nine CHA developments and enabled residents to "assum[e] their share of responsibility for the character of their communities." From the CHA's perspective, the councils were designed to be a small cadre of laborers, hierarchically organized, with "each level of command accept[ing] fixed responsibilities for chores necessary to the smooth running of the building."[42] The lowest level in the council hierarchy was the "floor captain," one for each of the sixteen floors in a high-rise, who was "empowered to schedule the use of laundries and to assign cleaning tasks" to other residents. Together, the floor captains in a building made up the Building Council, the group responsible for distributing additional tasks to tenants, including monitoring elevators during peak traffic periods before and after school, and supervising play in parks and recreational areas. A representative from the Building Council then served on the Resident Council, the committee that had some influence over the implementation of programs and social services throughout the twenty-eight buildings of the housing development.[43]

Almost immediately after its creation (by the spring of 1963 such groups existed in nearly every building), the council played a prominent role in Robert Taylor. In public relations activities such as hosting mayoral and gubernatorial delegations, or meeting with philanthropic organizations, council members were asked to speak to the guests (informal networks remained more salient for watching over children and for everyday communication and sharing). Through these activities, the council helped build public awareness of the housing development. Individual council members also cemented their own stature in the eyes of residents and the Housing Authority. Many were hand-picked by the CHA, and those who were elected campaigned on their ability to get things done. These officers assisted the Housing Authority by quelling tenant grievances, often with expedient apartment repair or small gifts. CHA project managers called on them to give lectures to new tenants regarding homemaker skills and apartment maintenance. They formed the vanguard of the CHA's "Tenant Leadership Workshop," which was intended to culti- vate practical leaders in public housing by training them to monitor activities in their respective buildings.

Individuals who served on the councils could receive practical benefits, according to Edna Harris, a council president in the early 1960s. "Our apartments was always the first taken care of, 'cause we'd just call up managers and they knew to make sure we was happy or else we could make their lives hell." In this manner, Harris went on to ar- gue, the stature and influence of the council members were quickly grasped by the residents. Indeed, the evidence of a strong or weak Building Council president could be seen in the uneven levels of main- tenance and landscaping among buildings: "People was destroying the place, true," Harris recalled, "but like me, I could make sure things was fixed, and so me and Ms. Walton over there next to me, we had our place looking nice all the time." Speaking to the differences, Paulina Collins, who lived in several buildings during the 1960s, argued:

> We here [at the 205 building] have always been kinda funny, you know, kinda different than 210 or 218 . . . We had Ms. Walton [a Building Coun- cil president] fighting for us for thirty years now. Right from the start, when the CHA wouldn't pay [this part of the housing development] no at- tention, Ms. Walton made sure that we'd had gardens, our lobbies ain't had no piss all over them, we'd had our trash picked up, our apartments was real nice . . . so, no, I don't have no complaints about raising my fam- ily in Taylor. But maybe that's because I did it in this building and not in some of the others [close by].

Other tenants echo Paulina's observations but make a distinction be- tween the power of the members of the Building Council and that of its progeny, the Local Advisory Council. "[Building Council presidents] couldn't get us no jobs, like the [LAC] that came after them" is a typical response to indicate that the power of a Building Council president was limited and was most effective in matters of landscaping and, on occasion, response times for apartment repairs.

By working with one another formally and informally to meet their basic needs, residents organized themselves in meaningful ways. Many of the relationships they created were rooted in geographic proximity; for example, residents on neighboring floors found a marginal advantage when working with one another to monitor the behavior of children, and those living in high-rises that shared a courtyard would plan social activities together. Through these everyday practices, tenants formed symbolic associations with their buildings.[44] Qualitative distinctions surfaced throughout the housing development on the basis of a single high-rise structure or a group of several adjoining buildings that had tenants who cared for one another. With urging from the CHA, tenants painted murals and signs on concrete walls to distinguish their buildings, planted gardens next to their lobbies, and challenged neighboring high-rises to do the same. These informal practices were accompanied by recognized distinctions in terms of the maintenance and sanitation in these buildings, the amount of influence of tenants with state agencies, and levels of crime.

The most general distinction among buildings in Robert Taylor was between the northern set of buildings that composed "Taylor A" and the southern group that composed "Taylor B." For much of the 1960s, the "A" group was recognized as having more active tenant groups (for example, councils) and less crime and violence than its southern counterpart. Because of their cohesion, the residents in the "A" section were understood to have better maintenance by the CHA, timely service by sanitation and parks district staff, and more responsive law enforcement. Numerous reasons may be discerned for the north-south bifurcation of Robert Taylor. Whereas residents themselves will point to relative differences in tenant representation, gang activity, and police protection, others have cited the CHA's own practices. The journalist Nicholas Lemann writes that the entire housing development was constructed in four stages, and "by the time the last stage—the seven buildings at the southern end of the project between Fifty-first Street and Fifty-fourth Street—was under way, the Housing Authority's tenant screening procedures had begun to fray." Buildings lacking effective screening had the youngest population, the highest number of poor and nonworking families, and less vocal leaders.

Tenants' identification with particular territorial units did not stop at the border of the Robert Taylor Homes. It was formed in large part through their engagement with external entities such as political groups (for example, ward organizations) that canvassed buildings for votes, and pastors who asked constituents to bring their neighbors to church events. Most important, tenants' ties to particular areas in the housing development were the product of their interaction with government agencies, from whom they received most of their resources and services. These interactions were sometimes marked by contention and differences of viewpoint, and over the course of the 1960s, tenants' own vision of what makes for a safe, viable community would grow apart from that of managing agencies. They expressed their differences most often through the council officers in their buildings. In this manner, tenants' attachment to their buildings was strengthened not only by pleasurable activities such as flower planting or picnics but also by using their available representation—the Building Council—to send complaints to, acquire information from, and resolve conflicts with the many government agencies that administered their building.

The term "social space," coined by Henri Lefebvre, captures the interactive relationship of individuals to their built environment. People do not live *in* spaces per se, such as neighborhoods or cities, but they actively produce them and invest them with meaning and significance through their everyday interactions. In the early 1960s, when tenants came to Robert Taylor, there was no self-evident or natural association among those who lived in different parts of the housing development. In fact, many of the earliest tenants identified themselves in varying ways, often less strongly with the name of the housing development than with the name of the immediately surrounding community—for example, "Grand Boulevard," "Bronzeville," or "Washington Park." Only by sharing common circumstances and challenges, and confronting similar representations in the media and popular discourse—most of which were negative—did the housing development create its own identities. Even then, tenants differentiated themselves in the more particular and personal terms of their specific floor or building.

The concept of social space captures a modern antagonism between the administration of space for rational planning and economic accumulation, and the use of space for everyday purposes, that is, the "inhabiting" of space.[45] The institutions that make up the state are forever concerned with managing space, planning and re-zoning, efficient and rational usage of territories, and so on. Their logic—that of "abstract space"—runs counter to that of the people who live in the space and who may value a particular territory for reasons that have little to do with its planning or economic development potential, but that have more to do with their connectedness to it. This antagonism surfaced in the history of postwar urban renewal: whereas the city saw little of value in the ghetto except its potential for development, those living there had homes, support systems, and peer and kin networks that could not be easily replaced or recreated in a newly built territory. In the 1960s, as tenants struggled with the Housing Authority and other state agencies to define how spaces could be inhabited—whether they could sell goods or retain boarders in their apartments, and whether they could use their apartments for political organizing—the antagonism arose once again in the context of everyday life in the Robert Taylor Homes.

The divergent viewpoints of tenants and administrative agencies would become particularly acute by the middle of the decade. The strain of living in the largest public housing development in the world was visible in the declining physical upkeep as well as in the rising rate of petty crime and vandalism. Yet forces in Chicago were only increasing the demand for housing at the Robert Taylor Homes. At the core was the city's large-scale urban-renewal program that displaced thousands of residents from their homes and pushed them onto the public housing waiting list. The CHA was deluged with poor and working-class families who needed immediate shelter.[46] The applicant pool for apartments was growing so quickly that the Housing Authority had to reformulate its own management strategy for the Robert Taylor Homes and accommodate the surge of applicants; that is, the CHA had to abandon its social-engineering blueprint for the development and forgo a "mix" of poor, middle-, and working-class families.[47] Federally imposed stipulations further constrained the CHA's flexibility by forcing it to give priority to poor families. For example, the Housing Authority could not refuse an apartment in Robert Taylor to any applicant who earned less than $5,200 per year in favor of a middle-income client.

The Housing Authority could have adjusted to the influx by relocating black applicants across the city, but to preserve the status quo in accordance with the wishes of city political leaders, the agency did not offer black applicants immediately available housing units in white neighborhoods.[48] Instead, it gave them apartments in Robert Taylor and told them to accept the dwellings or remain on the waiting list for an indefinite time. The net effect was that Robert Taylor's 4,400 apartments would house far fewer middle-class families than the Housing Authority had envisioned, and the agency's aim to include middle-class, working-poor, and unemployed households no longer appeared feasible.

The rhythms of settlement also brought into relief the effects of site selection and design, which had hitherto been abstract notes and drawings on architectural blueprints. For example, out of a laudable desire to meet the housing needs of as many individuals and families as possible, CHA designers had made the Robert Taylor Homes an unusually large complex relative to other public housing developments in the city; that is, "about three-fourths of the apartments have three and four bedrooms, and about 1000 of these have one oversized room large enough for three or four children."[49] Unfortunately, the Housing Authority had not correctly anticipated the number of janitors, maintenance personnel, administrative liaisons, tenant advocates, and so on that would be required.[50] They struggled to find the best means to hear grievances, communicate with households, make resources available, and conduct physical upkeep. All the while, they were susceptible to the changing political winds in Washington, which could reduce their operating budgets by millions, often without warning. As the 1960s marched onward, their own dependence on the national political climate, on the health of the nation's economy, and on the prevailing mores and habits of their clientele would dramatically affect their own capacity to manage the affairs of the Robert Taylor Homes.

To compound these problems, economic downturns had cast residents into the ranks of the unemployed, and the majority of employed, two-parent households were starting to give way to single-parent, unemployed households. The networks, associations, and organizations that had emerged to help respond to household needs were facing growing challenges that went beyond the surveillance of children playing outside. Families were facing job loss, employed families had moved out and taken their resources with them, and tenant collectives that were ostensibly designed to provide minor comforts could not legitimately be expected to handle the needs of a disenfranchised populace. There were fears that Robert Taylor would move in step with the socioeconomic stagnation of the neighboring black belt. Tenants, the Housing Authority, the city government, and the media all acknowledged the need for quick action in order to ensure a successful community within this two-mile stretch of State St. However, not everyone agreed on the appropriate steps to ensure the viability of Robert Taylor. As the CHA sought funds for building modernization, the tenant body moved in an altogether different direction to ameliorate their growing distress. The 1960s imprimatur of organized protest for justice and civil rights crept into the housing development to transform the nature of tenant association, formal and informal. Tenants joined together in solidarity, and the shouts of parents became the voices of empowered citizens. The female head-of-household stood at the political vanguard. Domestic life become political labor.

The Rise of the Local Advisory Council

In 1966, the Housing Authority counted 27,400 people living in Robert Taylor (most likely a conservative estimate when one considers the seasonal, temporary, and off-the-lease people who passed through). The sheer size of such a new populace in a narrow land tract caused expected concerns but did not by itself pose insurmountable problems. Although there were maintenance exigencies, residents were coping with their new surroundings, and they used the Building Council, MOMS organization, and various informal support networks as needed. The Housing Authority's own Board of Commissioners may have responded to growing public criticisms of high-rise developments with admissions that Robert Taylor "should not have been built," but their daily correspondence, to themselves and to residents, reveals that the housing development was basically intact and hope was not lost that a vibrant mixed-income community might be created.[51] In fact, given adequate schools and recreation centers, political leverage, and a healthy community economy, one could argue that the housing development would not have suffered many of the manifest problems of its population density, instead resolving them in a manner similar to that employed in the dense residential environs in the city's North Side, upper-class, predominantly white communities.

Toward the end of the 1960s, all this would change as Robert Taylor showed signs of distressed physical upkeep and tenant-management disputes that were not adequately rectified through existing administrative pathways. The CHA had lobbied the federal government for modernization funds, but state bureaucracy moved at a

seemingly glacial pace and offered public housing tenants little so-
lace. By the end of the decade, calls for more efficient administration
played only a small part in tenant demands: residents had reframed
their concerns in terms of the nationwide struggle of blacks for justice
and equity. Their leadership adopted the language of "community
control," that is, the *lingua franca* of 1960s urban social protest
through which the disenfranchised demanded a more central role in
local affairs, whether school administration or street sanitation.
Words such as "tenant rights," "citizen participation," and "empowerment" began to color the language in the homes and public spaces
of Robert Taylor.

Not only had residents' rhetoric changed, but the tenant body was
itself created anew as the housing development felt the impact of the
nation's economic downturns. Increasingly, tenants spoke as people
thrust from the labor force onto welfare rolls and into the ranks of the
unemployed. As for the CHA, not only were its federal funding
streams decreasing, but there was declining national support for
high-rise developments, which seriously reduced the agency's options to modernize, fix equipment, and plan for the future. Taken collectively, these changes to tenants and the Housing Authority
indicated that Robert Taylor was caught in the maelstrom of a national social and economic movement far beyond its control.

In the middle of the decade, public attention to Robert Taylor
grew in accordance with the increasing popular concern with unrest
in the nation's ghettos. News stories on Robert Taylor and several
other of Chicago's largest housing developments appeared in
Newsweek, Time, Look, and other periodicals, and most often the features portrayed the developments as exemplars of the alienated
ghetto. Whereas residents did not always think of themselves solely
in relation to the housing development, that is, identifying themselves only as Robert Taylor tenants, their sense of collective uniqueness, what the sociologist Ruth Horowitz calls a "community
culture," was spawned in part by their treatment in the larger society.[52] The public heard of the challenges to "project living" but were

not always aware of the complex household and interpersonal dynamics in Chicago public housing. Titles such as "vertical ghetto,"
"$70 million ghetto," and "Congo Hilton" were clearly intended to
prey on Americans' fantasies about black poverty and to arouse interest in the profligacy of government programs.

The earliest, most popular exposé of the inner life of the Robert
Taylor Homes was written in 1965 by M. W. Newman, a well-known
reporter at the *Chicago Daily News*. His week-long series on life in the
housing development set the standard for popular and academic reportage for years to come, but even his well-intentioned commentary
showed the circumscribed portrait being circulated about Robert Taylor. Newman began the series with a tone reminiscent of Victorian
portraits of Africa, India, and other colonial recesses. Not a boat but
an elevator afforded him passage through Chicago's "Congo Hilton":

> We're stuck with [this bungling and hellish way of life] for 40 years to
> come . . . You step inside the elevator. It's dirty and gray and cold. In one
> corner is a pool of blood. In the other, an empty wine bottle. You press the
> automatic button and hope nothing more happens on your way up-
> stairs.[53]

Newman combined statistics with stark description to substantiate
his claim that Robert Taylor was far removed from the general citizenry. The housing development was a "death trap [where] the dangerous life is routine," one riddled with crime, "vandalism," "public
drunkenness," "teenage terror and adult chaos," and missing entirely
morals, civic responsibility, and respect for neighbors.

Although the week-long *Daily News* series sounded an alarm and
called attention to Chicago's newest community, Newman's portrait
was filled with inconsistencies. A trope for one article was the ex-
ceedingly high crime rate in the complex, yet Newman wrote that,
"actually, the incidence of crime and violence within Taylor is less
than in the adjacent community, according to Robert Harness of the
Wabash Avenue police district." Newman had included the testimony of a police commander who stated that crime rates attributed to

Robert Taylor were inflated because administrative records group together the development with its more criminally active neighbors to
the east. Elsewhere, he characterized the housing development as "fatherless" and as a den of illegitimate births and disillusioned
youth—for example, he describes a young mother as "so unrealistic,
lost, [and] half-literate" that "she had dreams of becoming an airline
stewardess"—but he ignored the lifestyles of two-parent families, the
majority presence (60 percent), as well as the contributions of leaseholders who held full-time jobs (50 percent).

Newman's perspective was not completely one-sided, however.
His attentiveness to criminality also included the voices of residents
who "complain that it's hard to get city police protection," and he
made sure to point out that "there are not enough private guards on the
site." Ultimately, although human interest stories on Robert Taylor—of which the *Daily News* series was the best crafted—created empathy for the plight of the poor, they did not always grasp the many
forces that were affecting the quality of life in public housing. Just as
important, they did not give readers a sense of the means by which tenants and governing agencies were trying to work alongside one another
to address mutual concerns and build a habitable community.

By the end of the 1960s, the declining physical infrastructure and
the near ubiquity of hardships for those living in Robert Taylor were
much more visible. At the root of the changes was the deteriorating
material status of black ghetto dwellers. The heyday of postwar national economic prosperity was over. The economy was stagnating
and employment rates for workers at all educational levels were falling as a result of mechanization, plant closings and relocations, and
recessions.[54] For urban blacks who did not have access to education
or training, there was little chance to take advantage of emerging opportunities in the white-collar trades. Lodged in the unskilled, service, and operative sectors, they experienced far greater job attrition
than other demographic groups in the 1960s. The prospects for blacks
to reenter the labor market were minimal; only a few of those displaced would find immediate employment, and even fewer would

find work that paid a living wage. Many simply dropped out of the labor force altogether.[55]

At Robert Taylor, the economic shifts were most visible in terms of household formation.[56] To make ends meet, households began to adopt sharing arrangements in which friends and relatives lived with the leaseholder. Edith Huddle, a tenant who came to the housing development as a young adult in the 1960s, offers one of the most direct assessments:

> It was like all of a sudden, well, maybe two years or so, but you had people losing jobs and they would just transfer the lease to their woman who had a kid, and she'd go on welfare and then her man and everyone else would just stay there. People wasn't trying to get away with nothing, it's just that they couldn't afford to live on their own no more.[57]

There was a corresponding change in the domestic role of adult males: with no jobs, many men had to live secretively with their partners in order to safeguard federal housing and public assistance subsidies. Newman and other journalists saw an apparently "fatherless" world, but they did not pursue fully the relationship of welfare legislation to the limited public exposure of men; reporters were also largely unaware of the changing ways men could contribute socially, emotionally, and economically to the public housing household, despite being unemployed and working off the books.[58] These were men who, according to Edith Huddle, "we [women] had to hide but that doesn't mean that they still wasn't a daddy to our kids."[59]

Robert Taylor's households were also growing younger. The age of the heads-of-households moving into the housing development was decreasing: in 1964, only 33 percent of the people accepting apartments were under thirty years of age; by 1970, the number would increase to 55 percent. With younger household heads came fewer two-parent families, that is, the number of families that the CHA defined as "normal" ("husband, wife and at least one child") declined precipitously from 2,615 (60 percent) in 1964 to 782 (18 percent) in 1973.[60] Curiously, although households were becoming younger in the latter part of the 1960s, the CHA recorded nearly an unchanging rate in the "average number of minors per family" for Robert Taylor from 1964 to 1973. Moreover, the "average number of persons per family" showed only insignificant declines, and the number of families with eight or more children also remained fairly high. How could nearly half of the heads-of-households be under twenty years of age by 1970, yet family size not show a correlative change? Surely, with younger parents one would expect fewer children and thus smaller families. By contrast and somewhat surprisingly, the available figures suggest that Robert Taylor continued to contain large families, that is, the impact of younger heads-of-households appeared minimal.

The statistics masked the fact that whereas in the early 1960s single large (one- and two-parent) families moved in at disproportionately high rates, by 1970 large family sizes reflected the tendency for apartments to contain several families spanning two or more generations. Another important factor contributed to the move toward multigenerational living in the housing development: residents charged that the CHA was giving preference to poorer and younger applicants who the agency knew would be moving into apartments with parents, aunts and uncles, friends, as well as the children of these adults. As one tenant recalled:

> You see, [the CHA] was letting in younger and younger people, who didn't have jobs and who just wanted to be "independent," you know, have themselves a baby and get a check each month. People with jobs was moving out when the place started getting bad, and all we're left with are children raising children. And that's when the problems started . . . Now, we [the older residents] have to live with them.

The Housing Authority was not entirely at fault, however. It had intended to conduct thorough tenant screening in Robert Taylor by forming screening boards of CHA staff and tenant leaders who would review applications and ensure that each building had a mix of families with different income levels, single- as well as two-parent households, some elderly and some younger leaseholders. But the agency was inundated with new applicants owing to housing shortages in the city, and federal housing regulations stipulated that an available apartment be awarded to residents on the basis of need. Both factors hampered the CHA's ability to screen and place tenants effectively.[61] Because Robert Taylor had larger bedrooms than most other housing developments, one consequence of the rushed screening process was that apartments were awarded to poorer heads-of-households who came with their own children as well as with the families of their kin.

By the end of the 1960s, then, Robert Taylor had moved toward a predominantly out-of-work, young population—formally single-parent households but often multigenerational—composed of wage earners who were not on the lease. This demographic composition did not help the community-building process. In a mixed-income development, where more than 50 percent of households were employed, individuals differed in their needs, and those with resources helped neighbors by sharing or simply by acting as psychological supports, role models, and embodiments of hope. After 1966, however, tenants were not simply seeking amenities from the Housing Authority as renters. Instead, most were unemployed, ghetto poor, single parents, and welfare clients for whom state supports were imperative for daily sustenance; indeed, "from 1966 to 1974 the percentage of tenants [in the Robert Taylor Homes] on welfare would double, although the overall population would decline."[62] They were living surreptitiously, and any particular household might be hiding some combination of men, boarders, or income. Tenants were also vulnerable because, unlike their employed counterparts, they could not easily pack up, pay higher rents, and move into a private-market dwelling. Their only real choice was to ensure that their needs were met in the housing development. (It should be noted that even for the employed, Robert Taylor was an attractive alternative given that local housing stock was dilapidated and few decent units were available.)

The visible physical deterioration of the housing development brought this new population and their emergent concerns into sharp relief. From failing elevator systems to rat-infested laundry rooms,

tenants and government agencies found a seemingly endless list of
problems. Many infrastructural issues had not been anticipated by
CHA management. Internal CHA memoranda reveal surprise and
consternation over the inability of the physical structures to with-
stand human use. Housing Authority officials admitted poor judgment in the design and construction of the Taylor Homes, the result
of which was costly, prolonged rehabilitation: sprinkler systems
could not reach all areas, so underground water lines had to be constructed; poorly built gallery fencing on hallways led to several children falling to their deaths, so floor-to-ceiling wire fencing was built
(the enclosed galleries gave the feel of a penitentiary, so much so that
the moniker "Stateville" or "Stateville Homes" was conceived by residents to signify the similarity of their buildings to the Stateville Illinois State Penitentiary).[63] The CHA also attributed some dilapidation
to the tenants themselves. Overused or broken playground equipment became a physical hazard, and fencing was required to reduce
use of grass and park space. In addition to excess demand, Housing
Authority officials argued that growing vandalism and abuse of physical facilities had taken their toll on janitorial and maintenance staff.
Tenants tore up gallery fencing, compromising the protection of the
railing on the external hallways; burglars repeatedly broke windows
and doors; and children who were unable to wait for the elevators
urinated or defecated in stairwells (the problem of adequate
restrooms was so severe that Reverend Martin Luther King Jr. included them—in all play areas and one for every third floor of the
high-rise—in the platform of demands that he submitted to Mayor
Daley in his famous open housing protests in 1966). Taken together,
the design flaws and excess demand caused physical deterioration to
reach levels that surpassed the ability of the Housing Authority's
physical plant to keep pace with maintenance and repair.[64]

The CHA was hearing growing resident protests over lapsing
maintenance. The authority was aware that the buildings needed
"modernization"—the term used by public housing officials to refer
to both physical improvements and the need to include tenants in

management decisions—and they tried with varying success to appease the dissatisfied. Their record is mixed and reflects to some degree two different sides of public housing management. The Board of Commissioners, composed of people appointed by Mayor Daley to monitor the financial portfolio of the CHA, was busy responding to the dominant ethos of all 1960s federal social policy, namely, "maximum feasible participation" of citizens in the decisions that affect their communities. From 1967 to 1970, the federal government's pressures on states and municipalities to be more responsive to the voice of the poor meant that, in public housing communities, CHA Board members had to include tenants more centrally in their management decisions or risk losing their federal funding. In that four-year period, the failure of Board members to do so was the chief source of criticism from federal housing officials in Washington, D.C.

While CHA Board members begrudgingly instituted plans for "maximum feasible participation" of tenants, another wing of the Housing Authority was faring better in its relations with the tenant body. This was the arm of the CHA responsible for managing the developments, issuing repairs, planning construction programs, and working intimately with tenant groups. Staff may not have fixed every problem, but at the very least they were committed to ameliorating physical deterioration and appeared willing to keep the lines of communication open with residents. Correspondence between the CHA staffers assigned to these duties—engineers and management directors—and William E. Bergeron, the federal government's "regional director" of public housing, reveals a continuous assertive campaign by the CHA to acquire federal funding for repair and renovation. CHA staff gave Bergeron detailed budgets and work plans and kept him abreast of the problems that affected tenant quality of life. In their internal correspondence, CHA management staff appeared quite empathic when discussing the difficult circumstances faced by residents, and they repeatedly stressed the need for quick ameliorative action. If an eviction notice was sent to a tenant, officials were careful to list the date and times of the incidents that gave them no recourse except to initiate lease termination. The following letter from Deputy Director of Management Gus W. Master is exemplary:

Dear Mrs.____,
A careful review of your file indicates several very serious incidents of undesirable conduct on the part of your son . . . The latest incident was of such a serious nature that your son has been confined to Audy home [a juvenile detention facility] . . . It would appear that your son cannot adjust to community living, and under the circumstances, if he returns to the home, in all fairness to the other families and the community, we would terminate your lease. You may, however, remain in residency until such time as you receive a termination notice.[65]

Wherever possible, CHA management officials provided warnings to tenants regarding repeated vandalism, criminal activity, or incidents of behavior deleterious to other families. In many cases, the CHA project "managers" fought off their own superiors' desire to impose lease termination and monetary fines. However, because their clientele included several thousand tenants, these managers could not adequately assist each person, and so they relied on tenant spokespersons—including, but not restricted to, council members—for information about individual households. They worked actively with these individuals to pass on information to tenants and to plan future activities, and when they received grievances, they responded as best they could.

At the center of the dialogues between the CHA and tenant spokespersons over the physical condition of Robert Taylor was the female head-of-household, most often a separated or unmarried woman (and usually a mother). Many of these women were already involved in local affairs as Building Council officers, secretaries of tenant organizations, Bible-worship group members, and informal Mama's Mafias associates. They knew one another as neighbors and peers, and they were prepared to sit on the front lines of the emerging tenant movements, demanding an improvement in the physical condition of Robert Taylor.

Edith Huddle, Louisa Woodson, and Cathy Blanchard were some of the tenants who became advocates for Robert Taylor in the late

1960s. Their introduction into the world of public housing politics appears in part as an unintended consequence of their earlier, less formal efforts to develop networks and associations for social, psychological, and material support. But their paths also seemed to be guided by broader political movements taking place in Chicago and across the country. Sometimes tenants directly imported to Robert Taylor lessons from their involvement in broader struggles, and on other occasions, their work in the housing development simply took sustenance from the spirit and energy of the Civil Rights era. As their efforts to weave the social fabric of community in Robert Taylor gathered steam and became more formally politicized, their relationships with one another shifted from friends and neighbors to partners, collaborators, competitors, activists, and co-organizers. By tilling the memories of those who participated in the community in that era, one can discern the general contours of the political movements occurring in Robert Taylor and their relationship to the wider world of Civil Rights and organized ghetto-based struggle.[66]

Women who were members of the Building and Resident Councils in Robert Taylor worked most actively with the CHA to discuss maintenance issues. Most of their dealings were with the side of CHA management that included project managers, engineers, and janitors. They speak empathically of the day-to-day work these CHA workers put into maintaining the high-rises. But they were less willing to tolerate the actions of the commissioners on the CHA Board. In the late 1960s, they expressed dissatisfaction with this high level of public housing administration. Council officers worked hard to help households by relaying information to the Housing Authority, but they felt removed from the CHA decision-making process. Edith Huddle, the council representative in her building, speaks of this dilemma in the context of the benefits that council members received in return for their work with CHA management:

> Yeah, well, we was getting our apartments fixed quicker [than most tenants] . . . I ain't gonna lie. But you also got to remember that not all of us

was like that, some of us weren't happy with what was going on. A lot of us was also getting pissed off with the CHA because they were using us, and they wasn't fulfilling their promises to give us our fair share of control.

Council members were in a difficult position. On the one hand, they tried to meet the growing demands of the tenant body by working cooperatively with the CHA and quieting tenant dissension wherever possible. But they were becoming more critical of the Housing Authority because of their own lack of influence over resource allocation, tenant screening, eviction, and fines. Mary Catrell, a Building Council president, argued that once tenants' grievances turned from requests for social programs—for example, picnics and field trips for children—to improvements to the physical condition of the high-rises, council members could not offer them much help. Hence, council officers were unable to balance successfully their role as effective intermediaries between tenants and management.

Council members could not ignore the tenants' increasing dissatisfaction with their role. They were being criticized by their own constituents at the same time that they had become frustrated with their own limited influence within the Housing Authority. Not all tenants would manifest publicly their frustration with the council representatives in their building. According to Carroll Woodson, "most of the people in my end [of the housing development] refused to get involved because they thought they would get kicked out if they got [Building] Council members angry at them." Carroll Woodson and Louisa Lenard were part of the early contingent that publicized disrepair as well as the perceived impotent role of tenants in CHA resource allocation. In doing so, they challenged not only CHA management but also their own representatives on the Building Councils. They had great difficulty enlisting broad tenant support for their cause. Fear of retaliation by the CHA kept tenants passive. This changed in time, says Woodson, but "only when they saw that we was serious, that they could make a change and didn't have to worry about getting evicted—because if they got evicted the CHA would've had to kick us all out. Then, you know, they started jumping on board, complaining about all sorts of things that we didn't even know was happening in their apartments." In the same conversation, Louisa Lenard recalled:

> We saw friends of ours that were getting kicked out of their apartments because they were late on rent. But we knew lots of people who hadn't paid for much longer, but they was in good with the CHA or the councils so they were OK. And in the beginning we just made it clear to others in the building that we were upset, and we told our building presidents in meetings.

Woodson and Lenard found themselves in a slowly expanding movement to protest against the CHA's maintenance failures as well as those council members who worked alongside CHA staffers. To help build grassroots support for their criticisms, Woodson and Lenard joined other tenants in writing letters, posting flyers, conducting door-to-door outreach, and speaking at townhall meetings.

In an early sign of their own frustration with the CHA, council members organized meetings for tenants independent of the discussions co-sponsored by the CHA and the council. According to several council officers, their assertion of independence drew hostile reactions from the Housing Authority. For example, Edith Huddle says CHA staffers disrupted the biweekly tenant meetings she held in her apartment, threatening her with eviction unless she agreed not to organize future council meetings:

> I was one of the first people to tell [CHA Commissioner] Swibel and all them other cats [that] they couldn't prevent me from meeting [with residents]. I brought in the Constitution. I said, "I have the right to free speech." You know what they did? They tried to say that we was communists, subversives trying to overthrow the CHA! They said we couldn't hold no communist meetings in our apartments.

To avoid eviction, Edith Huddle moved her meetings elsewhere—for example, to restaurants, churches, and the police station "community" meeting room. Other Building Council officers followed her lead, but they did so at some risk, argues Mary Catrell: "We was taking a chance, because we could've gotten thrown out [of our apartments]. Remember, lots of us still was living with our mens and working on the side, so we wasn't exactly angels or nothing."

The decisions by council officers to break ranks with the CHA was no doubt motivated by growing and more organized tenant criticism of their role within the tenant body. When Carroll Woodson and Louisa Lenard publicized tenants' displeasure with the Building Councils in the southern end of the housing development, Edith Huddle and Kim Walton were two of the council members they singled out. Council Officer Huddle lived in the 210 building, next door to Lenard and two blocks away from Woodson. Council Officer Kim Walton lived in 205. The posture adopted by Woodson and Lenard was courageous because they criticized two of the most powerful council officers in the housing development, both of whom were popularly understood to be in good favor with the Housing Authority. To confront the two, Woodson and Lenard began distributing petitions and displaying accumulated signatures as evidence to allay the fears of those residents who worried that they would experience retaliation if they participated. As more residents signed, more felt willing to join in, which helped to bring others aboard, and so on. Woodson and Lenard organized tenant meetings and brought the petitions to Edith Huddle and Kim Walton to show the two council officers that tenants were willing to explore collective challenges to the CHA. By that time, both Huddle and Walton were themselves considering a more critical posture toward CHA management, and seeing that support existed among tenants for such a move, they forged an alliance with Woodson and Lenard.

In other areas of the housing development, residents formed their own opposition to the Housing Authority, but not always via a union of council officers and tenants such as the alliance of Huddle, Lenard, Woodson, and Walton. Michael Wilson, who lived in the northern end of the housing development, suggests that each building in that area mobilized against the Housing Authority to different degrees, and some lacked entirely any formal organization:

> It was like this, you see. You had people like Ms. Walton, my momma, they were all in good with the CHA and they was getting all kinds of shit from residents because they wasn't doing nothing. But no residents fought against them, because they was too scared. But in other buildings, residents just wasn't gonna cause no trouble because they didn't want nothing happening to them. So they was just left out of it, until the petitions started going around and they felt, you know, more comfortable, they started protesting and marching. Then, you had these buildings, it was like people was dead or something. No one gave a damn, even when people was protesting and meeting, these people was sleeping.

The use of "petitions" signaled a shift in the type of organized protest practiced in Robert Taylor. The petitions were effectively public statements in which tenants formally called into question the status of the council officers throughout Robert Taylor. They also signified that the tenants in Robert Taylor, like residents of other developments across the city and the country, were expressing their discontent and demanding what they perceived to be their rights. Indeed, some tenants were involved in the Civil Rights movements over citywide housing discrimination; others were helping to register voters, protesting school funding, and joining in national "sit-ins" and pickets of stores. Through immersion in these broader movements, tenants in Robert Taylor learned how to frame their own political platforms. What began as a "fight just to get services for our buildings," says Carroll Woodson, became "all about affecting how CHA was spending their money, because we started realizing this is our community."

The cross-fertilization was evident as public housing tenants throughout Chicago adopted the *lingua franca* of "community control," which by the late 1960s was well known in American ghettos. Across the country, the federal government responded to ghetto protest by developing community-based institutions that promoted resident participation in local affairs. These "neighborhood initiatives" were to serve as a "vehicle for assimilating socially and economically marginal people into the larger society."[67] They would rebuild the institutional sector of isolated communities, and with such institutions, the nation's disadvantaged would, it was hoped, gain access to external resources (grants, loans, and investments) that could support service provision, educational programs, and housing construction in their neighborhoods. A broad range of federal support was distributed to create such "community control," ranging from direct financing to allocations of manpower and legislative decrees. However, irrespective of the form of federal assistance, recipient ghetto communities faced a common challenge when using neighborhood initiatives: whereas ghetto dwellers preferred to create direct relationships with the federal government, city officials wanted all federal support in local communities to be managed by their own representatives—mayors, in particular, feared a loss of power should residents acquire unmediated access to federal funds. In public housing, this provoked a power struggle between city officials (including the CHA Board) and tenants, both of whom tried to use the Department of Housing and Urban Development (HUD) to their favor.

This triangle of tenants, CHA Board members, and HUD officials would define "community control" debates in public housing from the late 1960s until 1971. After 1968, tenants made more explicit requests of their Housing Authority and recommended their own changes to existing management policies. The particular concerns varied by housing development but could include a direct voice in capital expenditures, veto power over prospective tenant applications, and freedom to organize and meet with residents without the need to inform Housing Authority managers. The most important tenant advocate was the Chicago Housing Tenants Organization (CHTO), a network of tenants living in nearly all of Chicago's public housing developments (no recorded history of the organization exists, but most tenants recall the CHTO's birth as circa 1969). To publicize the condition of public housing, CHTO members sponsored marches and demonstrations, held meetings with Housing Authority management, and provided testimony to federal government committees as well as to the National Association of Housing and Real Estate Officials (NAHRO).

The CHTO's efforts to gain legitimacy as the voice of public housing residents were being supported by HUD's own housing programs. After 1967, HUD had initiated a massive "modernization" program across the country to respond to two sets of pressures: (1) "the serious deterioration and obsolescence of much of the older public housing stock . . . which local authorities lacked the financial resources to correct" and (2) the "growing discontent and alienation from the community of low-income people, generally, and of indifference and dissatisfaction with their homes among many public housing tenants."[68] Local authorities such as the CHA could apply for modernization funds to repair buildings and to put into place administrative structures that incorporated residents directly into the decision-making process.

In the late 1960s, the Chicago Housing Authority tried to comply with HUD pressures to increase tenant participation in public housing management. CHA Chairman Charles Swibel supplemented the Building and Resident Councils with Executive Councils and Executive Boards that were also composed of tenants. Swibel wanted to signify that tenants had moved up in the CHA hierarchy and were closer to the point of decision making. (An additional motivation for the CHA Board arose because HUD was considering a proposal to link formally its disbursements of federal modernization funds to signs of increased tenant involvement in local housing authorities.) In the meetings between public housing tenants and HUD officials, tenant leaders suggested that Swibel's "executive" councils and boards were not democratic given that tenants were not allowed to elect their own representatives to the two bodies. Swibel did offer elections, but he allowed only CHA-appointed tenant "officers" to elect the Executive Board and Council members instead of enabling the tenant body to elect the members directly. Eventually, Swibel admitted that this management structure was not democratic and agreed to put a new structure in place in which tenants could directly elect their representatives.[69] However, until he did so, he remained adamant that he would listen only to those on the Executive Council, since it "had been in existence for many years" and its members were "representative" of the tenant pool.[70]

At NAHRO's Fifth National Housing Workshop, held in Chicago on September 9–11, 1970, congressional leaders met with Chicago public housing tenants, their spokespersons, and tenants from housing developments across the country who were protesting the management policies of their respective local housing authorities. Tony Henry, the director of the National Tenants Organization, made spirited requests that the federal officials take seriously the demands of Chicago's tenants:

> The [CHA] has refused to give [CHTO] any kind of recognition . . . The director of the housing authority would only deal with the group of advisory councils that have been set up with the help of CHA, which meet at its call and behest and which, even the housing authority admits, are so ill representative of the tenants in the housing authority that they're going to call for new elections at the end of the month.

With no Housing Authority officials to answer to the panel, public housing tenants took over the platform and listed what they perceived to be the CHA's abuses and injustices. They stressed that the current "boards" and "councils" of public housing residents created by CHA Chairman Swibel were not representative of tenant composition. They also complained that the elections instituted by Swibel were a "sham" because residents were not adequately informed of the timing of elections nor of the type of power and authority that elected tenants could hold in the CHA management structure.[71]

The tenant struggles yielded several gains for residents of Chicago's public housing, but in some respects the victory was pyrrhic. The most tangible accomplishment was a "Memorandum of Accord," signed by Chairman Swibel on April 8, 1971, that allowed Chicago's public housing tenants to elect their own leaders directly. The document gave them considerable powers to determine both day-to-day

CHA operations and decisions over policies and expenditures for their respective housing developments. In order to obtain the "Accord," HUD pressured Chairman Swibel by threatening to freeze $8.2 million in modernization funds for the CHA unless the agency's Board agreed to institute changes to its management system.

The Local Advisory Council stood as the formal sign of the success of Chicago public housing tenants, but it was the new relationship that tenants had established with their federal representatives that would be most important as they forged habitable communities in the years to come. The federal government had made clear that it could intervene to force the CHA to accede to tenant demands and would be a watchdog over CHA management. The Local Advisory Council–Central Advisory Council (LAC-CAC) tenant management structure grew out of the 1971 Accord. In each housing development, tenants within a building would elect a "building president" to a Local Advisory Council, the board that offered input into the CHA's policies for that complex. And in each development, tenants would also elect a separate "LAC president" who would sit on Chicago's Central Advisory Council (CAC), the board made up of the LAC presidents of each public housing complex across the city. The president of the CAC would actually be a board member of the Housing Authority, with full privileges to attend the meetings of the CHA Board of Commissioners and vote on budgetary and management decisions.

Even before the first election of Local Advisory Council leaders on July 11, 1971, questions were raised as to the LAC's potential utility for public housing tenants. Residents fully expected the mayor and the Housing Authority to play an active role in affecting the composition of the LACs in order to create less resistance to the CHA's own policies. After the 1971 election, it appeared that they were successful, for the first cadre of elected tenant leaders did not seem to include many people who had vocally challenged the CHA's policies and programs: of the 732 tenants elected to CHA councils in 1971, 665 "were sponsored by the previous councils established by [CHA Chairman] Swibel."[72] Suspicion of election improprieties and CHA pressure tactics were bolstered with the election of the first Central Advisory Council president, John Marlow. As a precinct worker for the powerful Cook County Democratic Party chairman George Dunne, Marlow was one of the many street-level faithful who worked for elected leaders in exchange for patronage (in the form of a government job). Although he denied such accusations at the time, years later Marlow admitted that the CHA wanted to ensure control over the LAC-CAC and that the agency achieved this goal by limiting the information that residents received about the election and by sponsoring its own candidates: "[CHA] didn't want the radical group [of tenants] to take over the tenant councils. After years of looking back, I see where the CHA had put up a buffer," said Marlow.[73]

With the election of CAC President John Marlow and the overwhelming retention of tenant leaders who were already allied with CHA Chairman Swibel, controversy swirled as tenant leaders and the media accused the Housing Authority and Mayor Daley of co-opting the new management structure. Although there was precedent for such co-optation, the evidence did not fully support the tenants' accusations.[74] For example, tenant leaders at the time alleged that insufficient information was passed out to tenants concerning the rights and responsibilities of the new management system.[75] And, as Carroll Woodson argued, many tenants "didn't really understand that we had a lot of power and so they just didn't come out and get involved. [They] kept looking at the LAC like the councils that was there in the past, you know, they felt like they should elect the people who the CHA already liked because they might get evicted or thrown out if they didn't."

Tenant complaints regarding the noncooperative posture of the Housing Authority were not entirely founded; indeed, tenant leaders also shared a role in disseminating information to tenants regarding the new electoral process. Cathy Blanchard (a tenant leader who did not initially run for LAC election) suggested that current tenant leaders who chose to run for office in the new elections were insecure because they did not know what percentage of the tenant population actually supported them; thus many of them did not motivate residents to come to the polls and were themselves unwilling to provide accurate information to tenants: "These so-called [tenant] leaders," said Blanchard, "[they] knew that if everyone voted, then they may not get elected, so it wasn't just CHA that was hiding information, it was our own people that wasn't being straight with us. They just wanted people to vote who was going to vote for them."

———

Notwithstanding the fact that the tradition of Chicago politics seemed to have quickly penetrated the new public housing management with accusations of corruption, cronyism, and patronage, the blemishes could not take away from the significance of the new democratic management structure for the tenants of the Robert Taylor Homes. The Local Advisory Council framework may not have spelled an end to their struggle and hardships, but it did indicate that if the welfare of their families and their community was threatened, people in the housing development would come together to demand justice and improve the quality of life. Significantly, it was predominantly women who led the fight to better their communities through service on councils and by ensuring that adequate safe play areas were available, laundry rooms were clean, stair lighting was sufficient, and so on.

The Local Advisory Council was received with optimism, but also with some hesitation. The housing development had clearly passed through two phases, one relatively successful and the other problem prone, and no one knew precisely what the LAC would bring. Even the harshest critic of the Housing Authority would have to admit that before 1966, the original vision of public housing was being realized in Robert Taylor, that is, the development was a waystation wherein families of varying needs and capacities could decrease the sense of isolation they felt in the community in general and increase the self-efficacy of the less fortunate in particular. Tenants and CHA staff, on the whole, had amicable relationships, and the Housing Authority possessed the resources necessary to make repairs and meet demand as best they could. When they could not rely on external resources, tenants cooperated to put in place informal as well as formal methods to address their needs. At times, they formed associations and organizations to systematize their support functions, but more often, they relied on casual, non-institutionalized methods of caregiving and exchange.

After 1966, however, large-scale changes made it clear that the networks and associations that residents had devised would be insufficient mechanisms if they were to continue making public housing a viable prospect. Not only had their own personal circumstances changed with an economy that worsened the status of black urban laborers, but they suffered a new approach to public housing that seemed to be characterized by decreasing budgets and a local Housing Authority unaccountable to their interests. The LAC was the symbol of their successful struggle to ensure that their collective voice, produced through democratic means, would be part of the governance of federal public housing programs in the next phase. The council did not eclipse the strength of their informal associations, and they would have to continue cooperating with one another on a casual, peer basis in order to improve many aspects of their lives. It did signal that their friendships and alliances could be mobilized for more organized, political actions if events warranted.

The activism generated by these public housing–based social movements might appear minor given the extraordinary civil rights battles being waged in other quarters by African Americans, but it was not.[76] To be sure, unlike sit-ins and street marches, the protests by tenants of Robert Taylor and other Chicago public housing developments did not always provide them entrée into public political discourse; nor did they necessarily afford them the attention and support of their elected leaders. However, the movements by Edith Huddle and her compatriots were significant turning points in the black American experience. Their labors deserve recognition for thoughtfulness, courage, and willingness to demand that government and city work on their behalf. Their actions were as politicized as the more public street rebellions and demonstrations, but they occurred outside the political process.[77] Public housing tenants made their homes, the personal, into the political. They were heads-of-households, partners, mothers, citizens, and workers, many of whom had lost employed husbands, suffered their own job losses, and were left to make ends meet primarily with government support. (Although some men were involved, the struggles were predominantly carried on by women.) Their collective labors would make their home into a site of work, politics, and "reproductive" labor, that is, simultaneously a space for living and for protest.[78]

Although many of the issues that the tenants contested were specific to Robert Taylor and to the public housing lifestyle, such political activities were not entirely localized phenomena. The work of public housing tenants to improve their communities highlights the intersection of local politics and politics on a larger scale.[79] Tenants met with municipal and federal officials and listened as their leadership articulated demands in local and national media. Moreover, many cite a connection between their local support of tenant rights and their participation in social movements around the city. Whether they participated directly, watched intently, or lent their moral support, tenants catapulted themselves into the wider world through their involvement in, and observation of, home-based community politics. As they labored, participants experienced a sense of self-worth and a raised local consciousness common to many women in different spheres in the 1960s. Those in Robert Taylor did so not by breaking through glass ceilings in the corporate sector or in the campaigns of electoral politics. Instead, they fought for their rights and for the welfare of their households in the corridors and apartments of a public housing development. Time would tell whether their efforts to make a livable community in the Robert Taylor Homes would bear fruit.

2 | Doing the Hustle

By the dawn of the 1970s, the Robert Taylor Homes had become a familiar part of the Chicago landscape. The ceremonial tributes of black and white civic leaders that once welcomed the housing development had ceased, and Robert Taylor was just one of many settlements in Mayor Daley's "city of neighborhoods." Yet Chicagoans looked to the future of the Robert Taylor Homes with nervousness and skepticism.[1] In the public's eye, the image of the housing development had changed significantly from a waystation for many different classes of African Americans to a refuge for predominantly poor, single-parent households, most headed by females and many with boarders, hidden spouses, and relatives living off the books. In Chicago, news of public housing had been dominated by the contentious struggles between tenants and the CHA over management policies. Public housing residents gained a democratic victory—the creation of the Local Advisory Council management structure—but they had grown distrustful of city officials, and they were even becoming alienated from their own elected political representatives. Government officials, realizing the extent of resources that would be necessary to provide adequate services and upkeep, admitted that perhaps Robert Taylor should not have been built.[2] Similarly, on the national level, housing experts such as Catherine Bauer, who pioneered the movement for federally subsidized housing, agreed that high-rise complexes should no longer serve as a template for low-income housing. Given the political turmoil, it was difficult to understand how the promise of public housing as affordable and temporary shelter for the disadvantaged could be realized in places like the Robert Taylor Homes.

The new decade confronted the Robert Taylor community with mounting problems. With high unemployment, welfare rates near 70 percent, and half of its school-aged population dropping out, the housing development was an extreme case of the growing disenfranchisement of inner-city African Americans from societal institutions.[3] The employed families that once provided buffers to their poorer ghetto neighbors were no longer living in Robert Taylor, and for that matter, they had been slowly moving out of ghetto communities throughout Chicago. Household vulnerability, rooted in economic impoverishment, was exacerbated by an increasingly unsafe living environment, marked most visibly by rising vandalism and crime. Safety and security issues were rife, owing in part to the housing development's distressed relations with the outside world. Tenants were going through a period of strained relations with municipal police and CHA officials, both of whom suggested that the physical environment was inhibiting them from providing effective law enforcement in the twenty-eight high-rises.[4] This created resentment and a sense of abandonment within the housing development. Robert Taylor's troubled dealings with the police were not unlike what many predominantly black communities in the city were experiencing. The result was an inability on the part of the residents to control criminal behavior, provide redress, and procure effective law enforcement within their community.

Yet despite the mounting security problem and the few perceptible signs of hope that the Robert Taylor Homes would be a viable community, the residents of the housing development in the 1970s were very optimistic about their future. The residues of the 1960s empowerment struggles, in which tenants were awarded a greater role in public housing administration, offered at least a promise that "project living" would continue to be fulfilling and perhaps even improve in some respects. "It was the glorious seventies," "we were living large," "everybody had their little hustle going on," "it was the good life, even if we were living in the projects": these and other phrases are the stock of tenant recollections of the 1970s. Tenants in Robert Taylor were working with one another to improve their material welfare and to make their housing development a safer place to live. They were "hustling," to borrow a much-used term from that era, and their colorful endeavors involved intricate, and sometimes unstable and secretive, systems of sharing and exchange. Some helped them to make ends meet, others afforded security in daily intercourse, but all were part of the struggle to live "the good life."

Law and Order

In the early 1970s, black urban America was in motion. For the "advantaged" segments, civil rights victories had opened up employment opportunities in government and corporate sectors.[5] African Americans strode forcefully into the middle class, into City Hall, and into previously inaccessible non-ghetto neighborhoods, hoping to realize the American dream of prosperous communities that their white counterparts in suburban quarters had experienced two decades earlier. Politically, this contingent made some of their most noteworthy advances in that decade, their national leadership having moved from "rebellion to reform" by entering into municipal and corporate boardrooms where once they sat at the door.[6] For the less educated black, however, social mobility was not so evident. A sizable proportion of lower-middle and working-class blacks continued to toil as blue-collar workers in steel, railroading, meatpacking, and other industrial and manufacturing trades. But overall, black unemployment was still "two to three times that of whites," and blacks were "grossly over-represented in the low-skill, low-paying jobs."[7] For those who lived in ghetto communities, work was irregular and government subsidies were necessary to make ends meet.

Robert Taylor and other ghettos were a far cry from the social and economic firmament of the rising black middle and professional classes, but even they could boast some new resources and opportunities during the 1970s. To supplement welfare payments, ghetto dwellers turned to work that they hid from social workers, public aid officials, and Housing Authority managers. Those receiving government subsidies were forbidden to augment their income, but by exercising some caution, tenants in Robert Taylor could earn extra money from off-the-books and illicit exchanges. Black and poor, they stood on the lowest rung of the municipal political ladder, but in the new public housing tenant-management system (the Local Advisory Council), they had a liaison to the wider world that might work to help them meet their needs or exercise their political voice. In short, households in Robert Taylor were developing means to procure necessary goods and services in the absence of formal resources and poor relations with city political leaders. The good or service might vary, ranging from hidden income to receipt of a city service, such as timely apartment repair. But they were all part of a common effort on the part of tenants to live safely and securely in the housing development in light of the emergent social and economic hardships.

The viability of Robert Taylor was dependent on two activities, namely, locating material resources so that households could make ends meet and working with others to fulfill collective functions such as social control, policing, and law enforcement provision. Concerns regarding law and order in Robert Taylor were palpable early in the 1970s, and many of the earliest creative attempts to seek alternate means of ensuring the welfare of households, that is, those outside formal institutional avenues, arose in the context of policing and security. Indeed, if tenant struggles for "community control" in Robert Taylor defined the spirit of the 1960s, then the challenge of maintaining order in the housing development was the most frequently discussed aspect of social life during the 1970s.

At the start of the decade, there was nearly continuous public debate as tenant leaders joined with black city politicians and advocates (such as the Afro-American Patrolman's League, an organization of black law enforcement officers) to demand adequate protection.[8] With their new status as part of the CHA management, the elected LAC leaders pressed for better protection for residents, including increased police patrols inside buildings and quicker response times by municipal police.[9] The CHA and municipal police were sincere in their attempts to provide protection, and they tried to import into Robert Taylor some innovative tactics that were being used in other public housing communities. At times, tenant leaders worked directly with administrative agencies. But residents also developed their own, indigenous mechanisms to supplant the efforts (or lack thereof) of law enforcement officers, and thereby to secure their personal and collective safety.

Resident portrayals of law enforcement in Robert Taylor during the 1970s typically present an uncaring, dispassionate police agency serving a hardened community. The most famous is *Brothers,* a collective memoir about growing up in Robert Taylor during the 1960s and 1970s:

> It was hard out there in The Life, a Darwinian jungle, and you had to be stone cold to survive. You had to be prepared to kill if it came to that. You had to understand that the police didn't care who killed who in the ghetto, long as they were both black; the police just let the one on the ground die and bust the one still standing . . . [I]f you kept it in the neighborhood, brother against brother, you weren't going to do more than five, six years in the joint anyway.[10]

On several occasions, the authors emphasize the prevalence of aggressive tenant behavior in an environment of economic instability and minimal law enforcement. In another popular study of the Robert Taylor Homes, *The Promised Land,* Nicholas Lemann applies the "control and containment" theory of policing to the housing development. Lemann singles out incidents in the late 1960s and early 1970s in which residents fired at police (and at ambulance personnel and social workers) from the high-rises. The reasons for doing so are diffuse in Lemann's account, but tenants suggest that the charged atmosphere citywide between police and the black community, combined with tenants' growing distrust of government officials *in toto,* led to conflictual and sometimes violent exchanges when officials entered the housing development. As a result of their unfriendly welcome, police reduced their patrols and left Robert Taylor to cope with a diminished law enforcement presence for the next two decades.

The role of policing in Robert Taylor was following established patterns of law enforcement activity in Chicago's African-American neighborhoods, some of which could be traced to the early twentieth century.[11] By the mid-twentieth century, police activity on Chicago's South Side, like that in black neighborhoods in many large American cities, was characterized by an intimate relationship between law enforcement and illegitimate entrepreneurs.[12] Police directed underground commerce to the black belt, and African-American pimps, speakeasy owners, and policy kings—who managed underground gambling in the black ghetto—worked closely with black and white municipal officials to keep a watchful eye over commerce.[13] Both democratic machine leaders and black political brokers benefited from the lucrative underground trade, and only on rare occasions did law enforcement officials break up the ghetto's vice, bootlegging, and gambling operations (when they did, their action was usually politically motivated, specifically, a response to an order from a white machine politician to punish a black broker who did not cooperate with the machine). In this way, the ghetto community's receipt of law enforcement services was mediated by the nature of political relations between the ghetto and the wider world and therefore subject to any changes in the political climate of blacks and whites.

The existence of a black political broker who could mediate between the two worlds did not guarantee equity in the receipt of law enforcement services. Although police officials were intimately aware of underground ventures in the black belt, from the post-Depression years until the 1960s, "police continued to under-police black areas" in terms of adequate patrols and protection.[14] They responded infrequently to resident calls for help, offered minimal assistance, and at times harassed and brutalized blacks with little fear of censure or punishment. Blacks organized rallies to protest such lawlessness as well as the discriminatory hiring and promotional practices of police departments. But without the support of black leaders (especially those who were in a brokerage relationship with the ruling Democratic machine), there was little chance for public exposure of police injustice or redress. There was internecine warfare between blacks who demanded more responsible city services and their leaders who moved far more slowly on politically volatile issues such as policing. By the mid-1960s, police agents in Chicago were growing frustrated with an alienated population and with the social unrest that followed. A federal investigation would identify the police as a hostile presence in the ghetto.[15]

Periodically, in the late 1960s and early 1970s, city politicians would work alongside public housing tenants to fight police harassment and demand more effective, daily enforcement provision.[16] Police officials had upset tenants by admitting that they conducted only minimal patrols in public housing developments, responding only to "calls for help."[17] Housing Authority officials tried to rectify these lapses in service provision by immediately issuing promises of increased manpower allocations for public housing, but it remains difficult to gauge whether police activity actually improved (or increased) as a result of popular pressure and public outcry. That the promises and protests were repeated every few years does not itself indicate that law enforcement activity changed significantly during the 1970s.[18]

There were several types of law enforcement officers in the Robert Taylor Homes. City police were in contact with tenant leaders and responded to requests for assistance. Less often, they used "beat" patrols in and around buildings to meet residents. Some municipal police were assigned to special units, such as "gang intelligence," and they entered the housing development on potentially dangerous assignments during which they might encounter an armed group. Municipal law enforcement was accompanied by the Housing Authority's security personnel, typically guards who patrolled areas outside the housing development buildings.[19]

The allocation of municipal police and housing development security was not meeting local demand in Robert Taylor, but the problem of adequate policing cannot be blamed entirely on the number of officers. Law enforcement itself was not solely responsible for rising crime and insecurity, for they faced great difficulties trying to serve and protect Robert Taylor. Police explanations at the time pointed to the constraints imposed by the built environment. Law enforcement officials argued that they could not easily enter some areas and so were unable to respond to criminal activity. They did not feel safe approaching the buildings because they stood exposed in the external spaces—on several occasions, residents fired at officers and threw things at them from galleries and windows. Officers were particularly leery of the higher floors of the sixteen-story structures because of faulty elevators, temperamental stair lighting, and dark corridors that gave perpetrators a distinct advantage when police ascended. Neither tenant criticism nor CHA and police responses to it took into account physical attributes of the housing development that neither party could alter: tenants argued that police either were not present or did not respond quickly to calls for help; police pointed to the unsafe structure of the housing development rather than to any racial or class-based bias as a deterrent to their work.

For their part, CHA officials repeatedly told tenants that their vandalism and improper use of physical facilities—such as allowing children to ride on top of elevators—were compromising safety.[20] They responded to tenant accusations and legal challenges of improper security provision by arguing that tenant "carelessness," "negligence," and "indifference," and not necessarily maintenance or ineffective police protection, were responsible for their feelings of insecurity.[21]

In this context, a quasi-beat patrol evolved in which policing was intertwined with the social networks and authority structures of the tenant body. Indeed, it appears that a minimal level of collaboration actually characterized contacts between tenants and law enforcement agents. Specifically, some tenants developed a relationship with law enforcement either through their successful entrepreneurial activities, their position on the LAC, or because they had a relative or a friend on the police force. Police often turned to them during distress calls and in routine investigations. When presented with a list of prominent tenants in the 1970s, Ottie Davis could describe each individual's status with local law enforcement, including the nature of the relationship, whether any monetary or in-kind payoffs were employed, and the subsequent effect for overall community security. By way of summary, he stated,

> Back then, the community was real tight, you see, so you couldn't really just be making money without paying no cop 'cause everybody knew everybody. If you was selling, like I'm saying, you had to be friendly with folks [in law enforcement agencies]. See, most of these [tenants] I'm talking about was on [public] aid, so the cops was the ones who could keep [public aid monitors] off your backs if you was making money. Everybody got their little take, so you know everybody was happy. And if you was selling dope and you ain't had no cop protection, or you're not tight with LAC, then I call cops on you and make some money, you dig?

The entrepreneurs Judy Harris, who ran a "brothel and gambling parlor," and Momo Davis, who operated a car-repair service, were on Ottie Davis's list of residents whose stature rested both on their capacity to generate hidden income and on their ability to evade police investigation. Harris admitted to such clout, as did Tom and Jake Adams, and Kenny Davenport. Each revealed some form of informal association with a law enforcement officer—their claims were generally supported by other tenants—that helped them to reduce competition from other hustlers and to evade arrest and incarceration. For example, Tom Jenkins lived with his family in the 226 high-rise until 1976, when he left to become a city police officer. Tenants suggest that gang recruitment was absent and property crime and theft rare after 1976 because Tom and other police officers periodically met with his family and other residents. In the words of one tenant, "That's why my momma moved into 226. She heard Tom was a cop and she knew the building was gonna be safe. And it was until his folks moved out [in 1979], then all hell broke loose. [Why?] Because they didn't have no LAC leader."

Kenny Davenport and Ottie Davis point out that the brokerage mechanisms did not enable residents to respond to all the transgressions and illicit activities that affected their lives. Describing the cooperative relationships, Kenny states, "[The whole thing] was not really organized, you dig. It was just that you knew that if something went wrong, police may not take care of it right away, and if you really needed help or something, you didn't call police first." Informal relations with police were a practical means of working with a city agency that people generally distrusted and from whom they did not expect timely service. The deployment of a mediator or a broker became a creative strategy by tenants and their leadership to elicit a police response, in part an adaptation to a limited police presence but also a product of their prevalent belief that law enforcement was best approached through a local mediator. Althea Jefferson, a tenant, argued:

> People didn't like police, that's why you tried to call LAC before calling over to them. Black folk always been this way, we just don't trust them. It was like for the first time back then we had a way of getting them to come and help us. Not like today, you know, when the gangs just get in the way, you know, make the police mad at us.

In any high-rise there may have been a number of tenants who could influence the behavior of law enforcement. In Kenny Davenport's building, the first person to demonstrate such an ability was an elderly man who ran a gambling racket from his first-floor apartment; after he died, the mantle passed to LAC president Edith Williams: "Hell," said Davenport, "we never saw [the police] when I was growing up. You had to worry more about LAC if you was doing something illegal. Just look who caught me: Edith Williams, not the police . . . She was the one who called them to bust my ass." Slightly farther to the south, in the 205 building, Shadie Sanders proudly described the liaison service that her LAC building president provided: "As I keep telling you, [Kim] Walton ran things around here. Yeah, you could call the police, but you'd do better telling her. She'd call the police and they'd come right away."

Whereas entrepreneurs might have personally benefited from an association with police officers, their counterparts in the Local Advisory Council, whose day-to-day work brought them into regular contact with law enforcement personnel, translated their connections into widespread benefits for the tenant body. These elected leaders formed a first point of contact in police investigations, but the relationship was symbiotic. By currying the favor of police, elected tenant leaders could control entrepreneurial activity, assist households directly, ensure safe use of public space, and affect the traffic of strangers. All this could enable them to reduce the likelihood of loitering as well as property and personal crime. Police also benefited from this arrangement, says the LAC officer Edith Huddle: "[The police were saying] 'We can't stop crime around here without your help.' See, what they was really saying was that they couldn't do nothing inside these buildings, 'cause there was too many of us and they couldn't get around the building." Supporting Huddle's statements above, Lucille Rick argued that "police ain't interested in coming here for every little thing that was going on, so me and Edith and Caroline and [other LAC officers], we just tried to, you know, make sure that they came when really bad stuff happened." Tenant leaders wanted to retain control over social activity in and around their buildings, and law enforcement wished to be liberated from the difficulties of providing enforcement in a densely populated, vertically structured development. Louis Wood, a police officer who was assigned to the housing development, supports this view and admits to the benefits of using a tenant as a preliminary point of contact:

> We [in the police department] was under a lot of stress, you see, because the residents were criticizing us, Robinson [the president of the Afro-American Patrolman's League] was trying to make police work better. But no one understood how hard it was to go in these buildings. Everyone saw you coming in, so they could hide what they were doing. You had no choice but to call a resident, someone you knew, or maybe have them give you information. There was no other way to protect the people.

Their status as brokers did not prevent LAC representatives from vigorously pursuing a responsible police presence in Robert Taylor, which from their perspective included not only rapid response to emergency calls but also daily "walking patrols," additional black hires on the police force, and police attendance at community activities and townhall meetings. Their protests were supported by police admissions of neglect. One officer said quite openly to a reporter:

> There is no question that [Robert Taylor] do not get the same protection the more affluent and middle class communities receive . . . The area encompasses almost 20 city blocks but only two police cars are assigned to it as regular beats. On domestic calls the police often won't even show up. The only calls they seem willing to respond to are those in which they can flex their muscle, such as the report of someone with a gun.[22]

The willingness of elected political representatives to listen to tenants' cries depended, in LAC President Edith Huddle's view, "on whether they was up for election or not, because if they was, they just came down here all the time saying how they was gonna listen to us, make it safer." Notwithstanding her cynicism, throughout the 1970s there were intermittent attempts by these political leaders to call attention to security matters in Robert Taylor. Through protest and lobbying, tenant leaders were winning the attention of the nation's politicians. The publicity campaign received a jolt in 1974, when Congressman Ralph Metcalfe declared a "complete and total local, state and federal crackdown on crime in the Robert Taylor development." Congress responded by allocating hundreds of thousands of dollars to improve security at Robert Taylor.[23] In 1978, a $250,000 "holistic" crime prevention initiative was launched by the U.S. Law Enforcement Assistance Administration. That same year, $600,000 was allocated, and at one point, a House subcommittee "agreed to come to Chicago and investigate security problems at Robert Taylor."[24]

National exposure and increased federal funding legitimated tenant accusations that security had lapsed in the housing development and introduced additional resources into the community—much of which came in the form of expanded CHA security and municipal law enforcement patrols. Some of the federal support also targeted programs that attempted to enhance tenants' self-efficacy in security matters. As an example, the Housing Authority had developed a program in the early 1970s that paid tenants a modest sum to police themselves.[25] In these "vertical patrols," tenants walked through the buildings to monitor crime, knock on doors and conduct surveys of apartment conditions, and pay attention to strangers or people who loitered in hallways and stairwells. These patrol officers would then notify Chicago police of problems and provide them with witnesses during investigations.

The CHA's strategy to place responsibility for policing on the tenant body was not altogether novel. Since the early 1960s, CHA management had asked tenants to monitor behavior on their floors, report transgressions, inform police of violators and lawbreakers, and help protect children walking to and from school. In some respects, the federal support for the vertical patrols in the late 1970s was ironic because residents had already developed such procedures on their own. They had found ways to supplant ineffective law enforcement provision by relying primarily, and at times solely, on one another. The creative relations they forged with police were one example, but there were other, more elaborate indigenous enforcement schemes that were helping to maintain social order.

Indigenous Enforcement

Indigenous law enforcement in the Robert Taylor Homes was rooted in the social networks of residents. The ties among neighbors and friends had formed initially in the 1960s as residents helped one another watch over children. By the 1970s, they became important means by which to publicize incidents of theft, assault, or burglary, and to locate alleged perpetrators, whom tenants could then report to law enforcement personnel. In many of the high-rises, tenants developed interesting techniques to raise the safety levels for their constituents. In the buildings closest to Twenty-ninth St., that is, those under the watchful eye of Kim Walton, Edith Huddle, and Wyona

Wilson, tenants cite the most vigilant and sophisticated examples of indigenous social control, including community "watches" and reserve militias.

In the 210 and 218 buildings, for example, residents give credit to Wyona Wilson for creating a method of redress, a scheme that they praised and offered as evidence that "women always controlled men around here." Wilson noticed that numerous men were living in the buildings but were not being reported to the Housing Authority by leaseholders. With Judy Harris's help, she asked these men to locate individuals suspected of different transgressive acts, ranging from burglary to domestic abuse to "snitching" on the police. She asked the men to inflict punishment or obtain an apology—"which, to be honest," Wilson contends, "was harder to get from these wife-beaters." In her jurisdiction, a two-block area south of Twenty-ninth St., a tenant could report an infraction to either of the two women (or to LAC members), who would in turn relay information to the men, many of whom passed the day in open spaces. These off-the-books residents already lived in fear of the Housing Authority managers and so were eager to cooperate to safeguard their concealed status. Because of their extended tenure in the public spaces of the housing development (they had to use inner spaces with care since they were not on the lease), the men were privy to local information exchange. Typically, one of the men would respond by gathering other males to locate the suspect in question. Michael Minnow, an elderly gentleman who has been living in Robert Taylor off the books for nearly thirty years, recalls his tenure in Wilson's militia:

> Oh, you didn't want to mess with these women [Blanchard, Huddle, and Wilson]. Lot of us was living with our women, you know, but we wasn't on the lease. They was getting [public assistance], right. So we had to keep a low profile. So we did anything they wanted. Yeah, that meant we beat the shit out of niggers who was beating up women, or stealing, or just causing trouble. Hell, we'd be sitting in that parking lot and someone would come down yelling at someone else for stealing something. That's all we needed to hear!

Minnow revealed that the practice spread with varying degrees of formality to other buildings in the housing development (north and south of Twenty-ninth St.), and that present-day efforts by the LAC and street-gang members to help tenants locate and punish suspects simply follow from this precedent: "You know what [the gangs are] doing now, Prince [a gang leader] and his boys, helping these women find those niggers [who beat up women]? Shit, we done that a long time ago, and better!"

By employing personal networks and indigenous enforcement efforts, residents could deal a blow to several types of harmful or threatening behavior. For each, one can discern specific methods for enforcement and prevention: group patrols and watches were typically more suitable for locating incidents of fire, theft, and sexual abuse inside buildings; tenant leaders called public meetings to gain information on the whereabouts of suspected criminals; a phone call to a broker who had connections with police officers was the preferred strategy for rapid response to violent crime. As a means of deterrence, most procedures were suited for behavior in public and semi-private spaces. It was rare to hear of tenants who used them within apartments to prevent attacks from spouses or lovers (although once the incident occurred, they could use their neighbors to catch the offenders).

Tenants repeatedly mentioned informal networks of friends who inhabited public spaces in Robert Taylor for leisure, recreation, or to wait for prospective employers. These "watches" in the 1970s resembled the Mama's Mafias of the 1960s, that is, the networks of caretakers who supervised their children on building floors and in play areas. Describing the "watches," Judy Harris states, "We always couldn't stop niggers from stealing or beating each other up, but we wasn't living like animals, like they was in The Grave [three physically isolated high-rises known for drug trafficking and gang activity] down there. Everyone looked out for shit, 'cause we knew that you just had to if you was living up here. Anything could happen if you wasn't careful." Tenant leaders occasionally mobilized these public groups for their own investigations of criminal activity. Edith Huddle argues that a tenant leader knew "who was hanging out where and why, and we knew who we could call on if something was wrong." If, for example, a burglary occurred, Huddle would "make [her] rounds [in her building] and talk to the ones who was respected"—pressuring them to give information or cooperate in her own investigations. In this manner, through their repeated use by tenant leaders, the informal watchdog role of such men became an institutionalized part of the process by which residents maintained order.

Inside the five white buildings, in the semi-private spaces, the surveillance included the Mama's Mafias—the most casual means of surveillance—as well as the "tenant patrols," the more formal group administered by the Local Advisory Council with monetary support from the Housing Authority. For tenant patrols, the floor captains typically recruited volunteers to walk through buildings, making note of strangers in hallways, groups that loitered in stairwells, and rabble rousers in lobby areas. During their walks, tenant patrol volunteers might discover a woman who had been beaten or an apartment that was being burglarized. In some cases, the patrols and watches were closely linked to entrepreneurial activities: Judy Harris employed tenant patrol volunteers in her building to provide security at her brothel. For contract enforcement, Tom and Jake Adams hired tenant-patrol volunteers to watch the lobby of the 210 building and extract money from individuals delinquent in their auto-repair payments. And Paulina Collins, a tenant who sold homemade lunches, paid patrol officers in her high-rise to deliver her baked goods and collect receipts from customers. Moreover, the patrols continue to be invaluable means for tenants to observe social interaction and locate incidents of crime inside the buildings.

Indigenous enforcement was by no means universal, and predictably, in those regions of the housing development where there was greater tenant cohesion or where charismatic leaders worked arduously to help households, tenant enforcement was stronger and more effective. Consider, for example, the Twenty-fifth to Thirty-third St.

corridor. The two buildings near Twenty-fifth St. suffered a near absence of tenant enforcement: "I tried to help [people living near Twenty-fifth St.] when I could," said Kim Walton, who lived south of the street. "But gangs was just too strong and folks didn't know how to help themselves." In these buildings, LAC officers were inactive and many floors lacked a floor captain or advocate who could act as a liaison to the wider world. Citing similar reasons, residents of the three buildings that formed "The Grave" recall a fairly lawless space, where neither indigenous enforcement methods nor police and security personnel effectively provided protection for households.

Tenants do not portray their enforcement efforts as complete resolutions to Robert Taylor's security problems. Such schemes were unstable and could engender conflicts, especially when tenants confronted perpetrators directly and took matters into their own hands. At Judy Harris's brothel and gambling parlor, much of the conflict stemmed from the security personnel she hired (gang members and illegal boarders), many of whom would use their status as license to harass women. Unruly gamblers and burglars often accosted tenant-patrol members who walked through hallways, many of whom were single women and all of whom were unarmed. A personal tie to a police officer may have increased the likelihood of a law enforcement response, but it was by no means a guarantee. Many of the schemes depended on social relations that could change overnight, quickly eliminating any attached security-related benefits. In effect, the indigenous schemes were a trade-off for a community that suffered ineffective mainstream police protection. That is, tenants could continue to devise short-term methods that provided immediate assistance and redress, or they could put their efforts into guaranteeing a more committed city and CHA police presence. Charles Deacon, a CHA security officer and resident of Robert Taylor in the 1970s, says that this choice was "not really a choice at all":

Remember, police weren't really able to do much around here. It was just too many people, so you worked by yourselves. And yeah, you pissed off lot of police because you was trying to do their jobs, but really, lot of my friends [on the police force] didn't much care. Lot of them felt that you was doing them a favor because they didn't want to walk up in these buildings. So it was not really a choice at all for people living here. You just found ways to solve your problems and you hoped police would treat you better, later on.

For the tenant body in general, there appeared to be several advantages to internal policing. Many of the enforcement schemes were dependent on the active use of public spaces, and conversely, they also promoted continued use of those spaces. The existence of various collectives, including groups of tenants who sat together in parks and parking lots, small groups of gamblers or drinkers occupying areas in front of buildings, tenant patrols, and LAC members who monitored public traffic could foster the general feeling that local behavior was being observed and monitored. People in public spaces might be called upon to conduct security; alternatively, they might volunteer information or manpower—for example, notifying tenant leaders that they had witnessed criminal activity.

The indigenous enforcement schemes did not fully take the place of mainstream law enforcement. Indeed, law enforcement agents continued to have a visible presence in the community, albeit one that was a shadow of the role they played in the city's white neighborhoods. In this context, self-enforcement was an imperfect substitute, but one that spoke to the creativity and resolve that residents displayed to address their needs when formal resources were lacking. A less instrumental benefit of the innovative use of tenant policing was thus to provide a feeling of self-confidence. There may have been crime and vandalism during that decade, but individuals also expressed a deep sense of control over their local habitat.

Tenants' perception of themselves as able to take active steps to address conflicts and instabilities did not derive solely from their fulfillment of security-related needs. It resulted also from their innovative work to procure basic material resources for their households. Such labor required to secure their well-being, what residents refer to as their "hustle," included the generation of income as well as the creation of a safe living environment. The two were deeply related since hustles could include illegitimate and sometimes dangerous work, such as drug trafficking or prostitution, that threatened personal safety and required tenants to respond in some manner by resolving disputes and stemming conflicts. Thus it is not surprising that many of the same actors, such as the LAC, who played an instrumental role in helping to fill the gap left by a negligent police force would also exert an influence in the arena of "hustling."

The Underground Economy

There is no better word than "hustle" to capture the informal and clandestine processes of exchange, sharing, and support in Robert Taylor and other ghettos at the dusk of the Civil Rights era. The hustle was only partly an act of necessity. It was also an expression of determinism and self-efficacy, writ at the level of everyday community life, for those who did not have access to the opportunities opening up for more educated black Americans.[26] "You had to have your hustle on. Everyone was hustling around here, just like in the movies," says Kenny Davenport, describing his involvement as a high school graduate in the underground economies in Robert Taylor:

> Today, shit, I got to pay people to watch my ass, because people will kill you for nothing. Wasn't that desperate [in the 1970s], I guess, and gangs wasn't everywhere, controlling everything. You could make a little something, help out your family you know, and everyone was doing it. Shit, my momma, her old friends were hustling, selling cookies, walking around, sell[ing] their clothes.

For Davenport—who labored in the 1970s as a gang's hired enforcer, as a car mechanic, and as *the* pimp in Robert Taylor"—and other such small-time ghetto entrepreneurs, the compunction to hustle was reinforced by the aura of celebrity afforded such practices by Hollywood and the media. In the 1970s the pimp, the dealer, and the madame were popularized as the doyens of the black ghetto underworld in a genre of film and literary aesthetics called "blaxploitation," which gave to the purveyors of food, drugs, and labor in Robert Taylor an unexpected validation.[27] Hustling was a way to participate in the "American success dream," wrote the anthropologist Bettylou Valentine in her study of the Blackston urban ghetto. It was a dream "rarely realizable in the ghetto, [but] still strong enough to keep Blackston people hustling."[28]

Hustling was given credence by the glamour of films such as *Shaft* and the novels of Iceberg Slim (for example, *Pimp*) and Chester Himes (for example, *Cotton Comes to Harlem*), but its backbone for ghetto dwellers was the realities and the relationships of their communities. Without the presence of customers, lookouts, loansharks, suppliers, johns, borrowers, enforcers, and police officers, all related to one another via ties of enmity, transaction, and alliance, there would have been no basis for hustling and the lure of blaxploitation to make their way into the day-to-day world of the ghetto dweller. At the community level, hustling was not simply the act of exchanging a good or service, but also part of an "underground economy" of goods and services that would become central to the overall security, welfare, and identity of the tenant body.[29]

Hustling, then, was more than a blind adaptation to poverty; it was also a cultural practice through which individuals developed a sense of who they were in relation to their local community and to the wider world.[30] Hustling acquired part of its significance and meaning from popular cultural symbolism. Mythic figures, such as Richard Shaft, the protagonist in the blaxploitation film *Shaft,* were based on the lives of real ghetto hustlers (New York's "Bumpy" Johnson) and were known to millions of Americans, black and white, who looked to them as models. On Chicago's South Side, equally well known hustlers, such as the gang luminary Jeff Fort, had become celebrated icons of outlaw capitalism, looked up to by youth who saw them as part of the wave of blacks who overthrew the Mafia's historic control of the ghetto underworld. Hustling, as Kenny Davenport suggests, was a means to identify with these successful and widely admired black men and women. In an impoverished community such as Robert Taylor, hustling garnered attention and even praise because nearly all households were needy and a successful hustle was certain to benefit friends and neighbors. All housing development residents were close, socially and spatially, to people who actively benefited from underground dollars.[31] Even if they had not participated directly in these casual and covert schemes, they often did so indirectly, via household members who worked off the books or who had undue influence with public aid officials. Consequently, hustling was a significant part of life and survival at the Robert Taylor Homes.

A wide range of creative activities that generated income and yielded social support qualified as "hustles." Exchange of legitimate goods and services, such as car repair or homemade baked goods, was "underground" because residents did not report their income to government agencies, such as the Internal Revenue Service, police, and public aid. Other unreported income could derive from illicit goods and services, such as narcotics and gun trafficking, gambling rackets, street- and apartment-based prostitution, and bribery of government officials. In any single household, both could be present alongside socially legitimate forms of income (including public assistance), and any given resident might be involved in one or more forms of trading simultaneously.

Hustling differed according to its location. Trade within the buildings (that is, in laundry rooms, apartments, lobbies, vacated apartment units, day-care centers, stairwells, elevators, and hallways) was more private and so was not usually subject to police action. The most lucrative activities were organized gambling, prostitution, and the sale of homemade, stolen, and illicit goods. But tenants could also benefit from opportunities to earn income made possible by the CHA, such as operating the laundry rooms or selling sundry items inside the buildings. These, too, were subject to the ability of individuals to curry the favor of CHA officials and obtain work. Hence they too were part of the terrain of hustling. Typically, the CHA seemed to award part-time employment opportunities to an existing organization with which it was already working and giving small programming contracts, such as the LAC or Mothers on the Move in Robert Taylor, but individuals could occasionally influence the process through payoffs.[32] Remarking on how women made money in the early 1970s, Lucille Rick states, "Oh, don't listen if they telling you [that] you couldn't do a little something to get that job. I managed the laundry in my building for years, and it was because I was friendly to CHA, paid that man, Mr. Williams [the CHA staffer who managed her building], maybe twenty dollars a month from the money I made there. Then, he just let me do what I want with the rest. That's how it was, you just made your way, found you a little something to get by." Rick listed other tenants living in the buildings near her own high-rise who also used a similar favor or payment to a government official to win the position of laundry room manager, day-care operator, or convenience store clerk.

Outside the buildings, in the alleys, external lobby spaces, parking lots, sidewalks, and concrete expanses, another component of the underground economy flourished. On both sides of Twenty-ninth St., there were adequate open spaces for tenants to conduct car repair, sell homemade and stolen items, offer high-interest loans, and discreetly peddle illicit goods. The stores and recreational areas attracted customers and offered plenty of space for people to park their cars and shield their clandestine activities. Gypsy cabs waited outside stores, hairstylists came to the Twenty-ninth St. Elementary School parking lot with folding chairs and clippers, laborers stood on the corner of Twenty-ninth St. and Elm St. to solicit off-the-books work, and painters and those specializing in home repair advertised their services in front of a local hardware store. Several community stakeholders actively helped tenants find hidden income, but for a price: a local pastor helped to locate illegal social security cards for tenants who wished to avoid taxation, but he asked them to bring more people to his services; the owners of several small mom-and-pop stores staffed their facilities with off-the-books tenants and, by doing so, avoided theft and vandalism; and according to Kim Walton, "a friendly CHA manager would help you find part-time work for a little cash or if you washed his car."

Hustling included not only activities that might help households to get by in times of crisis, but also potentially destructive activities that threatened personal and household welfare. Drug and alcohol use only exacerbated the troubles of tenants out of work and psychologically ailing. Moreover, by violating the income-supplementation prohibition that accompanied government aid and public housing leases, hustling could lead to the removal of family members or eviction of entire households from their apartments. Certainly, the income or the services generated by secretive transactions could help mitigate poverty or fill the void where a formal avenue might be unavailable; however, there could be less welcome side effects of the constant presence of addicts, hawkers, customers, "shadies," and underground politicos.[33]

Some activities, such as drug distribution and prostitution, were detrimental for the community overall because they jeopardized the use of public space. The underground brought strangers into buildings, thereby creating safety concerns for a populace that controlled its environment through ongoing surveillance of public behavior. Arguments and physical altercations were common, and there was always the possibility that verbal disputes would escalate into more pernicious violence. These conflicts may not have been easily resolved through the brokerage schemes that were forming. It is understandable, then, that some tenants would feel that the growth of hustling was more a nuisance and a threat to peace and safety than a mark of progress for the community.

Tenants formed a moral compass to distinguish the myriad forms of hustling, but one that was not based solely on the nature of the activities, that is, whether they were deemed illegal according to the law. Some practices may have been illegal, such as payoffs to a police officer, but they could take place in such a way, with minimal public exposure, for example, that residents did not feel threatened; conversely, other practices, such as large-scale car repair in the parking lot, may have been fully legitimate, but they brought car and pedestrian traffic into common areas and so compromised safe passage. Just like any other system of exchange, hustling required at least a minimal set of rules, codes of conduct, and mutual consensus among those involved for it to operate in a predictable manner and not completely threaten social order. In Robert Taylor, such a structure provided a framework for the many different forms of hustling to become an established part of daily social life.[34] In the layout of the housing development, constituent buildings and regions had already been organized on the basis of types of resident groups, degrees of safety and antisocial behavior, and levels of maintenance and vandalism. These "social spaces," formed in the 1960s and 1970s, would contain the flourishing underground economy.[35] The older territorial distinctions would be reconstituted, all in ways that reflected the infusion of patterns of sharing, exchange, and income generation. As a consequence, tenants' exposure to the destructive and constructive elements of hustling and their sense of its threatening, permissible, and morally reprehensible aspects would be expressed not only as an attribute of the good or service being traded, but also as a product of where hustling occurred, who participated and in what manner, and whether and to what degree the activity was socially controlled.

As hustling settled into the social fabric of Robert Taylor, different areas of the housing development became known for particular forms of peddling and trading—people knew where to go to trade, sell, or purchase a specific good or service, whether material (for example, car repair) or political (for example, advocacy with a municipal official). The hints of a regulatory apparatus could be discerned as unique and sometimes peculiar methods of taxing, price setting, and codes of conduct coalesced. Moreover, tenants devised ways to respond to the social annoyances of hustling. For example, some individuals commanded influence and respect through their role in mediating exchanges or through their ability to police the underground and ensure safe areas of intercourse. They would mimic their mid-twentieth-century predecessors—the black "brokers"—by serving as a resource for households and a stabilizer of the underground activity in the housing development.

The activity occurring between Twenty-fifth and Thirty-third Streets illustrates the social, spatial, and political dimensions of underground activity in Robert Taylor. Notwithstanding internal distinctions, this region of the housing development had a reputation for inadequate maintenance and upkeep, high rates of vandalism, and poor political clout with the Housing Authority. The area was divided by Twenty-ninth St.: to the north, between Twenty-fifth and Twenty-ninth Streets, sat five white buildings; to the immediate south, between Twenty-ninth and Thirty-first Streets, there were five red buildings; and farther south there were three white buildings that constituted "The Grave." As a major thoroughfare, Twenty-ninth St. was important for the livelihood of tenants. To the west, the street led into a major freeway, a small police outpost (removed in 1980), and finally a predominantly white community. Within the two-block stretch of the Taylor Homes, the north side of Twenty-ninth St. hosted a commercial complex with two restaurants, a medical clinic, a grocery store, a beauty salon, and a winding contiguous parking lot that was a popular meeting place. Follow Twenty-ninth St. eastward and there were more stores, bars and lounges, social service agencies, and churches all the way to Lake Michigan several miles to the east.

Among the five white buildings to the north of Twenty-ninth St., the 205 South Main St. high-rise (hereafter "205") was the social center. Kim Walton, the elected tenant representative who served on the tenant-management board (that is, the Local Advisory Council), was an enigmatic figure who lived on the top floor of 205—"so that I can be closer to God if my people need me," she explained. As the "LAC building president," Walton took very seriously her role in shaping the quality of life for the approximately one thousand people in her building. She also accepts credit for socially integrating all five white high-rises north of Twenty-ninth St. Together with two other tenant leaders in that area, Shadie Sanders and Paulina Collins, Walton had organized recreational leagues, informal watches over children and strangers, protests against local merchants, emergency loan funds, and various social activities. Their early and active role in promoting the cohesion of tenants in the five white buildings would propel them into a position of power and authority, eventually facilitating their control over many of the hustling activities in their area.

To the south of Twenty-ninth St., the 210, 218, and 228 buildings, all colored red, formed the heart of another five-building collective—the 230 and 231 buildings sat on the periphery and bordered the high-rises that belonged to "The Grave." In those high-rises, Cathy Blanchard worked with tenant leaders Wyona Wilson, Louisa Lenard, and Edith Huddle to organize residents and plan activities in ways similar to their neighbors to the north of Twenty-ninth St., with whom they were fast becoming rivals. As with their counterparts to the north (Walton, Sanders, and Collins), their involvement in organizing social activities made them naturally suited to become involved in the hustling that took place in and around their buildings.

"Each floor [of a high-rise] had something going on," said Judy Harris, who was in her twenties and living in 218. Judy's brothel and gambling parlor was considered by numerous tenants who lived in that area to be a symbol of hustling in the 1970s, and it exemplifies the different roles individuals could play in an underground activity. In Judy's parlor, attendants conversed at a cash-bar and danced to music or lobbied LAC officers—and of course women came to find johns to escort to their apartments. Judy described the layout of underground activity in 218:

> Different floor captains had their tastes, so on the fifth floor you had soul food cooking, below that it was marijuana. You had gamblers between the seventh and the ninth, in the stairwells, and you could always find a game. And let's see, on my floor and up above you had people whoring and pimping like crazy, but I was the best one and drove all them out of business pretty quickly!
>
> Oh yeah, and you had [Louisa] Lenard making African-style clothing, and then Mary Watkins was making clothes for babies on the same floor,

and every weekend you could just walk up and down that damn floor and go clothes shopping. See, that was nice because lot of us didn't have cars so we couldn't drive to the stores. And people who stole stuff, like shoes or shirts, they'd bring their shit to that floor too, so you had like the Maxwell Street Market [a famous city flea market] going on right here.

As Judy Harris points out, the availability of homemade clothes and food within the building gave residents an opportunity to save on transportation costs—especially over succeeding years as stores closed and residents had to travel considerable distances to purchase these items—and they could use in-kind payments and barter arrangements in lieu of cash. These credit systems became invaluable when tenants were awaiting the arrival of their welfare payments: in the days before the checks arrived, "when money was tight," said Judy, "it really helped that you could pay folks with promises or maybe by giving them something you made, or something you stole, instead of having to give money."

North of Twenty-ninth St., Paulina Collins's "baked lunch" sales paralleled Judy Harris's "brothel and gambling parlor" as a popular symbol of the underground. Paulina had come to Chicago in the 1950s from rural Mississippi and moved into Robert Taylor in the early 1960s with two newborns. Soon after her arrival, she sold boxed lunches to supplement her public-assistance payments, doing so almost continuously until the 1980s, when she bequeathed the business to her daughter, Missie. In her building, she was not the only one selling lunches, but "she was the best." Paulina formalized her operations by hiring tenants in her building to help with the cooking and packaging (in exchange for free packing materials, she allowed a local mom-and-pop grocery store to send advertisements inside the lunches). Her customer base included tenants as well as janitors, construction workers, CHA management, and police officers. The floor captains in her building would take orders outside the local commercial complex in the morning and would return there with prepared lunches in the afternoon. Paulina formed relations with other entrepreneurs among the five white buildings, such as hairstylists and baby-sitters, and a symbiotic exchange developed wherein each advertised the goods and services of the others in her network.

Twenty-ninth St. had become an axis that differentiated underground activities occurring outside buildings. At times, entrepreneurs on either side would compete with one another by attracting pedestrians and cars that passed along that thoroughfare. An exemplary contest was that of Tom and Jake Adams's car-repair service to the south of Twenty-ninth St. and the repairs offered by Momo Davis—Ottie's brother—to the north. Tom and Jake are brothers who spent their youth and young adult years in Robert Taylor during the 1970s. They moved in and out of the legitimate labor force throughout the decade, most often to part-time menial positions, but they turned to car repair full time in the mid-1970s when the demand for their services grew. Momo Davis used the parking lots to the north of Twenty-ninth St. for car repair as well as for sales of licit and illicit goods. Momo's operation competed with Tom and Jake's repair service for local demand. Based in different parking lots, the two parties engaged in strategic price gouging, and they resorted to tactics "like spreading horse shit or used oil all over the lot so nobody would bring their car there!" Momo was in good standing with several tenants who had connections with municipal police officers, and in return for free merchandise, the tenants would help facilitate a police raid on Tom and Jake's operation. Police officers intervened on several occasions, but Tom and Jake always managed to resume their business by using the influence of their own tenant representatives. "We paid our LAC [representatives] real good, so they'd keep the pigs off of us," Tom recalls. In fact, he suggests, his LAC representatives and those in Momo's territory colluded with one another to raise the ante and extort greater "payoffs" from the two parties. Others report similar payments to LAC members, many of whom were already developing relationships with law enforcement officials as part of their overall task of raising security levels.

Although levels of surveillance and regulation varied from territory to territory, the officers on the LAC were the primary overseers in nearly every area. The watchdog role played by the LAC was a natural outgrowth of its creation in 1971 and its involvement in other matters of tenant safety. Edith Huddle, an LAC building president, said, "I didn't have time to help no one else but [the] 210 [building] because people in our building began having problems with their apartments and they wanted a lot of stuff done from us." LAC representatives saw themselves as responsible for monitoring safety and maintenance in their respective buildings, including how and for what purpose people used semiprivate areas and surrounding spaces. They saw the need to manage economic activities as an extension of that responsibility.

Thus, some LAC leaders developed an interest in hustling because it benefited their buildings and residents, but most of the time they themselves stood to gain from such activities. For example, leaseholders who did not accurately report household members would placate their LAC building officers with bribes or public support in elections in order to evade detection. As one LAC officer stated, "I didn't ask for payoffs from all these niggers in my building, only if they was living with their mens, because I was supposed to tell CHA about that, so I could've got in trouble. Lot of these men was making money, you know, hustling, but I didn't ask them for nothing, except to be quiet and respect me." Other tenant leaders demanded support or monetary kickbacks not only from unreported household members but also from gamblers, purveyors, and homeless people who used stairwells and insulated areas within the buildings.

LAC officers justified their actions by claiming that they needed to maintain a hospitable living environment. They could not ignore hustling, says Martha Harrison, an LAC officer, because hidden exchange was a potential threat to safe public intercourse: "It was your job, if you was on LAC, you had to know everything going on, and people selling stuff, trying to do their little hustle, you had to keep it all under control, that was your job." Although some leaders suggest that they intervened only to the degree that hustling affected the quality of life for their constituents, nearly all LAC officers admitted receiving some payoffs from their tenants and others who hustled in their jurisdiction. Certainly, many felt the need to oversee hustling as a way to protect themselves against accusations by the CHA that they were unfit to govern. If they were forcibly deposed from office, they would lose not only their status among tenants, but also their part-time wage and the opportunities to find employment for friends and family members that could result from their connections with CHA officials.

The payoff of tenant leaders—which included monetary and in-kind payments such as promises of babysitting or use of a car—was one of the earliest means to control the activities of underground entrepreneurs. The scheme followed the Local Advisory Council's bureaucratic hierarchy. The floor captains (usually appointed by the LAC building president) would monitor local entrepreneurialism and collect payments ("payoffs") from the entrepreneurs on their respective floors. According to Louisa Lenard, who lived in the 218 building, each floor captain would then "have to give some of the payoff to the [LAC] president [in his or her building], but they still got to keep enough to help out with their kids or buy some groceries or something." The LAC building president would keep some of the accumulated revenue as personal income but would also channel funds into the common pool that assisted residents during times of financial emergency, such as rent delinquency and bail posting. (In the 1970s, six buildings in the Twenty-fifth to Thirty-third St. corridor had such funds.)

By the middle of the decade, the "livelihood processes" of barter, sale, and exchange could be differentiated by space (where they occurred) and mode of regulation (for example, which tenant leader commanded payoffs, and the level of involvement on the part of the LAC).[36] In buildings with a strong leader and residents who were in close contact with one another during the political demonstrations of the 1960s, informal economic schemes developed more quickly and proceeded with less likelihood of police interdiction. Charles Deacon, a CHA security officer who worked and lived in Robert Taylor at that time, described the conflation of tenant representation and economic activity:

> The LAC wasn't just about getting apartments fixed. Take this area [looking at a map of the housing development]. Here [pointing to Kim Walton's building] you had everyone selling shit, working off the books, not reporting their income, and never getting caught because their LAC person was on the ball. But just a bit further away [north of Twenty-fifth St.], these people were busted every day because the [Housing Authority] manager may not be paid, or they weren't as organized, or maybe they were just more stupid, too—you can't rule that out. They could have been selling dope [out in the open], where the people over [in Ms. Walton's building] knew not to stand outside.
>
> That's really how it started once LAC came to power. And remember, [security guards and police] weren't making that much money and this place was a gold mine. Who cared if [tenants] complained about officers on the take, I mean, that's just how it was back then. They were poor, they made money, and we [law enforcement officers] made money.

The officer's statement is matched by other tenant assessments which suggest that influential tenant leaders (most often those in an elected capacity on the LAC) could both facilitate entrepreneurial activity by limiting competition and smooth relations between residents and law enforcement agencies.

Beyond the income that might accrue for some households, the underground economy did not seem to have consistent and widespread benefits for the tenant body as a whole. Disputes between entrepreneurs and the occurrence of illicit transactions threatened the safety of public space. One tenant wrote a letter to CHA officials, expressing her inability to move about the community and run errands because of such activity:

> I'm having trouble with these people on this gallery day and night . . . I speak to the [housing] office regularly but no respond [sic]. It is getting out of hands here, I have trouble like shooting fireworks in front of my door, gambling, smoking, putting radio speakers . . . in full blast, beating up my little one. I can hardly get the guards when I call.[37]

Clients who searched for prostitutes or who came to buy narcotics could become unruly and initiate physical fights—as they did on many occasions, according to Judy Harris, who hired friends to provide security at her brothel and gambling parlor. Residents were apprehensive about relying on tenant leaders to stabilize underground activity, given that their personal welfare, and that of other household members, might be determined by the capriciousness of the local LAC officer. Nor was there much recourse if one felt aggrieved or injured as a result.

Sometimes individuals who did not want to accede to a tenant leader's demands for payoffs argued and resisted. Tom and Jake Adams "[had to] start off by paying all sorts of people coming around saying, 'You got to pay me to work here.'" "Like who?" I asked. "Gang leaders, LAC, winos, CHA staff . . . You just had to pay them, because you'd get caught in a minute if you didn't." Judy Harris gave money to several people to ensure the success of her business: she made monthly payments to floor captains, the LAC building president in her high-rise, and local CHA managers. Neither the Adams brothers nor Harris submitted willingly. Their arguments with those demanding bribes lasted for years and were marked by verbal and physical altercations. These battles could be public, and they often made people anxious about their safety when moving around the housing development.

The long stretch of Main Ave. that runs through the housing development, a famous entrepreneurial arena in the 1970s, demonstrates the benefits and drawbacks of the underground for the average tenant. From the city park at Twenty-third St. to the row houses at Thirty-fifth St., there was a lively street market on Main St. where one could find "hooch, kooch, and reefer," according to Judy Harris. "Anything you needed." Individuals brought their licit and illicit wares there and erected tables for food and drink sales. Others simply opened up the trunk of their cars and spread items along the ground. Residents remember the strip as an animated space where hustling occurred at all hours, where even people who did not approve of the "hustling and pimping" nevertheless came to take pleasure in the traffic of strangers. As with a shopping mall, "individuals [came] to participate in a certain type of urban ambiance which they crave. They [were] consumers of this quasi-public space at the same time as they circulate[d] as consumers for the benefit of retailers."[38]

Yet even in areas of Main Ave., tenants described an unattractive atmosphere. Residents of some high-rises that bordered Main Ave. accused the LAC leaders in neighboring buildings of sending less desirable activities into their areas. Indeed, ridding one's own area of such behavior and moving it into another was one attribute of a strong LAC leader. For example, an LAC officer might use the public knowledge of her connections with law enforcement to tell drug dealers or late-night carousers to keep their activities away from her building. William Levins, a police officer who lived in Robert Taylor at the time, recalls particularly powerful tenant leaders who would pressure Chicago police or CHA managers to remove drug trafficking or gang activity from the parts of Main St. near their buildings: "Ms. Harrison, she was one of those people that, well, let's just say Main Ave. was like her backyard. You want to sell dope, you do it down the street, she don't care. But not near her building. She'd wake me up, three in the morning, to stop somebody smoking reefer who was too loud or something." In this manner, the economic activity was differentially placed on Main St.—for example, near the 205 building, Paulina Collins brought out their foodstuffs, and next to the 228 building, a basketball court housed carpenters and general laborers. But in some areas, the street market was more a space of aggravation and disruptive activities than an attractive arena to visit and do some shopping.

It was difficult for tenants to escape the problems caused by various forms of hustling in and around the high-rises. Their sense of security in their dense quarters had developed partly as a function of their capacity to interact with one another in external public spaces and in areas inside the buildings, such as galleries and lobbies. These were the primary places where children played freely and where tenants came to share information, learn of one another's needs, solicit services, and distribute resources. "If somebody slanging [selling dope], they're making money," Kenny Davenport liked to say, "but there's also somebody using, and nobody wants a dope-smoking user hanging around." That is, hustling of drugs may have brought needed income into Robert Taylor, but it also carried risks for the community. Tenants who were concerned that their use of public spaces was threatened by drug users, as well as by peddlers and merchants, made their feelings known to their leadership, who felt pressured to provide some semblance of safety and security.

Ironically, the work of the tenant body to mitigate the deleterious effects of hustling was itself a hustle. Indeed, safety, much like clothes, drugs, car repairs, and favors, was becoming an object of this economy that could be bartered and/or purchased. A tenant leader might offer a public aid official valuable information on the hidden income of neighbors in return for the bureaucrat's turning a blind eye to that leader's own hidden work and that of his or her friends. Men hawking goods might offer LAC members discounts because these tenant leaders could easily have put a stop to their business. A tenant could assist police in investigations, and in turn, ensure timely police response for those in his building. Individuals exercising such influence over household and public security commanded respect and stature in much the same way as those who chartered lucrative off-the-books economic ventures. They, too, were viewed as successful entrepreneurs, hustlers in the fertile subterranean world that was becoming integral for household livelihood. Despite the advantages of these informal security procedures, however, they, too, were unstable ventures that exacted a high toll in terms of stability, security, and the equal treatment of all tenants.

In describing the underground, tenants are mindful of the debilitating effects of hustling, from the use of informal means to obtain law enforcement to the opportunities to earn off-the-books income. They express moral reprehension for the payoffs, bribes, and general instability that hustling caused, but they stop short of negatively assessing most practices—even drug dealing. They accept that some of these activities are inevitable within a poor community with few other opportunities. Instead, their critical eye turns to particular individuals who could exercise some control over the broader consequences of hustling. They discriminate among their leaders and security personnel, specifically LAC representatives and CHA and police officers, who they feel had primary responsibility to make sure that hustling did not threaten household safety. They also offer invectives against the purveyors themselves, that is, against "drug dealers," "thieves," and "disrespectful folk" in the tenant body who brought violence or instability into the housing development. But when recalling such individuals, they point to the failure of the entrepreneur to organize his or her commerce in a responsible, controlled manner by obeying the commands of LAC leaders and CHA staff. In this manner, particular areas of the housing development are seen as more lawful or safe than others, not necessarily because they lacked disruptive individuals, but because in such areas there was a network of people who could control activities and minimize, albeit not completely, the negative effects of the hustling taking place.

From Tenant Leader to Tenant Broker

The consequence of a decade of hustling in Robert Taylor was the restructuring of tenant leadership. Politics and advocacy in the housing development took on a new flavor when access to policing, security, and underground income became a sought-after commodity for individuals and households. The opportunities to influence safety provision and hidden entrepreneurial activity afforded leaders several means by which to assist households. In doing so, they reconstituted local leadership and networks of authority as well as the specific mechanisms by which individuals and households worked with their leaders. The most visible change was the transformation of the LAC from an ostensibly democratic organ—a popularly elected representative body that was accountable to a housing development constituency—to a powerful broker that was the primary gatekeeper for residents seeking access to resources in the outside world.

When the LAC management structure was originally conceived in 1971, tenant leadership in Robert Taylor rested on one of two foundations. Some individuals worked closely with the Housing Authority as members of tenant screening boards, budget review committees, and public affairs panels. They acquired access to echelons of CHA management that proved useful when, for example, an apartment in their building required repair. In some cases, these leaders could boast symbolic support from tenants, but the relationship was primarily governed by instrumental exchange. As Cathy Blanchard argued, "[Those leaders] usually got our support because we knew they could get stuff done for us, not because we respected them or, you know, because they was for what we was for." The second type of leader—that is, those like Cathy Blanchard—gained support from the tenant body by organizing collective actions such as boycotts, rent strikes, and antigang drives, as opposed to providing a service or good. Such leaders were generally on poor terms with the government agencies and had few private-sector contacts, so their influence over service and resource allocation was minimal.

The oppositional leaders, that is, those who worked "outside of the CHA" and the broader state administrative structure, declined in number and in influence during the 1970s. Dissenters grew less prominent and dropped out of leadership roles altogether, while others remained politically active by changing their posture from working against the state to working through the state: "You see," explains Louisa Lenard, "we was all hopeful, you know, we expected that things was gonna be different, so most of us stopped clawing and scratching and just decided to work with the [CHA]." Edith Huddle's ideology of resigned pragmatism was a common theme among leaders in the 1970s:

> We still fought, but we wasn't trying to overthrow the CHA, you understand, we was working with them sometimes, fighting them too. It was a

lot different than marching because we picked up the phone, we didn't just wave signs and throw petitions and stuff at them.

Huddle's statement suggests that the fundamental change was to the process of criticism and political engagement itself, whereby those who opposed the status quo began working within existing structures. The basis of power for any local leader had moved from the capacity to mobilize residents in direct engagement with the state, which best characterizes the 1960s, to the capacity to fulfill the general needs of the tenants in one's building, whether this be regulating underground income generation or initiating innovative attempts to ensure safe conditions in one's high-rise.

Edith Huddle's assessment of politics in Chicago public housing points to an interesting parallel between "project living" in Robert Taylor and the black urban experience in general. Political brokerage in the housing development mirrored the work of those black urban leaders who moved from ghetto streets to the privileged world of City Hall and who, in turn, used their advancement to help their constituents.[39] In some cities, African Americans translated their Civil Rights victories into greater political power in municipal administrations. This political movement was certainly not widespread, and it is arguable whether the majority of urban African Americans derived great benefit, but the advance was nonetheless an important signifier of the shifting status of black Americans. Middle- and upper-class black leaders moved from the position of social outcasts *cum* critics of American institutions to some of its most earnest reformers and upholders—an economic as well as a political shift that the political scientist Adolph Reed perceptively described as "the triumph of the commodity form over insurgent black politics."[40] Whereas racial politics was once lodged in ghetto street protests and in factory union fights over hiring, strikebreaking, or equal pay, now black Americans were voicing their needs from a position of influence in the city's political and social arenas. They were one of several constituencies fighting for their fair share of municipal resources, and the new leaders were their primary advocates and representatives.

In Chicago, the emergence of an LAC-based leadership cadre within public housing was deeply intertwined with the broader political aspirations of the city's African Americans. As Chicago's black community used its rising numbers and increased political presence to challenge the reigning white-ethnic political machine and its hegemony over city administration, its leadership could not ignore Robert Taylor's approximately twenty-five thousand residents. The power of leaders on the South Side, where black social advancement was historically based, was rooted in their ability to produce a significant voter turnout, much as it had been since the 1930s, when they became the "swing vote" in Chicago mayoral elections. No wonder, then, that the voters in the Robert Taylor Homes were a sought-after voting bloc. For example, they were heavily courted by the rising black political leaders who belonged to the local 3rd Ward Democratic Organization. In practice, according to the Urban League historian Harold Baron, the same politicians demonstrated a greater interest in addressing the needs of the *non*–public housing residents in the ward than in attending to the problems of those in Robert Taylor and the adjoining housing developments in their district. Ultimately, the inclusion of Robert Taylor's tenants within this historic ward organization actually deterred the development of tenants' own political representatives who could advocate on their behalf. As Baron writes, "Pressured under the controls of the Housing Authority, the welfare system and the very successful 3rd Ward Democratic organization . . . the tenants of Robert Taylor have never been able to form any effective grassroots organization to represent themselves. Black militants, independent political aspirants and civil rights groups have all tried to and failed so far."[41]

Baron's assessment that Robert Taylor had impotent citywide representation may be valid. It is probably true that the housing development was not being attended to adequately by its elected leaders and that its own tenant brokers, the LAC officers, did not figure prominently in the contentious national debate over who or what faction would become the spokesperson for American blacks. Moreover, these brokers did not have any significant success in motivating tenants to vote in city and state electoral contests.[42] To offer an explanation, some LAC leaders argued that black and white citywide leaders energetically blocked their aims of political mobility beyond the field of public housing. As one LAC officer recalled, "Tenant leaders never got the respect outside of their community, so [city officials] would never take us seriously, and, you know, they never let us have no input on nothing unless it had to do with public housing."

Notwithstanding their circumscribed field of power, the public housing tenant leaders remained important in determining residents' quality of life. In the 1970s, leaders held a newfound power; their field of authority could include the resources of the Housing Authority, the behavior of other government agencies, and, less often, a promise of employment or service from an organization in the surrounding community. Their gains would be limited to the world of hustling, but their power signified to those living in public housing that the horizon of black mobility and autonomy was not unapproachable. Like their electoral representatives who had entered city councils, state legislatures, and Capitol Hill, the tenant brokers had one ear turned to the needs of their constituents and the other listening to external halls of power. The inclusion of public housing tenants into more formal political spheres was changing their own conceptions of what it meant to be political beings and what gains could be extracted through participation in, as opposed to direct challenges to, systemic institutions.

The presence of a powerful LAC by no means guaranteed that the quality of life for tenants would subsequently improve. Like the black brokers who preceded them, the LAC leaders were able to capitalize on a politically and economically disadvantaged populace for their own personal gain. The officers themselves were quite poor, and most did not work in legitimate jobs. Their meager wages as LAC officers, combined with kickbacks and payoffs from hustling, could improve

their circumstances substantially, and thus they had a direct investment in maintaining their power and remaining in office. It was not
always apparent that they were putting the needs of their constituents ahead of their own interests; nor was it evident that they could
bring improvements to Robert Taylor beyond intermittent enforcement services or resolution of underground economic disputes. Ad-
mittedly, the enforcement and quasi-regulatory services provided by
LAC members were not negligible, and it would be foolhardy to expect that the LAC officers could have secured improvements for their
constituents in the manner of a powerful mayor, congressperson, or
ward boss.

This raises yet another parallel to the historic ghetto-based broker:
like their predecessors, the LAC officers were also unable to improve
significantly the lives of their constituents.[43] The federal government's retrenchment program had cut CHA budgets, and policing and
city services continued to suffer in Robert Taylor and throughout Chicago's ghettos. As the 1970s moved forward, the LAC operated in a
climate that gave them fewer and fewer opportunities to ensure that
their tenants' needs were being met. Outside the sphere of hustling,
therefore, the LAC was not a reliable source of assistance. Its power
appeared to rest in part on tenants' fear of reprisal and detection by
government agencies. With few other resources available to tenants
and with members of their own households involved in hustling, it is
understandable that the LAC could wield a measure of power without having access to many resources.

———

The patterns of hidden work and the complex schemes for policing
social problems in the Robert Taylor Homes offer a clue as to how the
poorest sectors of black Americans coped with the growing impoverishment of their communities in the 1970s. At the time, social scientists and policy makers were diligently seeking to discover such
"survival strategies" on the part of the urban poor.[44] Some directed
their attention to large-scale social processes. These were the

staunchest critics of President Richard Nixon's highly touted "black capitalism" project, which they argued was not helping the ghetto to produce jobs nor providing it with any effective institutional basis of capital and credit that could jumpstart economic development.[45] Their colleagues observing ghetto households pointed to one after another behavioral "adaptation," emphasizing hustling, barter, kindred-based sharing "coalitions," and other techniques by which the poor generated income and sustained themselves.[46]

Only a few observers paid attention to ghetto communities and neighborhoods in toto.[47] Unexplored were the social institutions in ghetto communities other than kinship that governed the exchange of dollars and in-kind resources so instrumental for personal and household support. Few people asked whether ghetto survival had a community dimension. In the Robert Taylor Homes, survival and household support included not only sharing between families, but also forms of assistance that spanned the entire community. Such assistance encompassed the brokerage relationships of police and tenants, residents' creative self-policing techniques, and the underground activity that tenants drew upon to acquire goods and services.

What had formed in the Robert Taylor Homes was a complex "social economy," that is, systematic patterns of exchange of goods and services that had spatial, institutional, and cultural dimensions and so were more than simply "adaptations," that is, mechanistic behavioral responses to poverty.[48] Throughout the community, the flowering underground economy affirmed social relationships, many of which had been in place before the 1970s, by creating patterns of obligation, reciprocity, and expectation among tenants. Conversely, the established networks and associations facilitated the introduction and consolidation of material and social exchange among individuals, households, and buildings. As this burgeoning economy created social problems, tenants responded with strategies to restore safety and security, sometimes effectively, sometimes not.

In meeting their needs, residents affirmed their relationships with one another and with organizations and agencies in the wider world.

Moreover, as the economic anthropologist Marcel Mauss pointed out, the exchange of a good or service is an exchange of part of oneself; thus, residents of Robert Taylor were also shaping their personal and collective identities through their giving and trading. They affirmed their social bonds, created new associations, and left others behind. Although the identities that residents formed in the underground economy had a local character, in the sense of being rooted in the relationships of the housing development, they were completely saturated by the social institutions and reigning ideologies of that time period. Indeed, in some respects the cultural valence of hustling overrode its material significance, given that most underground ventures provided minimal earnings, were short-lived, and could sometimes be dangerous. Hustling did not afford a life of extravagance. Instead, as Paulina Collins has stated, money-making schemes gave residents a sense of belonging and respect: "We was living large, but we wasn't making much money. It's just that we was feeling good about ourselves and who we were, and what we could do." Like Collins, others described the underground as a set of practices enabling them to be effective and assertive—which they could not be by working in the menial mainstream jobs available to them. Tom and Jake Adams enjoyed "setting our own hours," and Judy Harris "liked the fact that I was in control of something in my life." In their small-scale operations, individuals realized an affinity with the popularly glorified madame, pimp, and street voyeur who had saturated the mass media and who were known throughout the ghetto.

The tenants' alertness to images circulating in the broader society and the will to craft their identities in accordance with ideals in the outside world signaled a dual process taking place in Robert Taylor and in urban ghettos generally. Ghetto poor were not simply withdrawing from the mainstream, although they were certainly excluded from full and equal participation in many institutional settings. They were forging a new place in American society. Their relationships with law enforcement agencies, to offer an example, were not wholly severed. Instead, police and other security personnel were involved

in the ongoing attempts to produce social order in the housing development, albeit in ways distinct from those that prevailed in other areas of the city. That is, tenants were simultaneously working
creatively with police to instantiate effective enforcement, criticizing
police and demanding better protection, and creating alternative
mechanisms that provided some measure of safety and redress when
police were absent. It would be possible to draw a similar conclusion
with regard to tenants' relationships with the mainstream labor market, namely, that they were not simply out of work but becoming new
laborers: economic restructuring had cast them out of the blue-collar
workforce and into a service sector. Even in the service sectors, they
faced great difficulty when seeking avenues of re-entry and tended to
work for menial wages either part-time or as general laborers; in the
interim, they supplemented their income with off-the-books work in
the underground. For better or worse, public housing tenants and
other sectors of the urban poor had built a fragile apparatus at the
level of ghetto communities, whose girders consisted of the many
forms of "hustling" that enabled them to get by when formal institutions failed them.

These clandestine opportunities, combined with infrequent main
stream resources, helped them to approximate what the sociologist
Lee Rainwater called "the good life." In any given community, the
benefits of this supplemental existence may not have been equally realized by everyone—the fortunate few on the LAC and the small
cadre of successful hustlers in Robert Taylor certainly had their elite
parallel in other, non–public housing ghetto quarters. But as one anthropologist of 1970s ghetto life noted, hustling was *the* avenue for
the poor to seek out the "American dream."

Because observers of ghettos in the wake of the Civil Rights era
had great difficulty capturing the double-sidedness of this dynamic,
they tended to portray the ghetto largely as moving away from mainstream America. For example, the anthropologist Ulf Hannerz began
his ethnography of a Washington, D.C., ghetto community by writing
that "to [the ghetto dweller's] largely mainstream way of life we will

devote rather little attention."[49] In this manner, both unemployment and underground work were labeled as "ghetto-specific" behaviors, that is, as modes of activity signifying withdrawal from the mainstream, as opposed to a new role within society. These observers were less attuned to the similarities and relationships that alienated communities such as Robert Taylor were building with the wider world.[50] They ignored aspects of daily life, such as the political work of building a habitable community and the role that hustling might play in this process.

They focused instead on "personal intimate life," which translated into an infatuation with individual behavior and household organization that they perceived to be distinctive or "ghetto specific": that is, "hanging out" on the street corner, public drinking, sexual promiscuity, domestic instability, and non-nuclear family formation became grist for their voyeuristic mill.[51] With their attention drawn to peculiarities, observers depicted the lifestyle of black ghetto dwellers as a partially self-generating "culture of poverty," a "shadow system of values," an "adaptive value stretch," these and other such phrases connoting a marked separation from, or approximation to, American mainstream culture. It was only a small step to then say that the ghetto dweller was culturally beyond the pale of this mainstream or, worse, an outright pathology absent of morals and civic virtue.

The means by which the Robert Taylor community met its needs during the 1970s do not suggest that a structure was in place generating pathology, failure, and a totally un-American way of life. Problems were present, but to some degree they were the outcome of a population trying to live up to the ideals of America. They were tenants seeking to recover democratic representation in the face of poverty and political inequity. The LAC leaders were mimicking their counterparts outside the community with their creative and sometimes questionable tactics to help themselves and their constituents, and many were seeking to emulate the rising fortunes of their middle- and upper-class counterparts, albeit in unstable and dangerous underground economies. Their material circumstances prevented them from reaching these goals: in the absence of meaningful, well-paying work, illicit income generation offered no solid foundation upon which to ensure personal and household well-being. Moreover, with tremendous neglect by citywide political leaders as well as by their formal agents of governance and social control, the LAC's evolving brokerage capacities offered no basis upon which to create a safe community or to organize for change in their everyday lives. Hustling may have been an "American success dream," but it had the potential to become a living nightmare if it got out of control. With the resurgence of street gangs lurking on the horizon, such was the concern for tenants of the Robert Taylor Homes.

3 | "What's It Like to Be in Hell?"

With a heavy sigh, Kelly Davis narrated a turning point in the history of the Robert Taylor Homes, "the time when it just got worse and worse." In 1988, she had been serving in her seventh year as the building president of the Local Advisory Council in the 230 South Elm St. high-rise. As the building's elected representative, she considered herself to be "the best friend a tenant had in 230." She fought for clean floors and well-lit stairwells and against security guards who harassed young women. With a cousin employed by the CHA, she boasted an advantage when repair schedules and work orders were distributed among the buildings. So it was with some regret and pain that she described the events of autumn 1987 to spring 1988, when her power to assist tenants was put to the test. "I let them down," she said, assigning herself blame. "We was doing well until then, it was our community. Then *they* took over."

"They" were the street gangs that roamed the housing development—specifically, the local factions of the citywide Black Kings (BK) family, a federation of neighborhood-based gangs. The BKs were unquestionably the dominant street-gang family in the Robert Taylor Homes, claiming "control" over twice as many buildings as their archrivals, the Sharks. Jon Lenard was the highest-ranking leader of the Robert Taylor Black Kings, and he lived in the 218 building, one hundred yards away from Kelly Davis. Lenard had pushed the BKs into local underground markets, specifically narcotics trafficking and extortion of stores and local hustlers, and he looked to the 230 building to anchor the gang's newfound entrepreneurial interest. In May 1988 Maurice Wilson, a tenant of the 230 building who ran a car-repair service outside his building, refused to "pay off" the BKs; he was already paying Kelly Davis for "protection" against police detection. Senior BK "officers" summarily beat him, sending him to the hospital. In the following days, two BK officers similarly assaulted two other underground mercantilists, and the gang let it be known that others could suffer a similar fate. They were the new kid on the block, and all protective services would be offered by *their* organization, not by Davis and the LAC.

Davis and the tenants of her building faced a dilemma in responding to these new threats. They could ask the police to arrest the gang members on assault charges, but officers could not realistically be asked to settle tenant-gang disputes over the control of illegal underground activities. Similarly, the CHA security guards and managers could pressure the gangs, but they could not legally support an underground economy regulated by LAC members. While the inhabitants of 230 debated their options, Davis sought assistance from LAC leaders in other buildings, all of whom were anxiously watching the happenings in 230. The proven techniques they had developed to assist families were starting to show signs of impotency in the face of entrepreneurially oriented gangs that sought to secure their position in the growing crack trade.

The gang's "corporate" ventures were producing various forms of violence and instability.[1] The potential revenue from crack economies escalated conflicts between gangs, and increasingly weapons were used during these disputes, often in public spaces where tenants and their children were present. The violent happenings in 230 were equally threatening, and many tenants feared that their own buildings might be the next target of Lenard and the Black Kings. At the same time, the rate of drug use and vandalism among tenants was increasing, and poor and needy individuals were turning their anger against others, including spouses and partners behind apartment doors and neighbors out in full view.

The 1987–1988 events between gangs and tenants were more than a fractious exchange between two parties with longstanding animosities. They had brought to the surface a number of concerns regarding quality of life that had been gathering steam since the beginning of the decade. Some concerns centered on the increasing public presence of armed youth who sold drugs and harassed tenants, yet the gangs' behavior was part of a broader inability of tenants to ensure their safety and welfare. This included not only diminishing control over young people, but also the growing neglect of police and Housing Authority agents in security and maintenance issues, and the inability of the indigenous enforcement schemes devised in the 1970s to make up for this gap. There was an overall decline in the quality of life of Robert Taylor taking place, and the tremendous improvements that tenants had fought for in the 1970s were now being threatened.

In 1987, to publicize resurgent gang activity and the declining safety of CHA developments, a *New York Times* editorial asked, "What's it like to be in hell?" For tenants of the Robert Taylor Homes, the answer would include not only the gangs' activities, but an array of changes that signified a period of crisis and speculation. What was popularly known as the "gang and drug problem" was a more total disruption to everyday life, and no one knew quite how the challenge of "project living" would be rewritten.

Living with "the Worst Managed Housing Authority in the Nation"

In 1982, when federal officials in the Reagan administration gave the Chicago Housing Authority the dubious distinction of being "the worst managed housing authority in the nation," the agency was at the nadir of its fifty-year history.[2] Maintenance in public housing had lapsed, millions of dollars were needed for modernization, thousands of households showed no hope of entering the private housing market, and violent crime was on the rise. But if it appeared that the conditions in public housing communities could not worsen, the remainder of the decade would suggest otherwise. By 1987, the nation's public housing budget would be slashed by 87 percent, at a time when America's urban poor had become a jobless population for whom subsidized public housing was a last defense against homelessness and abject poverty. These changes meant more than leaky faucets or rising rates of elevator malfunction. In Robert Taylor, what began as a decline in the built environment was compounded over the course of the decade as tenants felt a mounting insecurity concerning their personal welfare and the safety of their households. The techniques that they had crafted to manage themselves and that had helped to make the housing development livable, if not actually viable, showed signs of impotence.

In the early 1980s, the level of social problems in American ghettos, noted the sociologist William Julius Wilson, "had reached catastrophic proportions." Middle- and upper-class blacks had replicated the earlier white flight by establishing new neighborhoods outside of ghettos, taking with them valuable resources that helped mitigate the effects of poverty for their poorer counterparts. Inner cities appeared void of commercial activity, capital and credit availability was minimal, their institutional sector was eviscerated, and observers warned that the remaining population had grown "socially isolated," with few meaningful contacts with mainstream institutions. One needed to look no further than the domicile to see the turn for the worse that many inner-city blacks had taken.[3] Nationwide, the proportion of teenage births in the black community had risen from 63 percent (1970) to 89 percent, and nearly half of black families were headed by women who struggled to find income as well as support from their partners. The out-of-wedlock birth rate for blacks was five times that of whites, and increasing numbers of black children were being born into conditions of poverty. All these indicators were particularly acute within high-poverty areas.

Hardships in the household were matched by high levels of violence on ghetto streets. By the mid-1980s, homicide would become the leading cause of death of black men and women aged twenty-five to thirty-four—98 percent of these murders involved a black victim and a black perpetrator. Blacks constituted 13 percent of the population in cities, yet they accounted for more than one-half of the arrests for violent crimes occurring there[4]—over the course of the decade, the rate of black imprisonment rose sharply, at a pace nearly seven times that of whites.[5] As the imprisonment of black youth escalated, thousands of inmates were leaving prison walls and reentering ghetto streets with few employment opportunities or community-based institutions to facilitate a productive transition to civilian life.[6] While conservatives pointed to welfare dependency and a culture of poverty among ghetto dwellers as root causes of crime, liberals pointed to continued racism and inadequate education, and progressive voices documented harsh police practices and entrenched racism in judicial institutions. None would discount that American ghettos housed a segregated and concentrated poor population that was in a precarious position, living with considerable misfortune and turning some of their anger and frustration inward in destructive ways.

Public housing populations exemplified the vulnerability of the so-called underclass household. In Robert Taylor and other large Chicago housing developments, 90 percent of the population was out of work and receiving welfare, nearly 75 percent of households were headed by single females who struggled to find sufficient resources, and crime rates were the highest in the city.[7] For these individuals, a subsidized public housing apartment might have been one of the few stable aspects of their lives and one of the main avenues by which they could remain in contact with institutions in the wider world.

Early in President Ronald Reagan's first term (1980–1984), there were indications that the status quo of public housing would be called into question. The nascent signs were visible in his first major budgetary proposal, the Omnibus Reconciliation Act of 1981, in which he translated his philosophy of "New Federalism" into a new contract for American cities. His strategy had two premises: (1) give states unrestricted "block grants" as opposed to federal funds for specific programs and they can construct policies for metropolitan regions with flexibility and autonomy; and (2) government spending on social programs was needless and should be reduced given that the "private market" could make up the difference. Congress saved many programs that Reagan wished to eliminate entirely, but one department that did not rebound from imposed retrenchment was Housing and Urban Development. The Reagan administration sharply reduced HUD's overall budget, realigned the department's internal priorities (for example, by arguing that rural housing needs overshadowed those of city dwellers), and forced public housing to compete for support with other HUD programs. Citing the growing distress in cities, housing-policy experts quickly characterized Reagan's approach to subsidized housing as "a leap backward" and the "worst of all possible worlds."[8] The invectives were carefully grounded in statistical assessment and study, but their alarm over the radical cuts also reflected an anxiety about the rapid pace of change that Reagan's policies would engender for America's urban poor.

Reagan's New Federalism had staggering consequences for the housing options of Chicago's low-income population.[9] Chicago, like many other large cities, had experienced an upsurge in government-supported housing construction throughout the 1980s, but federal subsidies primarily benefited the city's middle and upper classes. For households with income below 80 percent of the median—roughly two-fifths of the city population—"only minimal funds [were] allocated by the federal government."[10] Ironically, despite its faith in the power of the market, Reagan's own Commission on Housing reported that "the private market has been unwilling to house many of the [low-income, single-parent, minority, and large] families," a moot observation given that the administration had already won congressional cutbacks to low-income housing.[11] By 1983, housing in Chicago's low-income neighborhoods was in short supply and much of the existing stock was old and decaying; in the large neighborhood that subsumed the Robert Taylor Homes, 80 percent of the housing stock was at least forty years old (the majority constructed before the turn of the century), and 70 percent of the units were "overcrowded" or "deteriorated and in need of major repair."[12] Despite substandard housing options, Chicago's poor black households paid almost 80 percent of their income for housing;[13] compared with whites, *all* of the city's black residents paid, on average, 8 percent more for the same housing unit while discrimination continued to limit their housing options to predominantly black neighborhoods and a few integrated communities.[14]

With HUD's funding for all housing programs reduced by 76 percent from 1980 to 1988, the CHA operating budget fell by 87 percent during the same time period, leaving little money for modernization of aging physical plants and apartments.[15] Forced to do more with less, the Housing Authority could not be blamed entirely for allowing the physical conditions of the developments to lapse even beyond the abysmal levels at the start of the decade. Overall, the CHA reported a $1 billion maintenance backlog, with 10,000 new work orders per month and more than 30,000 orders remaining to be fulfilled (some tenant requests were eight years old).[16] In 1988, the CHA estimated that $1 billion would be necessary to bring public housing up to minimum standards.[17] One of its requests to HUD for $724 million was considered somewhat humorous by the media and HUD officials because the figure nearly exceeded HUD's nationwide budget for such repairs.[18] Yet despite the state of severe distress, public housing programs had alarmingly long waiting lists. In 1980, 13,323 people awaited an apartment; by 1984 the figure had jumped to 24,000—in that year, 56,000 households queued for a CHA housing "Section 8" award that would grant subsidies for a private-market rent.[19]

Notwithstanding its fiscal constraints, the Chicago Housing Authority employed questionable management practices that could not be directly attributed to the Reagan regime. At root, the CHA had failed to devise an overall plan to guide its short- and long-term policies, that is, the agency had "no idea of what it would actually cost to fix up its physical plant," and its expenditure priorities had little rhyme or reason.[20] A routine apartment repair might result in cost overruns, and for no justifiable reason, the same repair might vary by hundreds of dollars in different housing developments. The cumulative effect of this fiscal looseness was staggering debt, which over the course of the 1970s had risen to millions of dollars. By 1987, the

agency owed at least $34.4 million to vendors, contractors, and util-
ity companies. Nor had the agency kept up with maintenance needs;
privately conducted investigations of apartments in Robert Taylor
uncovered CHA-approved work orders that had not been fulfilled for
months. The agency was proactively cutting money from its "Tenant
Services and Ordinary Maintenance Budget" while spending more
money hiring administrators and mid-level managers.[21] The City of
Chicago was complicit in promoting lax maintenance, as it failed to
prosecute the Housing Authority in its "housing court" for the hundreds of building-code violations it incurred.[22] Nearly continuous reports of the agency's poor management produced little empathy for
CHA officials' own cries that decreased HUD funding limited their
ability to conduct upkeep and maintenance.

By the mid-1980s, the media had linked the agency's shoddy management to corruption, scandal, and poor public relations. There was
an overall management problem, and neither the mayor nor CHA
commissioners were able to rectify matters. While news of CHA cost
overruns received nearly continuous publicity, critics discovered
questionable investment decisions and disbursement of high-paying
contracts that had benefited Board members and their friends in the
business world. Chicago's mayors were choosing CHA Board members who had little experience in management or in housing. Many
had little experience with government and could not leverage HUD
support; in one publicly ridiculed management decision, the agency
devised an "Adopt-a-Unit" initiative that asked outside institutions
to "adopt" families and help pay for the cost of maintaining their
apartments. Some Board members resigned either to avoid further
criticism or out of frustration.

The disarray peaked in 1986, when public accusations circulated
that the CHA had failed to renovate vacated apartments and was quietly emptying its high-rise complexes in order to prepare for future
demolition and the resale of the cleared lands to private developers.[23]
(Mayor Harold Washington once publicly admitted his wish to transform high-rise public housing into commercial offices and armed

forces barracks.)[24] By 1986, the CHA had "a national reputation for mismanagement and patronage," and "because its vacancy rate, its overdue rents and the condition of its buildings all fail[ed] to meet the standards set by the federal government for a well-run authority," HUD declared the agency "severely troubled," one of its poorest ratings.[25] In December 1987, a federal judge dealt the final blow by placing the agency in receivership until HUD could locate a new management team. To the general public, the 1980s drama of public housing appeared in the guise of budgetary crises, high-ranking administrative scandals, fiscal irresponsibility, and contentious federal and municipal battles for "local control." But for Robert Taylor's tenants, the real drama was the threat to their capacity to live safely and securely within their development.

Tenants acknowledge that their own behavior was also a factor that contributed to making Robert Taylor uninhabitable in the early part of the decade. They readily admit that participation in vandalism and crime had outpaced the capacity of janitors, police, and CHA administrators to maintain the physical integrity of the housing development. They are also careful to emphasize a burgeoning underground economy that had brought about exchange of gunfire, public drug use, and narcotics trafficking, all of which were contributing to the growing insecurity that they felt outside their apartments.[26] Their explanations for increased tenant involvement in such activities are peppered with allusions to the economic hardships that households suffered in the 1980s. Their accounts of violence among the young also emphasize the high dropout rates and truancy of a disillusioned youth population.[27] "People was messed up, wasn't no work," said Ottie Davis, describing the early 1980s. "I remember because lot of us couldn't find nothing, I mean nothing, and we ain't even had no families, shit . . . Now, how you going to expect anything else [but] niggers tearing up the fucking place, beating each other up. They going to take it out on each other." One resident, who had lived in Robert Taylor since 1962 and had reared thirteen children and sent them to college, made a similar statement to a reporter in 1980: "Things are different now, things are tense now. The young people have nothing to do. No jobs. No recreation. So they are rowdy. They don't go to school. They make trouble."[28]

Many tenants tempered these assessments by arguing that not all households turned to troublesome behavior when their material circumstances worsened. "It was a young person's thing, but not all of them," said Cathy Blanchard, tying involvement in crime to family status. "Some kids was just hanging out, they was bored, but that don't mean they was all criminals. Some parents, they wasn't respectful of nothing, you know? They just couldn't control their kids, just let them get into trouble, out of hand." Blanchard's distinction between a controlled, "respectful" household that limited the "trouble" of its kids and those who could not achieve this control is a common one. In fact, some tenants limit their own personal responsibility, as well as that of their friends and neighbors, and instead single out perpetrators living elsewhere in the development or belonging to other social networks. Senior residents offered another commonly invoked dichotomy: they distinguish law-abiding tenants, that is, those who arrived in Robert Taylor in the 1960s and early 1970s and had learned to work together to limit local transgressions, from newer and younger tenants of the housing development who were unfamiliar with the mores of the public housing lifestyle and to whom they ascribe destructive propensities. For their part, these newer arrivals were quick to counter that the LAC and police provided disparate enforcement in the housing development by favoring households that had already established ties to influential brokers, such as individuals with connections to the police or to powerful LAC officials. Even gang members active at the time freely cast aspersions on youth involved in *other* gangs, who in their minds were the real perpetrators of crime and unrest: Black Kings gang members blamed the Sharks gang for being thieves; those in the Sharks allude to the "wildness" of the neighboring Cobras, who in turn blame the "out of control" Kings for bringing crime into Robert Taylor.

In these narratives of rising social instability in the housing development, tenants frequently make reference to modes of social control that were available to them. Indeed, different eras are remembered for the type and level of social control over disruptive activities, whether maintenance-related or gang-related. The 1980s are usually contrasted with the previous decade, wherein social problems did not severely threaten the comfort of households because a network of individuals and groups limited tenants' excesses. Not surprisingly, given its role in the 1970s as an agency involved in facilitating social order in Robert Taylor, the LAC occupies a prominent place in their accounts of safety and security, both in the 1970s, when they felt a relatively greater comfort, and in the 1980s, when they began noticing a significant loss of control. At the end of the 1970s, tenants appeared quite confident of the future and of their collective efficacy in security-related issues. Most important, with the democratization of tenant management in 1971, tenants could elect their own representatives and respond to challenges in a unified manner.

By 1980, residents of the Robert Taylor Homes could point to some tangible benefits of an active and publicly vocal tenant LAC that represented their interests in CHA decision making and helped them to negotiate with government and civic agencies in the outside world. Their reliance on the LAC brokers was not an ideal situation. Yet at the start of the 1980s, the LAC did seem capable of performing a modest range of functions—most of which centered around ensuring public safety and locating social supports for households—that made "project living" less burdensome than it otherwise might have been.

The celebrated progress in tenant leadership waned after 1980, however. Even LAC officers argue that rising crime, gunfire, vandalism, and drug-related activity became a serious threat to their capacity to ensure safety in public spaces. Out of frustration, the LAC officer Edith Huddle wrote a letter to her CHA manager in 1984 in which she listed problems with public space and acknowledged tenants' own destructive activities:

> We got to do better not to throw things away on the ground and not break glass everywhere. Our kids are shooting each other and people don't feel

safe. [The LAC] is working every day to make people understand these things and to deal with the violence . . . [But residents] cannot bring their children to play [areas] because the swings are broken and there is glass everywhere. Our families don't spend the day outside because the place is filled with garbage that is not picked up. It smells and comes into the apartments and we cannot eat our dinner. There is no place for people to spend time, only in the hallways and lobbies, and people want to get out and enjoy themselves because it is summer now. It seems like it's getting worse every year.

Beyond the annoying smells and limited leisure options, if tenants could not spend time with one another in public spaces, they suffered the possible loss of an important method of self-enforcement, namely, casual observation of one another's activities in and around the housing development.

To voice their frustration, residents turned their critical gaze to elected tenant representatives who served on the Local Advisory Council. Moses Harrison, who lived in the 218 building, offered a common appraisal of his LAC representatives: "No one expected them to fix up all the apartments, but after a while we was getting pissed when they wasn't even listening to us and not even trying to do something for us." Tenants alleged that LAC and CAC officers were responsible for the declining state of affairs. That tenant criticism of their leadership would escalate over the course of the decade is understandable; however, only part of their anger can be tied to any demonstrable negligence on the part of floor captains, secretaries, building presidents, and other LAC officers. Some of the frustration with these officials may have been provoked by the unprecedented media attention given to the CHA from 1980 until 1988, which had few positive things to say about the management of the agency. There were weekly reports of CHA corruption, overspending and resource depletion, management turnover, fiscal irresponsibility, and "creative bookkeeping" techniques that allowed maintenance to slip while the number of administrative and managerial staff increased.[29]

In this atmosphere of scandal and mistrust, the local LAC officer, who received a modest part-time wage and who could use his or her influence to win part-time jobs for friends, was beginning to look more like privileged CHA management and less like a tenant advocate.[30] Judy Harris, a neighbor of Moses Harrison in the 218 building, laughed as she described the relative comfort of the LAC officers in her building: "People had holes in their walls, they ain't had no water. And then you went to [LAC building president] Cathy Blanchard's apartment or where [LAC floor captain] Melinda lived and you see new furniture, new stove, hell, they had nicer places than people living outside the projects!" The media supported rising tenant anger by openly criticizing the LAC as fortunate beneficiaries of an archaic patronage system who "[had] first crack at jobs [and could] influence the distribution of services within public housing developments."[31]

Although it was impossible for the LAC to enact fundamental improvements to Robert Taylor's physical infrastructure, tenants had grown accustomed to the LAC's playing a relatively active role in their lives, especially in matters of security. Their expectations were high because some LAC officers candidly publicized their own role as security providers. Shadie Sanders, Edith Huddle, and Wyona Wilson, for example, claimed responsibility for winning substantial federal support for enforcement services in the early 1980s. In a wide range of moral and legal activities, from locating burglars and police informants to hiding household income, the LAC certainly played an important role. Events in the 1980s, however, called into question the numerous procedures of protection and redress, and the tenant body grew impatient for better protection. If LAC officials had accepted the credit for devising the security measures, who better to criticize if these failed to offer peace of mind.

The swelling tenant frustration with Robert Taylor's elected leadership is best understood in the context of the Housing Authority's own attempts to enhance security in the development from 1980 until 1987.[32] At the beginning of the decade, the CHA appeared ready to overhaul its enforcement strategies. Mayor Jane Byrne had commissioned a study of public housing security in 1980 for Chicago's high-rise complexes.[33] Using the Cabrini-Green Homes, a high-rise public housing development on the city's north side, as the case study, the commissioned report evaluated the physical layout of high-rises and offered several recommendations for planning and security improvements within all CHA high-rise developments. The report relied on Oscar Newman's writings on "defensible space," in which the urban planner had articulated several influential ideas on workable city planning and habitation. His treatise, which emphasized visibility and openness, ease of surveillance, and residents' collective ownership of their shared space, undergirded the CHA's reconstruction of its security approach for much of the 1980s. The commissioned report used the "defensible space" concept to distinguish between "basic and enhanced security":

> Basic security emphasizes the resident's ability to control his or her own living environment, given a supportive physical design. It is universal and can be applied to any housing development, even those without any identified security problem. Enhanced security is intended to provide additional security measures with less reliance on the individual resident. Instead, it demands a more structured organization of manpower and security devices such as security patrols and electronic monitoring equipment.[34]

In the 1981 report, the conceptual distinction between "basic" and "enhanced" security buttressed a practical, twofold approach to security provision: physical renovation of public spaces to promote surveillance and safe passage, and the support of policies that "strengthen the residents' control of their living environment."[35] Physical changes for Robert Taylor included the walled enclosure of the ground floors of high-rises in order to focus pedestrian traffic at a central entrance.[36] Over the course of the decade, the CHA would experiment with (and in some cases install permanently) video cameras, lobby intercoms, emergency call lighting systems, and metal detectors and turnstiles in the lobby area. Moreover, its security guards were directed to pay particularly close attention to the lobby area during their "perimeter patrols."[37] The agency was less diligent in following the 1981 report's more mundane recommendations regarding architectural innovations, such as well-lit entrances, the use of graphics that would enable residents to create a sense of ownership, and clear separations between spaces of leisure and passage.

The CHA initiated several strategies to promote "resident participation." It allocated greater funding for the organized tenant patrols and fitted them with communications equipment and distinctive uniforms. Although the tenant patrollers would receive a small wage, the Housing Authority also requested "voluntary" cooperation from the general populace in a "resident identification system" wherein all tenants were asked to carry identification cards and to report visitors to CHA officers at a lobby station. In perhaps its most creative scheme, the CHA introduced plans for "misdemeanor courts" within the high-rise buildings at which minor transgressions would be adjudicated and punishments meted out by county judges; the courts would provide jobs for tenants employed as clerks and bailiffs. The Housing Authority added new regulations such as fines for tenants whose "activities threatened the health, safety and welfare of other residents"; the agency's hope was to use citations as evidence to support eviction of households with misbehaving tenants.[38]

There was one important dimension to physical security outlined in the 1981 report that the Housing Authority did not pursue vigilantly.[39] Commissioned studies of housing development habitability mentioned many public-space activities that could support a productive role for tenants in providing local security. These included adequate outdoor bench seating, a vibrant local commercial sector, sufficient civic and social services, delimited and accessible recreational areas, and the transitional spaces that promoted interchange of the tenants with the surrounding community. However, in their security and rehabilitation plans for Robert Taylor, the CHA did not seem to take seriously suggested programs that could engender safety in these indirect ways.

The agency's refusal to pay attention to public-space issues stemmed partly from a nationwide shift in law enforcement strategies for urban poor neighborhoods, the seeds of which were sown in the early 1970s. Until that time, a "liberal" apparatus of institutions, programs, and government agencies—what social scientists called "mediating" institutions—worked to reform and then integrate convicted offenders into the social mainstream through probation and parole, job training and placement, and rehabilitation and medical treatment. Much of this treatment was rooted in the community, in the form of agencies, centers of employment, clinics, and social workers that not only helped to buffer poverty, but also strengthened the public life of the ghetto by actively weaving disadvantaged individuals back into their communities and into the larger society. In the waning years of President Nixon's administration, with the street rebellions on the minds of the American electorate, this approach received less political and popular support. Federal funding for mediating institutions in the ghetto, ranging from job training centers to social work programs, withered and there was little buffer between law enforcement agencies and the citizenry. By the dawn of the Reagan administration, funding priorities for policing in inner cities shifted almost wholly to the use of law enforcement techniques such as mass arrest, infiltration and covert surveillance, and surprise interdiction that disrupted public space, rather than policing it in a manner that promoted its usability.

For public housing communities, this turn to punitive social policy manifested itself in HUD's redirection of resources to the development of security initiatives that relied primarily, and at times exclusively, on law enforcement and surveillance. This climate meant that CHA could acquire few funds for law enforcement initiatives that sought to rectify the lapsing use of public spaces by tenants and that promoted "eyes upon the street" and other casual forms of enforcement. While youth and young-adult truancy and loitering increased, and correlatively crime, vandalism, and gunfire escalated, the CHA failed to consider the maintenance of popular transitional areas between public housing and surrounding areas as a central part of an overall security strategy. Instead, they focused their efforts almost entirely on paramilitary and surprise tactics, so much so that by 1989 they had redirected much of their security budget to the maintenance of a special CHA police force whose jurisdiction was Chicago public housing.[40]

In effect, the CHA's initiatives augmented the sense of separation that Robert Taylor and other high-rise developments felt from the rest of Chicago's neighborhoods.[41] The agency's interest in formulating specific security measures for high-rises was segregating the complexes from the wider world. Calls for a separate CHA police force (whose creation Chicago's City Council supported with additional proposals to assign Chicago police officers to public housing), state-of-the-art electronic and physical design surveillance, and controlled visitation and curfews did little to empower tenants nor to integrate the developments into surrounding communities.

Even when the CHA reinforced its law enforcement apparatus, it did not pay attention to the ways in which police officers historically provided enforcement and protection in the community. Police had stopped conducting daily beat patrols in the housing development in the early 1970s. They preferred to rely on relations with tenant leaders, using the "brokers" to find information on crimes and to develop appropriate responses to transgressions. Officers active at the time indicated that many early forms of gang activity—that is, before they expected members to be older and armed with weapons—could be controlled to some degree. They felt comfortable calling on families and handling the truancy or petty delinquency of their children in informal ways. (The comfort levels of police officers would change over the course of the 1980s as the gangs became armed and invested in drug economies.) The Housing Authority could have designed its own security guard system to act in a similar manner, visiting households and working intimately with tenants to act as a community resource. Instead, until 1986, the CHA refused to allow the guards inside buildings, for reasons it did not carefully spell out, and even after that year, it would only allow them to move through the lobby areas—they still could not call on households.

This security posture was unfortunate because tenants had been relying on the more informal means of maintaining safety to reduce their architecturally "advanced xenophobia"—Jane Jacobs's term for the insularity of "housing projects."[42] In addition to casual relationships with formal agents of social control, unfettered use of public space and social activities that encouraged interaction between Robert Taylor and surrounding areas had shown their value in the 1960s and 1970s: gatherings of friends, underground economies that attracted consumers and producers, self-enforcement and surveillance schemes, and so on, all enhanced safety by creating an awareness of local activity and interchange with individuals in surrounding neighborhoods. The simple presence of groups of people within and outside buildings, some of whom may have made note of public behavior, exemplified the "eyes upon the street" and "defensible space" approaches to the maintenance of social order that Newman and Jacobs celebrated in their respective writings.[43]

The CHA's negligence with regard to these security components was also ironic given that, for much of its history, the agency had taken seriously measures that addressed public space and that minimized the physical separations of the large public housing complexes. After 1980, however, the agency seemed intent on treating public housing as a unique ecology, that is, as an identifiably distinct and quasi-independently functioning environment that required its own specific security posture.

In 1988 the Housing Authority admitted that its special security provisions were "a waste of money" and promised in the future to make residents "a part of the process . . . The residents have to be the eyes and ears of the whole system."[44] By that point, however, the eroded sense of security among the tenant body had soured relations between tenants and the CHA. Not only did tenants protest against CHA policy directly, but dissension was brewing in the tenant body against their own leaders, whom they held partly responsible for their state of affairs. This erupted in a small tenant protest in 1986 against the elected LAC leadership in several of Chicago's largest developments. During that year, a tenant contingent wrote letters to Congress, formed counter-organizations (such as the "Concerned Citizens of Ida B. Wells," a low-rise public housing development), and publicized reports of inadequate leadership and irresponsibility on the part of their LAC members. It was the first such organized demonstration since the late 1960s and the first public challenge to the LAC in fifteen years.[45]

The 1986 effort was short-lived, however, and never moved into the majority of the public housing complexes. The energy of the incipient movement was dissipated because the federal government placed the CHA in receivership several months after the tenants' protest began. But even before the takeover occurred, tenants who organized the movement failed to acquire significant grassroots support in the tenant body. As a consequence, the extant LAC leadership was not overhauled; nor was the system of tenant representation altered even slightly. In Robert Taylor, the LAC survived the coup. "Ain't nobody who was in power before wasn't in power after," said Kim Walton. "They made all this noise about how we wasn't doing nothing for 'em, but they didn't get none of us, no one left, not one person."

By the mid-1980s, changes in the behavior of youth groups and the campaign waged by local law enforcement agencies in response to them provided an additional source of frustration for tenants. The unruly behavior of idle youth with little connection to educational institutions and labor markets had been a source of frustration earlier in the decade. By the mid-1980s, the disparate acts of "vandals and thieves," says Kenny Davenport, had become greater in number (crime rates in public housing rose 41 percent from 1983 to 1984 and 39 percent from 1985 to1988), and the perpetrators themselves assumed a more organized presence. They formed more close-knit gangs, used guns to settle conflicts, and were "shooting, harassing people to prove you're a man, you know."[46] Tenants accounted for escalating gang activity in the mid-1980s much as they explained the general rising levels of crime and instability: disenchanted youth expressed their frustrations through "gangbanging" and shooting.

Tenants also cite law enforcement agents as partially responsible for the resurgence of the local gangs. Although the majority acknowledge that police were not realistically capable of eradicating the growth of youth violence and crime, they argue that law enforcement agencies in Robert Taylor could have taken better measures in response to incidents of violence, and they point to the distinctive law enforcement approach that CHA Chairman Vincent Lane (1988) developed as exemplary of the poor decision making of the CHA and the police. Tenant leaders had convened several meetings with residents and law enforcement officials to request that they eliminate their use of "mass arrest and bail" tactics, and replace them with patrols inside buildings and throughout the grounds of the development.[47] In a tactic also known as "mob action," police officers would conduct a surprise attack on an area, making numerous arrests and questioning those they apprehended to learn about gang dynamics and drug-selling patterns in the housing development. One police officer who was active at the time explained the reluctance of his department to patrol the development and forgo the use of surprise tactics:

> It was just before crack came around so you had lots of these gangs stockpiling weapons. Now, you can't expect officers to walk around out there in the open. We're too exposed to the gangbangers in the high-rises and, believe me, they shot at us many times. What folks call mob action, you see, that was the best tool we had because we could get to a bunch of them and surprise them.

A few tenant leaders, such as Louisa Lenard and Kelly Davis, were empathetic to these arguments, but they too expressed frustration at the inability of Robert Taylor to acquire policing in the manner of other city neighborhoods.

Alongside his predilection for curfews and limits on stays for visitors, CHA Chairman Lane instituted a highly controversial technique known as "Operation Clean Sweep" in the high-rise complexes that was premised on the "mass arrest and bail" procedure. The so-called sweeps were surprise searches of apartments, typically conducted before dawn, in which a team of law enforcement officers would furtively enter a single high-rise without search warrants to locate gangs, criminals, unreported household boarders, and illicit paraphernalia (for example, drug-producing and -packaging equipment). The sweeps split Chicago's public housing tenants, pitting those who favored suspending constitutional rights during crisis situations against those who wanted more holistic approaches that combined tactical law enforcement with daily enforcement. For its own part, the Housing Authority justified the paramilitary efforts as "emergency" responses to the increasingly frequent gunfire exchange between rival, economically competitive street gangs. For the remainder of the decade, public debate over the use of Operation Clean Sweep was defined by the theatrics of political posturing, legal maneuvering, finger-pointing, and poorly substantiated accusations that involved not only tenants and the CHA but the mayor, state legislators, and advocates such as the American Civil Liberties Union and the Fraternal Order of Police.

The unfortunate consequence of the attention garnered by the use of sweeps was to overshadow the complex security-related problems in the housing development. Before the sweeps, tenant leaders were busy attending not only to high-profile activities, such as organized gang activity, but also to less well publicized behavioral patterns, such as public drinking and drug use among the tenant population, youth vandalism and harassment, and the overall decline in the safety of public spaces. Afterward, gangs became their primary concern, which did not please all tenants. One complained that "everything was about gangs, that's all you heard about from CHA, and there were people ain't had no sink or hot water for months. What about that? No one wanted to hear that, just gangs, gangs, gangs." Their claims were not unfounded. By 1988, CHA and police officials inundated tenants continuously with press releases and programs that touted security improvements. Reports of mandatory ID cards, curfews, video surveillance, emergency searches of apartments, "mob-action" dispersal of gang members, budgetary increases for security guards, and similar measures made it difficult for tenants to introduce into public discourse more basic issues like the compromised state of the buildings.

"It was just out of control in 1987," recalls Edith Huddle, "and it wasn't just the gangs." Huddle and other tenant leaders describe a community in disarray in the mid-1980s, owing both to mounting levels of destructive behavior among the tenant body and to the incapacity of the CHA and law enforcement to make an effective intervention and ensure the safety and welfare of households. The social-control problems caused by ineffective management and tenant unruliness would become even more intense as tenants coped with the expansion of the local Black Kings street gang, relatively dormant since the early 1970s but slowly growing in size through recruitment of local youth and young adults. What began at the start of the decade as sporadic shooting, petty crime, and loitering would transform itself into extortion and outright gang warfare as the gangs sought to protect their narcotics-trafficking operations. With an already distressed physical infrastructure and a populace impatient with its leadership and its landlord, this Black Kings resurgence would stretch the community's resources and the capacity of administrative agencies even further.

From Social Delinquents to Supergang

There was no shortage of media attention paid to the gang and drug problem in the 1980s. Journalists and scholars emphasized the wealth generated by the drug economy (which the urban gang purportedly monopolized), called attention to wayward youth who had chosen delinquent over mainstream career paths, and portrayed entire populations held hostage by the newest rampant outlaw capitalist, the drug-trafficking gang member. In these reports and exposés, the gang developed a superhuman mystique. To the reader, the marauding street bandit appeared to have arisen from nowhere, for there was little information provided as to the gang's growth and expansion. Americans living outside urban poor spaces could find little that resonated with their own experiences. Those in "gang-infested" communities were perceived as victims who confronted an alien presence rather than as parents, social workers, uncles, schoolteachers, and pastors who had relationships with gang-affiliated youth. The role of the community in the activity of the gang and the face that the gang presented to its community were absent from popular discussions of the inner-city gang. Consequently, communities such as Robert Taylor were commonly viewed as disorganized and largely helpless to combat an apparently unanticipated troublemaker.

In contrast, tenants of Robert Taylor Homes recall with considerable clarity and emotion the Black Kings' resurgence in the 1980s. The increase in number and public visibility of gang members was commonly noted, and some people offered explanations for sudden changes in the nature of gang activity.[48] Hardly anyone—gang or non-gang—believed that the Black Kings' advance was a completely deliberate strategy or the product of foresight and commercial acumen on the part of the local gang leaders. Most portrayed the gang's ascent as a chaotic process in which the recklessness and ambition of gang members reached levels that the community could not control or redirect in productive ways. They described a community facing social-control problems that could not be effectively broached through some combination of internal policing and the external resources available to them. "Everything around here was a mess. No one trusted each other, we wasn't working together," recalls Paulina Collins. Gang activity became a problem because tenants were already vulnerable personally as well as in matters of collective security. They saw the rise of the Black Kings as inextricably linked to the general decline of the community's capacity to create a secure environment.

The Robert Taylor community was witnessing one in a succession of changes to the landscape of "gangland." Whereas for much of the twentieth century black street gangs were small, localized adolescent peer groups engaged in petty delinquency, as the 1960s unfolded ghettos turned from "spaces of misery" to "spaces of revolt."[49] Gangs increased in size, boasting several thousand black ghetto males, many of whom had remained members into their young-adult years. These local groups were loosely knit entities, not highly organized assemblages able to implement a set of practical goals, such as drug trafficking. At the end of the 1960s, the Black Kings was one such group, based in Chicago's west side.

The greatest expansion of street-gang activity was a direct result neither of poverty nor of the burgeoning crack economy.[50] It was an outgrowth in the 1970s of the increasingly large population of incarcerated black youths. Prison officials, using gangs to help maintain social control, effectively enabled gangs and their leaders to organize—often members joined simply for protection against indiscriminate physical harassment—and to consolidate, form alliances, and grow in number and strength. In the late 1970s and early 1980s, members returned to ghetto streets and found few legitimate work opportunities but increasing opportunities to sell heroin, cocaine, and marijuana, and to join car-theft rings and extortion rackets. Senior BK leaders recall an older core of members involved in these economies. The city's black street gangs became more cohesive as entrepreneurially motivated members turned to the lucrative crack market, but until then most gangs remained loose-knit youth collectives with sporadic involvement in underground economies.

Into the early 1980s, this pattern defined the Robert Taylor Black Kings gang, a relatively independent federation of individual "sets," that is, balkanized factions, each based in a building or a small number of buildings, ranging from fifty to more than two hundred members. Members of different BK sets had few dealings with one another or with members from other Chicago communities. Most of the city's Black Kings were teens or young adults in their early twenties. All the sets sponsored social activities, such as late-night parties, but the sets differed greatly in the regularity of their meetings, the strength of peer associations, and the attachment that members felt (and displayed) to the group. The Black Kings' presence in the housing development was a social nuisance, tenants argue, for members were mostly petty delinquents who participated irregularly in violent and criminal activity. For these young people gang activity was disproportionately composed of peer interaction, loitering, truancy, and cruising.

Until the mid-1980s, the Black Kings fostered group cohesion primarily through various "collectivist ideologies" such as "family," "nation," and "black brotherhood." Enshrined in literature and oral teachings, these terms were used by members in speeches and casual conversation to emphasize a shared mission and to lend meaning to their activities.[51] Where written and verbal pedagogy is insufficient, Anthony Kline, a BK member active at the time, notes, the use of fines and physical force has always been justified to ensure solidarity: "The Lit[erature of the Black Kings] says you never violate [physically abuse] your own, you always try to take care of it by being up front, but if that don't work, niggers know we'll beat their ass."

The BKs had never consistently displayed entrepreneurial tendencies, and they did not seem to possess the collective shrewdness necessary to manage a large economic operation.[52] After the late 1960s, when Illinois youth were incarcerated in large numbers, the Black Kings formed an organizational network primarily with their black counterparts linking members in prisons and jails with those on the streets—researchers referred to this web as a "supergang."[53] As late as 1985, supergangs were primarily in prison-based drug economies. Evidence of any collective presence in street trafficking—beyond individual members who were trading—was provisional, as only a small proportion of BKs participated in illegitimate revenue generation.[54] These "independents"—typically young adults—labored with considerable autonomy, usually alone or in small groups, and they moved back and forth among narcotics trafficking, stolen-parts sales, extortion, burglary, loansharking, and so on as opportunities became available. Few BKs merged their small-scale ventures into the overall structure by employing other members or by yielding their revenue to the gang's general funding pools.

The birth pangs of the Black Kings' collective commitment to underground economies occurred "around 1985 or so," says Ottie Davis, who watched the advance not only of the BKs but also of his brother Momo, who led the Sharks' advance. Tenants recall that crack cocaine entered the housing development around this time. BKs with connections to suppliers capitalized on the increasing local demand to control the sale of the commodity within the Twenty-fifth to Thirty-third St. area (the Sharks were working in the remaining areas of Robert Taylor).[55] Tenants' descriptions, and those of BK members, suggest that the gang's ascent was not planned in a deliberate manner, but was a haphazard movement inextricably linked to other community dynamics and to the entrepreneurial energies of BKs in other parts of the city.

It is not entirely surprising that tenants would perceive the gang's advance as fortuitous or as tied to other community and social developments. Any street gang's persona will be shaped by its role in the "local and larger neighborhood," to borrow the sociologist Martin Jankowski's phrase, and because the gang encounters skepticism and hostility from other actors, a degree of unpredictability and serendipity regarding its own movement must be expected. In addition, there is the social and psychological diversity of the gang itself. Gangs are not self-evidently homogenous, well-disciplined cadres but composites of individuals with numerous, divergent, and often competing interests and expectations that tenuously cohere. In the face of both external challenges and "defiant individualists," the gang is really an interesting organizational achievement, given that it must continually find ways to resolve these instabilities.[56] Moreover, the expected variation of interest and opinion found among the several hundred members of Robert Taylor's Black Kings gang was enhanced even further once the organization made an unprecedented move toward entrepreneurial-criminal activities.[57]

To facilitate both the gang's new mission and increased heterogeneity, the BK leader Jon Lenard accepted counsel from his brother Grady, two older BK members with whom he had gone to prison for armed robbery, and two younger members, Anthony Kline and Jamie Caldwell. Lenard's inner circle labored to make the Black Kings an entrepreneurial force. They organized periodic meetings of set leaders and persuaded each one to make drug distribution a priority. They sponsored collective activities among all Robert Taylor BKs, and they introduced specific roles for members—for example, "lookout," "enforcer," and "runner." As Anthony stated, "Lot of these folks was real young or was just hanging out, they wasn't gonna start slanging [dealing] ever, shit. But if they didn't, then *we* sold [crack] in their buildings." In addition, they exercised diplomacy, though physical punishment usually won out over persuasion, and created consensus among members with divergent interests and varying levels of tolerance for risky economic ventures.

The threats to the organization's integrity became salient as the BKs entered Robert Taylor's underground economy. The entrepreneurial turn was based not on the commitment or interest of a majority of BK members, but rather on the muscle of several older and higher-ranking BK leaders who pressured Lenard to monopolize local narcotics sales in the housing development.[58] The use of the gang for material gain was a realistic possibility for a senior class who had made contact with a drug supplier, for example, or an auto-theft ring. As one member active at the time stated, "You wasn't in it for the money, and wasn't much going around anyway, it was just niggers acting crazy, bored, or fucked up." The highest-ranking imprisoned Black Kings leaders and their paroled delegates urged Lenard and the Robert Taylor BKs to take over local narcotics trafficking from independent entrepreneurs and to subsume their ventures into the BK structure. "We had a choice," says Grady Lenard, Jon's brother and a BK officer at the time. "These niggers [who were our own leaders] said we could start selling dope, making money for 'em, or we could quit, you know, just leave and they [would] find new niggers to run the shit. They knew folks was getting high, and they wanted their cut."

The pursuit of illegitimate income by the Black Kings gang brought new challenges for BK leaders and slowly reconfigured the organization's identity and members' relationships to one another and to the community. For example, the increasing number of youths who used the gang to earn money sparked jealousies and competitiveness among members. Collectivist ideologies, such as "BK Nation," which emphasized the fictive-kin relation of members, did not always dispel rivalries, arguments, and fighting among BKs. They were written in the 1960s, when the Black Kings had little involvement in economic activities, and they did not contain any specific references to revenue sharing and profit redistribution. To resolve conflicts, BK leaders typically visited each BK faction. This was an unsystematic process whereby each leader used corporal punishment and verbal directives indiscriminately.

The drug selling of local youth provoked widespread concern among neighbors, families, and friends. However, Black Kings' tenets had few references to external relationships; thus, little guidance existed for responding to angry residents, storeowners, pastors, and other stakeholders who criticized their drug trafficking. The BK literature compelled members to be "responsible to our people," and, in fact, some teachings expressly prohibited the BKs from "dealing dope to black brothers and sisters," but few members paid much heed to these proscriptions. Only a small percentage of older members acknowledged the conflict between acting on behalf of the community and contributing to its demise via narcotics trafficking, public violence, and weapons use. Most brushed off suggestions that the gang might be injurious to the community, and senior members referred to economic hardships and the lure of drug-related income as the group's primary motivations. They suggested that members who eschewed trafficking in narcotics as well as "political niggers" who wanted to steer the BKs away from entrepreneurialism gradually and voluntarily left the organization because they realized that the gang was foremost mercantilistic.

As Black Kings members moved into the economic underworld of Robert Taylor, it appeared that another, implicit ideal guided their actions, namely, that black people would ultimately benefit if BK youth were organized, but the former should never be allowed to obstruct the latter's progress. Not surprisingly, this dictum contained the seeds of potential antagonism, especially if the larger community in question did not wholeheartedly welcome the actions of the gang. As the BKs reoriented themselves to an economic horizon, the tenant body resisted. This, in turn, forced the BKs to take stock of their own behavior. "We was doing new shit and folks was pissed," says Grady Lenard, who aspired to lead his own BK faction. "We had to deal with stuff we never did before. We had to organize." The need to "organize" became particularly acute when the BKs threatened the viability of household income by branching out into loansharking, gambling, and "street taxation" of hustlers. Yet BK leaders did not respond to the brewing tenant opposition because they did not feel threatened: "We had guns, you gotta remember that," said Anthony. "We beat the shit out of folks who fucked with us, why you gonna worry about them?"

Tenants agree that neither the citywide BK leadership nor the leaders in Robert Taylor made any sincere attempts to address the gang's changing role in the community. "They just didn't get it," said the tenant Judy Harris, referring to the Black Kings leaders. "You can't take over shit from people that's been selling drugs, making food, fixing cars and shit, for years. You can't come in and just tell 'em you gonna take over their shit. They gonna fight back." Tenants understandably protested against compromised safety, gang members' harassment, and the rising levels of crime and addiction. They were especially disdainful because the Black Kings had started as a historic youth-based organization involved at the grassroots in Chicago's African-American ghettos. To some degree, they were able to empathize with the leaders of the Black Kings because they understood youth as a difficult time of development, a sentiment likely to be found in most American communities. This implies not that tenants tolerated the excesses of gang members, but only that the Black Kings' behavior was comprehensible to them.

In the case of Robert Taylor and other African-American ghetto communities, tenants speak of the gang as having an intimate, although not necessarily harmonious, relationship with the community. The gang is an institution whose twists and turns attract popular interest. Tenants' specific historical references are not local, however, but are to the more infamous Chicago gang families. Tenants remember the Blackstone Rangers, the East Side Disciples, and the Vicelords (all based outside of Robert Taylor) as rowdy and militant, but also as defenders of poor black neighborhoods from "strangers" and other gangs. The gang is also used to illustrate the tension between the black community and the city. Gang members' altercations with police are, after all, not unlike the charged interactions of many black Americans with law enforcement, and gang-police altercations are never far removed, in time or place, from police abuse or harassment of other blacks. Similarly, tenants will say that gang members' unemployment and underground income are common to other ghetto youth. Although they clearly do not condone the gang's behavior, tenants characterize the Black Kings of the 1980s not as a foreign invader but as a distortion of collective youth energies that carried the potential for social change. "It's always been folks like Prince and them," said Kenny Davenport, "always been young people who get pissed and say, you know, it's time to help black folk out. Gangs, remember, were part of the Civil Rights movement around here."[59]

As the Black Kings embarked on their entrepreneurial turn, the Robert Taylor community spoke of this shift in the overall context of declining household safety. For the tenant body, the onset of "gangs and drugs" was the most recent episode in an ongoing struggle to maintain a usable and controlled living environment, albeit in the case of the Black Kings, criminal and violent activities played a more prominent role than in past years. "We had a security problem," said one local activist, Althea Jefferson. "It wasn't just that gangs was shooting, dealing drugs, it was police that wasn't doing their job, CHA wasn't working with us. It was a lot of things going on." The "security problem" captured a complex state of affairs that involved tenants and other groups and organizations and could not be reduced

solely to an increase in youth rancor; indeed, some form of youth rebellion had existed in the housing development since the 1960s.

Tenants point to numerous threatening and socially disruptive BK
activities that combined to reduce the general well-being of households. Tenants were less willing to sit on benches and occupy street
corners when gang members were present. Drug selling in these
spaces threatened their comfortable passage. Inside the buildings, the
gang sold drugs and held meetings in vacated apartments, occupied
lobby areas, and prevented tenants from accessing elevators. Tenant
frustration also stemmed from the more discreet intrusions of Black
Kings members into their long-standing support systems. BKs threatened the secretive "payoff" arrangements between LAC officers and
underground entrepreneurs; BK officers told tenants who earned income off the books to pay them off directly instead of compensating
floor captains, secretaries, and other LAC officers. Black Kings leaders also used monetary disbursements to curry the favor of tenants,
once again challenging the nearly two-decades-old patron-client relations that LAC officers had fostered.

Tenant response to the Black Kings' practices was motivated by a
need to protect well-worn techniques that for two decades had helped
them curb social problems. Tenants complained individually to CHA
managers, police officers, and political leaders, but the Local Advisory
Council stood at the vanguard of their collective response. LAC leaders
and tenants met with one another, as well as with CHA and law enforcement personnel, to discuss the gang's activities and devise intervention strategies. Tenant leaders report minimal law enforcement
support. Even those who had developed brokerage relations with police, and who could influence the response times of particular officers,
were unable to parlay this influence into attention to gang-related activity. These leaders argue that the police feared armed gangs and so
were hesitant to respond to calls by powerful LAC brokers. For many,
their capacity to act as police liaisons became restricted to domestic
abuse or incidents of theft and burglary, wherein an officer might continue to help them locate a perpetrator or recover stolen goods.

These leaders also point to tenant behavior as partly responsible for the decreased security conditions. This is somewhat predictable given that the leaders were defending themselves against accusations of ineffective leadership from both tenants and the media. Their primary complaint is directed at tenants who stored gang members' drugs, weapons, and cash in exchange for a small payment. However, they also cite growing drug use and addiction as well as tenants' own involvement in vandalism and harassment of passersby. Tenants who used drugs were less likely to support their anti-gang initiatives or simply too psychologically distressed to become active participants. Thus the likelihood of a unified response against the gangs—or against the CHA—decreased.[60] "People was using that stuff to forget about things," said Kim Walton, an LAC building president. "They was miserable and they was just buying the drugs. You couldn't get ten people to come to a [tenant] meeting. We tried to get them to march with us, but no one came."

The gang's behavior was certainly a critical cause of the community's problems, but it acted in concert with a negligent Housing Authority that did not ensure that all apartments were in habitable condition. LAC leaders lobbied the Housing Authority heavily to assist them in developing a response to the gang's practices, but they had little success. By the mid-1980s, the CHA's priorities had shifted away from the empowerment of residents and the maintenance of usable space in and around buildings, and toward more decidedly law-enforcement-based approaches that broke up the gang's activities and arrested its members. For example, in the past, disturbances inside the buildings were typically reported to LAC officials, who in turn asked CHA managers to remove squatters from hallways, stairwells, and vacated apartments—in the ideal case, the managers then rehabbed the dwellings and resettled them with new families. Not surprisingly, LAC officers argue that the powerful LAC members had greater success than others in enlisting these Housing Authority resources; their buildings had markedly lower vacancy rates.

Throughout the 1980s, the CHA allowed vacancy rates to rise (either through failed apartment upkeep or through the glacial pace of tenant relocation into available units), and CHA officials instructed security guards not to leave lobby areas; the colonization of apartments, hallways, and galleries by gang members and drug users grew as a point of concern. Even though CHA officials agreed that leaving apartments vacated led to increased gang activity, tenant leaders could not acquire assistance from them when gang members broke down doors and converted apartments into crack dens, party rooms, and meeting places, or when BKs partied and caroused on the galleries and threw items onto the ground below.[61] At the time, the Housing Authority addressed the tenants' outcries either with admissions that CHA managers were not performing their jobs effectively, or by suggesting that their security personnel were more successful if they patrolled the entryway to a building, thereby leaving interdiction in the high-rises to police and gang-intelligence teams.[62]

It was clear that the CHA had placed its hopes on the use of law enforcement–based "suppression" tactics; few additional measures were in place to stem gang activity.[63] Several LAC officers had offered alternative security suggestions to CHA personnel, such as expanding usable public spaces and placing restrictions on parking in grassy areas, where gangs often conducted meetings or "hung out," but they had little luck convincing the CHA to act on them. The net result was diminished public intercourse, sporadic gatherings of individuals in common areas, and the reduction of casual community surveillance known as "eyes upon the street."

Reports of gang members bribing CHA officials compounded the tenant leaders' difficulties.[64] CHA management did not deny that their managers and security officers were being paid off by gang members, and in perhaps the most harsh public accusation of his own personnel, CHA Chairman Vincent Lane concluded that gang members reduced the effectiveness of his security force to "two dead flies."[65] "You couldn't do nothing if you was LAC once [gangs] got a hold of CHA folks," explains Judy Harris. "Gangs started giving their own money to [CHA guards and managers]. Then they wouldn't work with us no more. Shit, sometimes they let gangs sell drugs wherever, beat niggers up, wouldn't do nothing for us." The gang's potential to replace the LAC was limited because gang members could never provide all the same services, such as acting as liaisons with the police and granting access to institutions in the wider world. However, gang leaders' bribing of CHA staffers decreased safety, both directly by cutting off an avenue of enforcement and indirectly by compromising relations between tenants and the CHA.

Undeniably, the LAC officials themselves played a complicit role in the diminished effectiveness of CHA personnel. For more than a decade, LAC leaders had positioned themselves as the primary liaison to the CHA, and in the eyes of some, this self-defined task included the use of payoffs and influence to win favors from various CHA officials. Leaders defended these relationships as a necessary compromise, that is, they were faced with poor law enforcement services and so a personal tie to a CHA official might make up for absent police protection. In the words of one LAC building president who admitted to serving her own interests, "It was one hand washing the other, and gangs turned all that around, messed it all up. Lot of us [LAC leaders] had worked long time to get these [CHA managers] to help us, maybe give them something, a little something for it. Wasn't that easy no more, 'cause these folks [in the BKs] could pay them lot more. Wasn't fair." The gangs had disrupted LAC members' off-the-books arrangements with Housing Authority officials. Thus, LAC leaders may have expressed dismay at gang activity and CHA staff relationships for "security" reasons, but it was clear that their concern was also with securing their own power over the residents and ensuring that they could use their political office for personal gain.

Tenant leaders remark that 1987–1988 as a whole was a turning point for the Robert Taylor development, indicative as it was of tenants' withered capacity to build a habitable community in the face of so many parties that were engaged in compromising, questionable, and criminal activities. At that time, the BK leader Jon Lenard was sending two officers, Anthony Kline and Jamie Caldwell, to the

BK-controlled high-rises to extort money from underground entrepreneurs and to punish those who refused their requested "payoffs." Typically, Anthony and Jamie would hire tenants as informants, paying them to monitor illicit economic activity in the building and to notify the leaders when payoff schemes formed between the local LAC building president and his or her constituents. To stop the gang's intervention, tenants pleaded with adults who had direct ties to the younger BKs and interrupted family gatherings to lobby parents and uncles. The LAC building president Kelly Davis and Amy Madison, both based in the 230 Elm St. high-rise, argue that these were once effective means to promote vigilant social control by parents and guardians. However, as gangs became entrepreneurial and more organized, adult control diminished considerably—Kelly Davis noted that their attempts were stymied because tenants whose children were in gangs were becoming reliant on the extra income that BK members brought into the household.

The tenants' valiant efforts met with verbal threats by BK members until the spring of 1988, when senior BK officers assaulted several men living in 230 for their refusal to make the payoffs to Anthony and Jamie. "It was tough after that," says Kelly Davis, referring to the nearly fatal beating of Maurice Wilson by gang members in broad daylight outside her building. "That's when we knew it was for real, we needed help, that's when all the bad stuff [warrantless, surprise apartment searches and mob action] with CHA started happening too. Hell! We was fighting each other, fighting CHA, fighting the gangs. It ain't never been the same since."

The beating of Maurice Wilson by several BK leaders with baseball bats caught the attention of tenants throughout Robert Taylor because it signaled a new *modus operandi* for "project living." From the perspective of an LAC officer in the 230 building, *"No one* knew what to do, you know what I'm saying. We ain't never seen nothing like that, young kids beating up people for nothing, people shooting each other. These were our children! Maurice [Wilson] was a good man, too, didn't deserve to be beat like that. We couldn't control them no more." Gang members and tenants both wanted to resolve the conflicts between them, but for slightly different reasons. For the Black Kings, the conflicts with tenants were inopportune because the organization was busy battling its enemy, the Sharks, for control over drug distribution in several buildings in Robert Taylor. For the tenants, a new set of security-related threats in the form of gunfire and week-long gang wars had manifested itself, and they needed to find altogether different techniques for maintaining a safe and secure living environment. As CHA resources declined, as gangs reportedly bribed CHA personnel, as public space became uninhabitable, and as the LAC grew ineffective, the traditional security measures failed to provide adequate protection.

By 1988, numerous areas in Robert Taylor had witnessed hostile encounters between gangs and tenants that were not being met with effective mediation—although the confrontations were not always as dramatic as the beating of Maurice Wilson. In most areas of the housing development the conflict stemmed from actions that affected ease of intercourse within public space (for example, loitering by gang members) or that destabilized the coping mechanisms that tied households together in systems of sharing and support (for example, gang members' disruption of tenant patrols).

Although each building probably had some type of tenant intervention in response to BK activities, residents suggest that effective social control was generally limited. There were some adolescents who might be dissuaded altogether from joining the gang, but tenants felt impotent in the face of older leaders who recruited with tangible displays of income and consumer power. These young-adult BK leaders would use force against their critics, so tenants had to tread carefully when confronting them. Tenants responded to their new challenges largely in fragmentary ways, acting on their own with their children and hoping that schools or other institutions might deter youth from gang involvement. There was little unified action, that is, there was no large-scale movement to lobby the CHA, as there had been in the late 1960s, and tenant leaders did not coordinate their efforts with one another to form a unified front. Occasionally they met with police and CHA municipal officials, and in some buildings an LAC officer might have devised a particular relationship with the local BK gang leader. In exceptional cases, such as in the 205 building, where Kim Walton reached an accord with Anthony Kline to limit narcotics trafficking to certain floors and specific times of the day, residents took advantage of the détente by running errands or using playgrounds. However, in most buildings, it appeared that residents simply adjusted their daily patterns to accommodate times when public gang activity peaked.

Differences of opinion had quietly surfaced in the tenant body regarding the community's new "corporate" gang presence. There were no distinct political camps, but some issues displayed a partisan character. Even the relatively straightforward decision to make gang-related activity a priority, which by that time was commanding the energies of local leaders, administrative agencies, and advocacy groups, could not generate consensus or equanimity. Some tenants simply believed that gangs unfairly overshadowed other pressing issues such as police ineffectiveness, entrenched unemployment, and poor apartment maintenance.

One of the most contentious issues dividing tenants was news of households that fashioned secretive agreements with Black Kings gang members. For example, in exchange for a small monthly payment or escape from physical harassment, people may have promised gang members the use of their apartments to hide narcotics. The temporary benefits could include decreased abuse of household members, but the proliferation of such individual contracts would jeopardize unified tenant social control. Few people claim that such arrangements were common. Nonetheless, tenants' descriptions of the 1980s are rife with such tales. "Folks was looking for anything, they was desperate back then," said Ottie Davis. "Think about it, what would you do when these niggers had guns, was dealing drugs, would kill you if you opened your mouth? Hell yeah, you'd be trying to make them happy, you promise these fools anything to leave you alone."

The gang's sporadic payments to tenants and their threats of physical abuse were serious, but they were the early stages of a more ma-
ture and invidious street-gang presence. It was not Jon Lenard and his
aging, thirty-something friends who were pushing the BKs vigorously
into the tenants' lives. It was a younger group, led by recent high
school graduates, including Anthony Kline, Jamie Caldwell, and
Prince Williams, who took the entrepreneurial spirit of the Black
Kings more seriously (much to the delight of their superiors, who removed Jon Lenard from office and replaced him with Caldwell). They
were on their way to disciplining the membership, helping the BKs to
shed the guise of a wild youth gang and present the image of an outlaw capitalist cabal. In doing so, they heightened the anger that tenants felt toward gangs and tested the traditional empathy that "poor
black folk" in Chicago had for this marginal youth group. As the
gangs moved decidedly into the drug trade, their resemblance to the
earlier BKs lay in name only. The distinction many tenants draw between "gang wars" in the 1960s and 1970s and "drug wars," which
characterized the 1980s, highlights their perception of this change:
"It used to be *gang* wars. It's all *drug* wars now."

———

Social observers of the "underclass" experience point out that the
1980s was a traumatic period for the urban poor. Some social problems grew entrenched (low labor-force participation) while others
cropped up anew (corporate gangs). As the happenings in Robert Taylor indicate, the decade is only partially rendered through measures
of unemployment or homicide rates. It was the process by which the
urban poor fought to secure their homes and their communities in
light of these changes that really marks their extraordinary plight during the 1980s.

The particular struggle of the Robert Taylor community bore witness to a complex set of changes, some occurring in the confines of
the housing development and others taking place in the halls of state
and industry, and all coming together to redefine the experience of

"project living." The rise of the BK supergang captured popular attention and attracted the resources of administrative agencies. However, a range of issues, from maintenance to ineffective tenant leadership, had created what one tenant called a "security problem." This problem involved the inability of many actors, in the housing development and outside, to ensure that residents received protective services and that disorder and crime, when they did occur, could be addressed and resolved appropriately, with minimal consequences.

Since the 1960s, the possibility of making the housing development viable was premised on the provision of sufficient resources by various government agencies. It would be foolhardy not to link the worsening situation in the 1980s to the massive resource declines that the Reagan administration—and the supportive socially conservative American electorate—brought about through cutbacks to public housing funding, through retrenched funding for programs that affected the lives of ghetto dwellers, and through a stubborn refusal to ensure that the changing American economy did not abandon the needy and the working poor.[66] Most alarmingly, the federal government slashed the CHA's budget by 87 percent during the decade. And given the correlative government reduction in direct funding for urban transportation, social services, economic development, and housing construction, there was little chance for organizations in the surrounding ghetto communities to make up for the shortfalls.

The CHA could have taken steps to realign its policies and address the early signs of instability. Independent consultants recommended that the agency make heightened law enforcement one part of a more holistic security approach. They suggested that decreasing the social and physical isolation of the development from the broader community would have as valuable—if not more valuable—a long-term impact on safety as the use of surprise, paramilitary-style law enforcement tactics. The CHA failed to incorporate many such proposals. By the end of the decade, mismanagement, scandal, corruption, and poor decision making at the CHA warranted a federal takeover.

Another facet of Reaganomics, its support of the American creed of individualism, contributed to the declining quality of life. "Greed is good," proclaimed Michael Douglas in defense of corporate downsizing in the movie *Wall Street,* which featured the yuppie icon and investment banker Gordon Gecko. This mantra, when placed alongside the ideology of personal responsibility with which Reagan defended his refusal to direct government money to the poor and needy, defined the former president's "bootstrap" public-policy view. It received considerable support not only from Republicans but also from a weary middle and upper class of liberal and left Americans no longer willing to support "handouts" for the poor.[67] And to complicate matters, the social conservatism of a yuppie population was paralleled by similar attitudes within an advantaged black class—sometimes called "buppies"—who themselves expressed many conservative views on social policy and matters of personal conduct in the ghetto.

The equivalent of "greed is good" on ghetto streets could be found in the declarations "I got mine, "I'm getting mine," and other internalizations of crass consumerism and self-interest that appeared most vividly in rap music and film. Dangerously, for ghetto dwellers, the retrenchment of government and the "bootstrap" mentality did not coincide with ample legitimate opportunities to live out the yuppie/buppie lifestyle; indeed, welfare provisions, sporadic menial-labor opportunities, and a growing illicit underground market defined sustenance possibilities. These economies did not spawn large numbers of underground Gordon Geckos, that is, a new ghetto petite bourgeoisie rooted in drug trafficking and off-the-books work, but numbers and success stories were not altogether important for a community seeking to ensure its well-being. A high-profile, dangerously unstable avenue of illegitimate gain had made an indelible impression on the ghetto population, particularly on young people who had channeled their frustrations with an irrelevant and poorly funded educational system into experimentation with the glorified world of drug running. Most of the large U.S. cities suffered an entrenched drug market that was helping to destroy the community fabric of the ghetto. Unlike cities such as New York, where large city-wide gangs had a relatively minimal presence, in Chicago and Los Angeles, mobility in the underworld was dominated by street-gang members, and their numbers continued to grow as more youth turned to them seeking opportunities for mobility. There was little question that the corporate "supergang" had become one of the most serious challenges facing Chicago's poor as they struggled to control their young people and reproduce habitable communities.

Despite intense popular attention to the drug-running street gang, America remained ignorant of the ways in which communities responded practically to burgeoning drug economies, to the gangs who controlled them, and to the youth who were attracted by them. As important, Americans were not cognizant of the fact that these problems were being neglected by the very government agencies responsible for helping to protect ghetto communities. In Robert Taylor, the Black Kings gang used rampant drug distribution, threats, abuse, and the colonization of public space to exploit a tenant body that was in a socially and economically precarious position. BK leaders based in the housing development explain their entrepreneurial actions as the result of pressures from their own, higher-ranking leaders, but to forge their path they intimidated residents and took advantage of their vulnerable social and economic status. With law enforcement agents providing them with minimal assistance apart from "suppression" programs that did not yield any reductions in gang violence or crime, tenants' last line of defense was the "hustles" and self-help mechanisms they had devised a decade earlier. Yet in their drive to become outlaw capitalists, Black Kings members had begun disrupting these networks and associations through which households supported one another. The gangs demonstrated a willingness to use weapons, bribes, and physical punishment to co-opt or threaten tenants who stood in their way. As in any other American community, it was not realistic to expect that tenant reliance on one another and their self-help schemes could continue to provide safety in the face of an armed and threatening group and an insignificant police presence.

In addition, by replacing the LAC as the erstwhile regulator of underground economic activity, the gang had expanded its role and purpose in the community. Yet it was not entirely clear that the gang's manner of regulation—most often physical force combined with expensive payoffs—could provide some of the modest benefits of the LAC. At the least, some LAC members might still be able to influence police activity or keep government agents' eyes away from tenants' hidden income. Moreover, as these leaders argued, their own status rose in the eyes of CHA officials when they showed control over tenant behavior, which could lead to other potential benefits and services, such as apartment repair or elevator maintenance. This may not have been the preferred mode of public housing management for most residents, but they certainly preferred it to a street gang that tried to conduct security-related functions.

Given their history in the 1970s, it is plausible to assume that LAC members could have worked together more effectively in the 1980s to ensure that the gang's advances were met with adequate opposition. However, this conclusion should be drawn cautiously. LAC leaders explained that they were in a state of shock in the 1980s and largely unprepared for the marauding street-gang brigade that would abuse them, or worse, if they resisted. We cannot discount their personal fear of gangs; nor should we expect them to perform a role that stakeholders in most American communities with decent police protection were not being asked to assume. As one tenant leader aptly stated, "[Controlling the gang's drug selling and violence was] not our job, and we was getting lot of heat for not keeping these kids in line. These [gang members] was thirty-year-olds dealing drugs, they wasn't little babies skipping school. It was the police's job." The absence of formal agents of social control does not excuse the LAC members' own steps to protect their personal interests by forging arrangements with CHA officials (bribery) or gang members (accepting payoffs). Nonetheless, such questionable practices must be viewed in the context of the gang's extraordinary powers of intimidation and law enforcement's equally noteworthy ineffectiveness when making any realistic assessment of the LAC's possible interventionist role.

I entered the Robert Taylor Homes at the start of the 1990s and in the aftermath of this decade of tremendous change. I encountered a population in the wake of a debilitating period of upheaval, but also one poised at the onset of renewal. Tenants had witnessed the metamorphosis of the gang from a grassroots youth organization that had always been delinquent but on the precipice of being a potential resource base, to an organized criminal enterprise with diminishing signs of promise. They had just seen the breakup of a number of important mechanisms by which they were able to make "project living" viable, although not necessarily fully enjoyable, for much of the 1960s and 1970s. But if defeat was at their doorstep, it was not always expressed in their faces. Especially among older tenants who had lived through the Civil Rights era, there was measured optimism that the community might come together as it had done in the past to address personal and collective hardships. Interestingly, many located the cause and the solution to their problems in the younger generation of households that had moved into the housing development. As Paulina Collins once said reflectively, "Us old folks, we lived through worse than this. We just have to teach our babies not to be so down all the time. Gangs and drugs, yeah, but it ain't the end of the world. They gotta fight, it's up to them, really."

In the same conversation, Collins admitted that the specific nature of the struggle had changed in the 1980s. The fight for a habitable Robert Taylor was going to require more than the ongoing battle to secure city services and police protection. Few tenants could gauge where they would find the strength or the resources to live "the good life." They did know, however, that the Black Kings gangs and an underground economy anchored in the exchange of narcotics would be with them as they entered the next decade. They knew that the probability of making Robert Taylor a community worth living in would be predicated on their ability to handle the corporate gang in a unified and effective manner.

4 | Tenants Face Off with the Gang

In late summer of 1990, under a bright blue Midwestern sky, several hundred people gathered in front of the 236 S. Elm St. building to watch a basketball game. Several hundred more stood on the galleries of the sixteen-story high-rise, watching and eating. Under a bright yellow canopy, the players took relief from the midday sun, drinking water and replenishing themselves for the second half. Music blared from car stereos, young girls skipped rope, and children took turns yelling into the loudspeaker. The return of the players signaled the resumption of the main event, but in this festive atmosphere, audience and performer were interchangeable. People cheered the two teams, signaling their respective allegiances as the players joked and jibed with the audience, responding with gesture, speech, or, on occasion, a feat of athleticism that demanded tribute. On the surface, this was a street carnival of the type Rabelais might have envisioned, where individuals suspended their routines and habits, forgot their hardships, and led "their second lives, organized on the basis of laughter."[1]

These recreational tournaments were signature summer events in the Robert Taylor Homes. At this particular festival, billed as the "BK Superfest" after the sponsoring group, people came to watch the final game of a month-long tournament between factions of the local Black Kings street gang. Four "BK sets" were competing for local bragging rights. In the championship game, the "Twenty-seventh St. Black Kings" fought "The End" for the title. The crowd, as well as the team members, sported hats and T-shirts emblazoned with the gang's titles and insignia and exchanged shouts of superiority for the BK set "representing" their high-rise.

At the Superfest, the Black Kings passed out free food and beverages to the crowd. The gang had consolidated its control of a lucrative crack cocaine trade and was now redistributing some of its revenue to the tenant body. For Kenny Davenport, a long-time resident, the gang's charity was a cautionary sign that "the gangs are trying to take over around here; lot of people can't see that." Davenport and his peers watched in disbelief as tenants consorted with "murderers and thugs"—one of Davenport's descriptions of the BKs. Some passers-by stopped to announce their horror or their support for the event: "Why are you complaining?" one man yelled at Davenport. "Ain't like anybody else doing stuff for folks." "That's right, at least they're giving back to the community," someone else responded, to which Davenport's peer, Ottie Davis, retorted, "These niggers [in the gang] ain't giving us nothing but trouble."

The occasional sharing of wealth by a street gang was not itself at the root of the tenants' concern; indeed, the BK's celebration, albeit grandiose, had historical precedent in youth groups—progressive, criminal, and militant.[2] Instead, residents' concern was directed at the behavior of the young Black Kings leaders, who orchestrated public displays that ranged from time-worn promenades to showcase personal wealth—for example, cruising in a new sports car or walking with bodyguards—to recreational tournaments and parties for other BK members and, on occasion, for the entire tenant body. The young gang leaders had become local politicos, each a statesman who inspired fear in some, awe or repugnance in others, but interest in nearly everyone. These were bright individuals whom many tenants expected to move outside the housing development eventually and find work in a meaningful job; they did not expect to watch them suffer the fate of other young people who shunned mainstream employment and turned instead to the underworld to earn a living.

If they had been content to amass their personal fortunes or to consolidate the commercial capacities of the gang, the leaders may not have attracted such attention—although they may still have been hated for their actions. But each was zealously pursuing a larger role in the community, one that materialized as a result of their frustration with unsatisfying legitimate work and the personal affirmation they received in gangland. In the words of Prince Williams, the Black

Kings leader, they wanted to "better the community," albeit not as elected leaders might, but rather as powerful lords who deigned to provide for the needs of their tenants. As if they were heeding a noble calling, they claimed that "folks around [Robert Taylor] been fucked over all their lives," and that they were "trying to help people that no one cares about no more." These leaders were trying to win legitimacy from the population while managing a criminal and dangerous entrepreneurial venture. To be saddled with outbursts of gunfire, rampant drug distribution, and extended periods of gang violence was itself a sizable burden for an economically destitute community with few resources. But then to confront the perpetrators of these disruptions and to find that they aspired to a legitimate role in the social life of the housing development, and had the organizational wherewithal to launch their campaign, was far more disturbing.

The new orientation of the Black Kings leadership was part of a more extensive set of changes in Robert Taylor at the close of the 1980s. Many of the most important shifts stemmed from the redefined role of the Chicago Housing Authority. Newly appointed CHA Chairman Vincent Lane had made security a top priority and had created a separate police force to patrol the housing development and to lead the agency's use of "sweeps" and other surprise anti-gang initiatives. "Public housing security is at a crisis state," said Lane, "where the gangs are in control of some of the buildings. We, the CHA, aren't in control."[3] Lane's new tactics split the community, pitting supporters of law enforcement against those advocating a more holistic approach. Tenants had grown more modest in their expectations that the Housing Authority would meet the physical needs of the housing development. Their ability to influence CHA maintenance schedules had been reduced, although not eliminated entirely, and only a few could boast brokerage relationships with police and CHA staffers.

Tenant leaders found their constituents to be weary and unable to sustain involvement in community affairs; leaders attributed the increase in tenant apathy to gang intimidation, crack cocaine and heroin use, alcohol abuse, and the introduction of new, younger households with no experience in local politics. They voiced uncertainty as to whether they could continue to perform their role and help the tenant body. They were not acting in as cohesive a manner as they could have been; they were at times speechless when asked to name organizations that could come to their aid; they did not know quite how to rekindle tenants' spirits; and they were not sure how to interpret the new claims of the Black Kings leaders that they were helping the community. To paraphrase the philosopher Antonio Gramsci, in the Robert Taylor Homes the old order was dying and the new had yet to be born.

Leveled Aspirations and the Turn to "Gangland"

It is not unusual for leaders of a "corporate" street gang to desire stable relations with neighborhood residents. Yet the question arises, Why take pains to "better the community"? If only to ensure their revenue from drug sales, the leaders could have relied on bribery and intimidation and perhaps an occasional good deed, such as retrieving stolen property for residents. Indeed, this was the *modus operandi* of previous street-gang leaders at Robert Taylor. To varying degrees of clarity and thoughtfulness, the BK leaders articulated an agenda that politicized their "social bonds" to the community, one that they believed should not be reduced solely to personal gain.[4] "We want folks around here to respect us, understand we're trying to do good," said the BK leader Anthony Kline. Their words, filled simultaneously with allusions to autonomy, wealth, community welfare, and family security, appear at odds with their criminal enterprise, which fostered insecurity and compromised safety in Robert Taylor. Whether they were well-meaning, self-serving, or simply hypocritical, it is worthwhile to take a closer look at the gang leaders' aspirations and their perception of the gang's role in the community in the early 1990s.

Whereas in the mid-1980s some Black Kings members still had no real desire to earn underground income, by the end of the decade,

they had either left the gang or moved to the organization's peripher-
ies. The BK's raison d'être had become that of illicit revenue generation. The gang's primary economic role was that of drug trafficker, but
it also regularly involved extorting storeowners and bribing
non-gang–affiliated underground entrepreneurs. The organizational
realignment toward petty accumulation meant not that all of the approximately five hundred BK members in 1990 were actively involved in narcotics sales and "street taxes," but that the nucleus of
the gang's activities and resources was directed at maintaining an
economic operation. The "core" group of nearly two hundred members had some regular involvement in underground economic activities as dealers, lookouts, runners, producers, street tax agents, and so
on; a peripheral group replaced the core members when the latter relocated, were jailed, or stopped trading.[5] Nearly all the core members
were over eighteen because most of the BK leaders did not feel that
younger "shorties" (gang members) could be trusted with responsibilities such as holding cash and cooking and packaging crack cocaine.[6]
As the shorties aged and became potential "core" members, the leaders entrusted them with specific duties, such as keeping drugs on
their person, to see whether they were comfortable with entrepreneurial pursuits. There were always shorties who preferred to remain
peripheral members after such experiences, and for them, BK
affiliation meant participation in impromptu gang fights and peer interaction in social and recreational activities.

The BKs claimed 70 percent of the drug market in Robert Taylor,
nearly 1.5 miles of the 2-mile stretch of territory, while the Sharks
controlled the remaining area. Apart from a few buildings that appeared to move back and forth between Sharks and BK affiliation
every five years or so (no resident could find a reason for the vacillation), the BKs operated in a territory that they had controlled since
the 1970s and that grew only slightly (by three buildings) because Jon
Lenard and his leadership cadre began selling crack to the tenants before the Sharks leaders could do so. The youths living in the three
buildings swore allegiance to the BKs—switching if they were

affiliated with the Sharks—to avoid harassment and abuse by the newly arriving BKs. Tenants perceived the incoming BK presence as a security threat because the gang members who were already there, most of whom spent time idly in the lobbies and surrounding areas, were being replaced, according to Ottie Davis, by "[BKs] who were making cash . . . niggers who'll beat your ass if you get in their business." Their LAC leaders established relations with neighboring LAC leaders who lived in BK territory, such as Edna Baxter and Patricia Cowens, thereby bolstering their support base should negotiations with BK leaders become necessary.

Consolidating their narcotics trade took the BKs several years and involved many members. But the leaders who were in power in 1990, namely, Anthony Kline, Jamie Caldwell, Prince Williams, Mason Watson, C-Note Miller, and Grady Lenard, accepted much of the credit for the organization's corporate turn. Their boasts are not without some merit. In systematizing drug sales, with Prince's help, Anthony and Jamie reconstituted the Black Kings by creating four sets, one for each building or set of buildings, led by C-Note, Mason, Grady, and Jamie—Jamie was the highest ranking of the four. This configuration made the day-to-day activities of the rank-and-file members more routine. Placed in sales groups of four or six people and assigned to specific locations, members sold narcotics at all hours (most of them also worked in legitimate jobs). Smaller teams secured their turf with patrols of the perimeter. Each set had a four-to-six-person officer body that created timetables and shifts for the sales and security teams and that collected street taxes from underground entrepreneurs. The "set leader" oversaw this activity and monitored developments, such as an arrested member in need of bail or legal defense, and shared information with other leaders weekly. The entire membership met once or twice a month in a public area, church, or social-service agency. An agenda for a typical meeting covered, in order: attendance, dues collection, sales reports, arrests and injuries to members, discussion of superiors' directives, notification of border disputes (typically with the enemy Sharks gang), and physical and monetary punishment of members who violated group by-laws.

The BK leaders also claim responsibility for incorporating non-criminal activities into the gang's repertoire. Trafficking, extortion, and attempts to bribe tenants, CHA security officers, and law enforcement officials were part of their daily labors; however, the leaders also monitored the behavior of strangers who entered the housing development by car and on foot, a behavior undoubtedly shaped in part by the need to safeguard the teams of drug sellers who stood in building lobbies and outside areas. It was not common, but also not entirely unusual, to see BKs helping tenants in their buildings with a small cash disbursement. During the summer they routinely hosted cook-outs and passed out free food and beer. Throughout the year, they offered the use of a car for errands, and they assisted tenant leaders in their search for apartment burglars. This behavior was not a regular occurrence around 1990, and its altruism may have been secondary to the need to watch over law enforcement and ensure that drug sales proceeded smoothly. Nonetheless, the occurrence of these activities, however infrequent and whatever the motives involved, was significant because it led tenants to draw parallels between the BKs and earlier youth organizations in the housing development that also had some noncriminal connection to the populace. The involvement in violence, weapons, and drug trafficking made the BKs' persona historically novel but not wholly unrelated to their predecessors who had led youth gangs in the housing development and who had made an effort to participate in the general affairs of the community.[7]

Tenants had few misgivings that, at root, the Black Kings were primarily interested in revenue generation and would not hesitate to use intimidation and violence to maintain their income. However, the strong personalities of some BK leaders and the occasional distribution of food and clothing, such as in the BK superfest, penetrated the collective consciousness and led to discussions among the tenants regarding what the future would hold with this new leadership class at the helm. Tenants were scrutinizing the actions and the biographies of the leaders in order to understand recent developments, and to see where, how far, and in what direction the multidimensional pursuits of the gang might take the BKs and the community as a whole.

Although each of the new BK leaders possessed traits that drew the attention of tenants, Prince Williams was the most charismatic and carefully watched. Prince was a college graduate. He stored his diploma and additional mementos of his accomplishments at his mother's apartment in Robert Taylor. He had even held a white-collar corporate job, and his choice to keep an apartment in a middle-class black neighborhood, where his girlfriend and child lived, and his intention to find a house "in the suburbs" for his mother were visible carryovers of his earlier mainstream lifestyle. Many of the other Black Kings leaders could also boast personal accomplishments. They did not all sit at the top of their high school class, but each had matriculated; not all were college graduates, but many had attended college; and although they had spent time in jail, they also had worked at length in legitimate jobs. Anthony Kline, a tall, stocky, and charming BK leader, was a basketball star in high school, class president his sophomore year, captain of the varsity football team, and had ambitions to transfer from his junior college and play at a university. Mason was a local chess standout who traveled with a youth group to participate in regional tournaments and who eventually competed in academic quiz competitions. Jamie Caldwell was co-captain of his high school basketball team and received a partial scholarship to a local college. Each of them appeared active in church and local recreational leagues.

Why, then, were they investing so much time and energy in the gang when other avenues were open to them? The fact that they had opportunities to leave the ghetto and pursue legitimate careers that carried far less risk of injury, death, arrest, and shame suggests that, at some point in their lives, they may have weighed their options. Their biographies and the characterizations of their friends and families offer information that challenges conventional wisdom regarding the outlook of ghetto youth and the ways gang membership might affect their development. It was clear that their own ascension in the gang was not a retreat from the community, but a redefinition of their role in the social and economic life of Robert Taylor, a process in which neighbors, friends, and family—to varying degrees—played a role.

The individual decision to join a gang has absorbed scholars of street gangs for nearly a century. Well into the postwar era, researchers advanced either structural or cultural explanations. A structural account usually pointed to the ineffective function of social-control agents such as neighborhood-based organizations (church or family) or macro-social institutions (the labor market), the result of which made a community "socially disorganized" and a target for gang activity. A cultural explanation looked "inside" the gang member and tried to locate a root cause in either a psychological trait, such as a propensity for delinquency, or a lower-class lifestyle generally. Those influenced by the sociologist Robert Merton incorporated some cultural components into their structural account by arguing that in the context of poverty, the gang member was using illegitimate avenues to pursue conventional goals—that is, no separate culture existed for those in the gang, just a different opportunity structure. And in another combination of structural and cultural factors, researchers suggested that gang members may have shared some unique attitudes or values, but that these were subject to redefinition as their experiences changed; thus, the gang's usefulness for individuals was situational, and the acceptance of gang activity as normative could change as situations changed.[8]

These analyses shared a vision of gang activity as a youth phenomenon.[9] Over an ideal life course, individuals "exited out" of the gang—the term used by researchers—soon after adolescence, formed families, developed friendships beyond the gang, and left "gangland" to enter the legitimate labor force. Typically, they exited to blue-collar work that demanded little training and only minimal educational achievement.[10] In this manner, a community's capacity to control gang activity relied on the aging of gang members and their maturing out of such activity.[11]

In the Black Kings gang, the process had shifted. As with other "underclass" gang formations (researchers sometimes referred to the BKs as a "corporate" gang), their activities focused around the generation of income in underground economies. These revenue sources played an important role for the livelihood of members because there were few other employment opportunities for which they would qualify, given their low levels of education and training. Thus, into the 1980s, young-adult members were not leaving the Black Kings and moving into the labor force. (Even exceptional people such as Prince and his peers who had partially reduced their involvement in the BKs nevertheless returned to the gang and had become full-time gang leaders as they neared their thirtieth birthdays.)[12] Once again, structural accounts of this relatively recent change emphasized eviscerated institutions, such as the church, schools, and family: continued gang involvement was an *adaptation* to weak labor markets and retrenched government services caused by the departure of traditional centers of employment and the declining support for liberal social programs.[13] Cultural readings pointed to the psychological profile of individuals who yearned for the raciness of gang life, who sought the support of like-minded peers, or who used rational calculations to determine that gangland offered more economic benefits than the mainstream.[14]

Prince and other BK leaders certainly made adjustments to the lack of legitimate opportunities in the broader society by climbing the BK organizational ladder, and at times, they admit to a preference for gangland. However, their extended tenure in the Black Kings was not a blind, passive adaptation to constraints such as poverty. Nor were they so strategic that they rationally determined that gang activity was optimal for personal growth and development. As Ruth Horowitz discovered in her own study of gang members in a Chicano community, their biographies fell somewhere in between: their lives were an ongoing drama in which situations and events arose that were not always predicted; their actions were not always fully informed; and their politicized views of the obstacles that American blacks faced in getting ahead spawned their pessimistic attitude toward, and "refusal to compete" in, society's "rigged" mobility game.[15] It would be mistaken to think that they were either destined for, or pursued willfully, the life of a gang leader.

The notion that aspirations reflect "an individual's view of his/her own chances of getting ahead" may provide a way to understand how gang leaders exercise their own will even though they are socially constrained.[16] Some of the BK leaders had the choice of pursuing a more sanctioned path, but all eventually ended up living in the ghetto and forging their identities in gangland. Most important, they did not end up in Robert Taylor because they had no ambition or sense of the good life. Rather, their gradual move away from mainstream career paths and into gangland was probably shaped by their perception of which path was more likely to fulfill their aspirations.

Youth aspirations are not formed solely by family and peers. Municipal and market settings, civic life in the neighborhood, and larger institutional arenas such as media affect an individual's view of the world and how he imagines his place in it.[17] Gang involvement "is never an individual decision alone."[18] For gang members, the wider community can be a field of antagonistic social interaction, colored by the persistent need to respond to altercations with storeowners, law enforcement and truancy officers, family members, and so on, all of which shapes the individual's tolerance for gang activity.[19] It is important to note, however, that youth can also have non-contentious relationships with these actors. Through both forms of intercourse, they are exploring their ambitions, constructing their identities, and otherwise ascertaining the likelihood that they will get ahead in different social spheres.[20] For the BK leaders, consideration of legitimate career opportunities versus those in gangland was influenced not only by their own preferences and vision of getting ahead, but also by their interaction with others in and around the housing development. In the past, Robert Taylor's inhabitants had ways of coping with troublesome youth. This history of experience, part of the community's broader struggle to create a habitable environment, drove its specific responses to Anthony, Prince, and the other BK leaders, who in turn behaved in ways that took into account their reception by the wider community. A more concerted focus on the community as a significant association of individuals, groups, and organizations, one with its own knowledge and historical momentum, helps to explain better the forces that shape youth development.

The aspirations of the Black Kings leaders appear at first glance to be much like those of many American youths. Anthony Kline grew up in Robert Taylor and continues to live there, although he uses his illicit income to contribute to the household needs of his girlfriend and their children, who live in a neighboring community. His willingness to tolerate the risks of drug trafficking and to use force when necessary in his underground trading is belied by his unassuming presence. Anthony recalled his post–high school goals, which were similar to those of the other leaders:

> I thought I was going to get out, you know, get out [*What do you mean "get out," do you mean leave Robert Taylor?*]. Well, maybe, but really just get a job, stop running, stealing shit with my friends 'round here. Maybe play college ball, you know, just do something fucking different. I had this girlfriend, she was gonna have my baby, man, we was going to be a family.

Most of Anthony's targets—a well-paying job, a "sports car," children, "respect"—were rooted in the same idealized male role that most Americans envision.[21] Unlike most Americans, however, Anthony confronted barriers to the pursuit of these goals through socially legitimate means; some were external, such as the lack of exposure to well-paying jobs, and some were psychological, rooted in fear or personal frustration with the opportunities immediately available. Whatever the factors, Anthony was unable to sustain contact with schools and employers, and, as important, he claims to have been gradually disillusioned with the notion that social mobility would become a possibility if he stayed true to mainstream avenues.

For the other leaders as well, pessimism resulting from feelings of impotence and vulnerability, presides, and the course taken often reflects that outlook. To understand the nature of this pessimism, it is necessary to explore two other aspects of the BK leaders' aspirations, both of which may not resonate with other American youth. One of them is a thirst for power and authority over others, an expected objective given their stature as gang leaders. For most of them, this appears as an interest to control the behavior of others in a systematic way, such as a gang war or a drug-selling venture, but for some, it can be a stated preference to participate in organized fighting, whether with fisticuffs or with high-powered weapons.

Another relatively unique attribute is the "fact of blackness," to borrow the philosopher Franz Fanon's inimitable phrase, which manifests itself in the leaders' testimony as the intractable barrier of race in America. Their social standing as black Americans who live in the "projects" and in the "ghetto" affects their expectations of success. The ghetto, in this usage, refers to Chicago's contiguous poor neighborhoods, but it also marks a perceived social distance from blacks who they feel are fleeing their lower-class counterparts, literally by seeking refuge in middle-class spaces and figuratively by disassociating themselves through moral high-mindedness: "We're all niggers," Prince likes to say. "Just because you got a house and I live in the projects, white folk still see you as a nigger."

The BK leaders, along with other Robert Taylor youth, strongly emphasize the race-based limitations on black mobility in the United States. They do not forgo the dominant symbols of success—for example, a house and a family—but politicize them in such a way that their pursuit justifies the use of non-mainstream paths. At the end of the 1980s, their reading of the American mobility structure was by no means fanciful.[22] "Underclass" neighborhoods could not offer mainstream paths of economic advancement, but they certainly did well to showcase a burgeoning underground economy, consisting of illicit activities and licit unreported work, in which youth could "learn the ways of capitalism."[23] The social and economic conditions giving rise to burgeoning street gangs earlier in the decade continued to figure not only in the alienation of youth from social institutions, but in the increasingly prevalent attitude among the young that the gang was an employer—if not preferable to many menial work opportunities, then certainly an option of last resort.

The BK leaders understand economic mobility in terms of three forms of income generation: gang-dominated drug economies, "shit work" for low wages in the service sector, and inaccessible "downtown jobs," which they see as high-paying, relatively secure positions.[24] Their own post–high school employment paths suggest that the underground economy and "shit work" were the most common spheres that they explored. Some of their "legit" opportunities, such as Prince's corporate-sector employment, Mason Watson's job as a factory supervisor, and Jamie Caldwell's college scholarship, carried the potential for career development. Most, however, were menial "dead-end" jobs that provided a subsistence wage but no real chance of growth, security, or the possibility of independence. Moreover, the need to earn a livelihood or their inability to see immediate benefits of a gradual ascent hindered sustained enrollment in college. With the exception of Prince, the others experienced a two-to-four-year period of post–high school vacillation, a movement back and forth in which short tenures at a city college or in legitimate employment were combined with stints of equal duration in petty crime, incarceration, narcotics trafficking, and involvement in the organized activities of the Black Kings gang.

As a result of pressure from his mother to augment the household income, Jamie Caldwell left college to work as a full-time janitor, giving up hopes of a bachelor's degree and a well-paying job. At times, he regrets this decision and characterizes it as a turning point, "when I started getting involved with [the BKs], and couldn't get out." Mason Watson, the most rambunctious of the BK leaders, enjoyed being a gang leader primarily because of the opportunity to engage in fighting. "I loved beating up niggers whenever I wanted," he once said. "Loved that power, man." In what he described as an ideal life—"what I dream about"—he would earn income outside of the gang ("probably run a little business") and use the gang primarily for social pursuits. He worked at six-month intervals as a general laborer (cleaning, parts delivery, and mail sorting) and taught chess at a local community center. Grady Lenard, sharing Mason's disdain for the entrepreneurial side of the gang, also preferred the opportunities for petty crime and fighting that the BKs offered. He worked in a warehouse and was promoted to a supervisory position after eighteen months, but after selling marijuana to his co-workers, he was jailed on the first of his two narcotics convictions. C-Note worked at menial jobs (car-parts delivery and food preparation) for short-term periods and supplemented his income with marijuana distribution. Anthony Kline attended a local junior college, spent one year in prison, worked part-time as a general laborer in construction, and simultaneously entered into an apprenticeship role with a citywide Black Kings drug dealer.

In explaining his decision to opt out of the legitimate labor force in his twenties, only Anthony admitted to the fear of "working downtown" in an unfamiliar area. The others enumerated different factors: lack of respect and autonomy in available work, failure to see the work-related benefits of their education, and white privilege that denies blacks job-promotion and career opportunities. Prince is noteworthy given that his story would be a success in terms of the "achievement" ideology and its purported blindness to racial status: with a bachelor's degree, Prince moved from Robert Taylor into a black middle-class neighborhood, worked as a professional, started a savings account for his child, and assisted his mother with her material needs. Unhappy with his "downtown job," he allocated greater time and energy (usually at night after work) to helping Anthony Kline and the Twenty-seventh St. BK set consolidate their entrepreneurial trade, eventually withdrawing from the corporate sector entirely. As he explains:

> You can't take [downtown office work] for too long. You can't be black and make it downtown. I know that sounds like some bullshit, because

lot of niggers work there. But you ask them, they'll say the same fucking thing. You get a nice job and shit, but you never get no power. White folk never give that up. Man, shit, I control hundreds of niggers down here [in Robert Taylor], I help out a lot [of them], a lot [you] just can't help. My life working at that desk, shit, I was a nigger like them other niggers: always gonna be working for some white boy stupider than me, ain't gonna get that promotion, they always give it to white folk first.

Mason Watson and Grady Lenard underscored Prince's observations by suggesting that the underground is more welcoming to black entrepreneurial aspirations than is the corporate and small-business sector. Of course, their role as gang leaders adds some bias to this view.[25] Both Watson and Lenard cite the opportunity for self-determinism in the gang's economies—surfacing as the capacity to mobilize peers in pursuit of illicit revenue—as a strong motive for initial membership in the gang. "We just wanted to run an organization, you know," says Mason. "It's a power thing really, 'cause maybe you got fifty or a hundred niggers that you can say is under you." In their view, the pursuit of a socially dominant goal like power via the gang is not unconventional. That is, given the choice of menial work, which compromises their masculinity and their capacity to make ends meet, and the path of the "shady" entrepreneur, the former is not necessarily a more laudable career choice. Prince states that the larger world has placed them in a "catch-22" dilemma:

> You can't win. You slang dope, they say you're [a] criminal, but you sit in [McDonald's restaurant] and they say you ain't trying hard enough, you gave up. So how the fuck can you say what I should do if you haven't stepped in my shoes? I'm making a living, I'm taking care of my family, and you *still* get down on me.

Gang activity, in Prince's view, enables the leaders to fulfill what they feel to be at the heart of the male role, namely, earning money, respect, and autonomy, and providing adequately for one's family.

When asked to account for their decision to tolerate the pressures of leadership and the gang's rigid organizational hierarchy, they usually refer to their power as leaders and to the income they can earn, which surpasses service-sector work and most of the blue-collar jobs for which they qualify.[26] But they also cite the gratification they receive from working in the community in which they were raised. They are close to their peers and families, and, as important, in the course of their affairs they do not travel much outside the predominantly black neighborhoods where they feel more comfortable. As Mason Watson says,

> See, lot of these niggers just don't like the feeling they get working downtown, ain't no black folk there, so that's why lot of us look for work in the ghetto, man, it's just that you with your people. Do you think white folk would take a job around [Robort Taylor]? Fuck no, they want to be with their people. So why you expect black folk are doing something else?

Watson's observation of patterns of segregation was shared with the other leaders. It forms part of a broader chant based on the ideal that blacks should not leave the ghetto behind. The leaders account for their own place in the ghetto in self-congratulatory fashion as a willful decision to "stay close to our people," in the words of C-Note, the youngest and the most militant of all the leaders.

Notwithstanding their self-congratulatory and otherwise laudatory comments regarding gangland as a potential career path, the leaders sometimes characterize their role as middle managers in the Black Kings in ways that contradict their assertion that the outlaw life offers space for self-determinative labor. The leaders were caught in a street-gang movement that they did not fully understand and over which they had little control. This ultimately intensified their involvement in gang and community, in ways that did not always enable them to be in full control of their lives. Indeed, they describe their move from gang member to gang leader in terms of a significant loss of personal autonomy, and much of their disdain for underground economic involvement stems from their own subordinate position in the citywide Black Kings gang federation. They may have enjoyed being free of around-the-clock "strict supervision" by citywide leaders, but imposed monthly drug-sales quotas and orders from superiors to engage in violence were some of the new, laborious tasks that filled their day.[27] With new responsibilities, they could no longer dictate how much time they devoted to the gang—Anthony and Jamie eventually quit their part-time jobs in order to manage the gang's business, as did Grady Lenard, whose original interest in gang leadership was for status and occasional income supplementation. They must continually answer to higher-ranking BK superiors, who make surprise visits to Robert Taylor in order to ensure that drug dealing continues apace. On numerous occasions, the leaders have been verbally and physically assaulted for "violations" that range from missing monthly payments to allowing younger members to instigate gang-related fights in school. Although the punishment is conducted in private by their superiors, the leaders cannot hide their black eyes, bruised bones, and shame from the other members and the broader community.

The leaders' decision to join the gang and remain members cannot be separated from their families' scrutiny of their behavior. Parents, uncles, aunts, and other guardians were the sharpest critics. With the exception of Anthony Kline and Prince Williams, both of whom paid the rent for a privately subsidized apartment for their girlfriends, all the leaders lived in Robert Taylor and (even Kline and Williams) spent the majority of their time with their families in the Robert Taylor development.

The conversation inside a leader's home did not always focus on his role as a gang leader. More frequently, the discussion involved general commentary on gang-related events in another part of the city, and household members' sharing details on the lives of individual BK members in Robert Taylor—at any time, some member was arrested, jailed, or involved in an unstable family or personal situation. If a tragic incident had occurred locally, such as a gang war's preventing safe passage for the leaders' families and friends, then emotions in the household could flare, and family members exhibited far less tolerance of the youth's role as a gang leader. In such cases, it was not unusual for family members to chastise the leader and throw him out of the home temporarily. The leaders' families typically used these occasions to plead with them to take concrete steps, such as finding employment, that would enable them to reduce their involvement in the gang. The following conversation occurred in Anthony Kline's home after the BKs were rumored to have killed a member of the Sharks gang:

> "You killed that boy, I knew that boy," said Michael (Anthony's uncle) to Anthony, greeting us at the door. "You shot him dead."
>
> "I didn't shoot him," said Anthony, lowering his head and walking over to the couch.
>
> "You know what I mean, boy, don't play games with me. You want to come see his family?"
>
> "Anthony, how could you do that, when is this going to stop?" said Anthony's mother.
>
> "Stop? Those niggers [in the Sharks gang] started it. I said I ain't done nothing."
>
> "You better get yourself organized, you got to deal with this. It ain't right," said Michael, who walked out of the room and into the kitchen, shaking his head.
>
> "Yeah, well, you can get the fuck out, nigger. Get the fuck out of my house, you bitch. I'm bringing home money around this motherfucker, you ain't making shit. You can't even feed your own family, shit. You just a bitch."
>
> "Anthony! Don't ever yell at your uncle like that. You go and find out how that boy's family is doing, you give your money to them. You want to deal these drugs, you just make sure you ain't killing nobody."
>
> "Ain't that easy, momma," said Anthony. "You know that."
>
> "Ain't that hard either, baby," his mother answered. "Put your mind to it, I keep telling you that, just get out [of the gang]."

As the conversation suggests, the gang leaders' actions served as occasions for family members to discuss the general conditions of "project living." In a household in which personal hardship was acute and in which numerous boarders struggled to make ends meet, the air was often heavy with tension and stress. The need to maintain the home as a refuge from the grind of everyday life meant that in the apartments of gang members, people sometimes discussed the gang as they might a socially sanctioned club or association. The need to ensure the households' material well-being meant that the gang members' illicit income was not always a topic of conversation. Each of the leaders paid almost all the grocery expenses of their respective families, and they routinely gave family members money for a variety of pressing needs, such as hospital bills and public transportation. In this context, the extraordinary gang-related behavior of a family member might be the spark that allowed everyone in the household to express frustration with his or her inability to maintain an acceptable distance not only from the violence outside, but also from the morally and legally problematic activities that entered their apartment.

Parents and elder kin of the other leaders would often argue that their children and nephews were limiting their development by remaining gang leaders. Grady Lenard's father, who lived in a nearby community, lamented Grady's decision to continue "banging" with the BKs. "Grady had a job, still keeps working now and then. Cleaning that asbestos. He got kids now and I try to tell him he needs to stay working, stop dealing the drugs and banging with these niggers." From parents' perspective, Chicago's gangs had always mixed criminal activities with noncriminal ones, but the BKs were too invested in drug trafficking to be a potential contributor to social order. Many acknowledged that Prince, Anthony, and their peers wanted to make a positive contribution, but felt that the ability to do so as BK members was eclipsed by the gang's involvement in drug economies.

The criticism of their families contributed to the leaders' sense of who they are, and therefore it cannot be dismissed as a factor that might sustain their gang involvement. The criticism generally came not from family members seeking to exile them from Robert Taylor, but from kin who were interested in redirecting their energies, though they were themselves benefiting from the leaders' illegitimate income. None of the leaders had much sustained contact with broader social institutions apart from the police, an employer, and, on rare occasions, a pastor or minister. Thus the continuous interrogation inside the home becomes one of the few means by which they receive the moral instruction of the mainstream.[28] But given that this feedback comes from a poor household reliant on the income they can provide, the message the leaders receive is that theirs may not be an acceptable path, but it is one necessary to some degree for household sustenance. Most leaders respond to the sum of these forces in pragmatic terms; according to Anthony Kline, "They don't want me doing this shit [dealing drugs and participating in street-based violence] forever. I know that, shit, I don't want to be running like this myself. But you see what I'm bringing in. I'm buying my sister's diapers, paying for all that food, the television. I can't quit, you know, it ain't that easy. I got to find me another hustle if I'm gonna stop slanging dope."

The gang involvement of the BK leaders was influenced by many complex factors, including their own personal aspirations, their early exposure to different pathways for reaching their goals, and the response made to their behavior by other, equally disadvantaged people in their households. This does not excuse the leaders' engagement in a world of violence and criminality; nor does it absolve their families when they tolerate some of the leaders' behavior. It does, however, signal that there is a moral universe present in the lives of the leaders and their families and that living according to their ideals is not easy in their circumstances.

Gang activity affords them space to "be a man." It is a life that is not far afield of the classic rags-to-riches American success stories, particularly the idealized organized crime narratives in which immigrants rise above their slums but remain closely wed to people living there. Like ethnic immigrants, the leaders want to leave poverty behind and gain independence, and their experiences as job seekers—and as observers of other aspiring ghetto dwellers—have not provided evidence that the legitimate labor force will support their dreams. Their frustration and their preference for remaining among their peers lead them to withdraw to the ghetto and to the drug trade.

This is not a dramatic decision, but one reached over the course of their lives, and one they revisit. They continually pay the price for choosing the nonsanctioned path, whether this is the castigatory welcome of family members, the knowledge that there is a social stigma attached to their work, or the awareness that they cannot be middle-level managers of a criminal enterprise forever. Moreover, as they assumed increasing responsibilities in the gang, it appeared less likely that the young adults were going to reduce their involvement in the BKs.

Pas de Deux of Gang and Community

"See, when you put an animal in a cage and then let it out, it'll kill you," said Kenny Davenport. "That's what you doing to these kids, treating them like animals, so don't be surprised if a man breaks out now and then." His parable articulates a widespread feeling among Robert Taylor's tenants: when the road to social advancement is rocky, young people will turn to rage to make their way. But what happens when they do not simply "break out" when they are frustrated, but rebel by pursuing their ambitions in a fairly organized manner, through an alternate, socially illegitimate, and dangerous avenue? How does a community in which people empathize with the plight of youth nevertheless cope with their destructive behavior as part of a street gang?

Such was the dilemma for Robert Taylor when the BK leaders charted a path of personal growth in the gang that embraced the larger housing development. With their decision to accept leadership positions, the public presence of Anthony, Jamie, and the other leaders became more prominent, and they began to think of themselves as something more than simply traffickers and outlaws. They associated service provision to the broader community with part of "being a man." This did not translate into a clear vision of entering community civic life; instead, they took a serpentine route, handling situations as they arose and taking pride in their public visibility. Their perception of their role as individuals who wanted to "better the community" became well defined in the process, and so too did the broader community's understanding of the actions necessary to live securely amid this new youth presence. In effect, the BK leaders' notion of *noblesse oblige* caused tenants' empathy for "troubled youth" to be diluted by anger and disgust. The result was a complex animus toward gang leaders on the part of the community.

Many people in and around the Robert Taylor development had observed—and, to differing degrees, participated in—the development of the young men from children to gang leaders. As neighbors, friends, teachers, kin, antagonists, and victims, they cite the BK leaders as examples of "youth in this community" who have gone astray, who have been discarded by mainstream social institutions, and who could not resist the temptations of the underground economy. In the words of their high school principal:

> See, folks think you got good and bad around here, but you got good and bad in the same person. That's what you see if you stay around here long enough. Anthony and Prince, they're decent kids and they can do good things if they put their minds to it [*Even as gang leaders?*] Yeah, they still take care of people, but they're lost, so they don't see that life isn't about what you do until you're thirty. That's what the problem is around here. Kids don't see that what it takes to be successful when you're forty, that's something different than twenty.

From the perspective of many tenants, the path away from education and into the underworld is not unique to gang members, but is indicative of the vulnerability of all youths who grow up in the Robert Taylor Homes. The full-time ghetto-based gang member is only the most highly publicized young person to share these failings and troubled circumstances.[29]

Given that tenants understand the plight of youth who develop associations with gangs, it should not seem incongruous that occasionally people would extol the leaders for having succeeded within the gang's opportunity structure—as opposed to singling them out simply for joining a street gang—and for wanting to help needy households. Deacon Harness, an ex–Black King member, observed that "when [Prince and his peers] started organizing themselves, even just to sell candy to make money, or stay in school when everyone else was dropping out, it was like they knew that they was different, that they was going to lead the other shorties around here." Gang affiliation, then, is not always a remarkable event for local youth, but rising to the top of the organization commands attention.

Tenants' interpretation of the Black Kings' actions as destructive but also worthy of some acclaim was due in part to the number of roles that the BKs performed and the ways in which tenants experienced the effects of a corporate street gang. As in the past (that is, before they became focused on drug trafficking), BK members continued to be nephews, friends, and neighbors of tenants, and so could not escape daily routine contact, the lion's share of which had little to do with gang matters. Even the majority of the antagonistic interaction between gang member and tenant, much of which did not radically differ from previous years, did not escalate beyond the social-control capacities of tenants. For example, BK members' conducting drug sales in public space provoked fear and could lead to hostile interaction with tenants who wanted to use that space, but any actual confrontation almost always was mediated by a third party (the LAC was the common intermediary), and the more fleeting verbal debates generally subsided. The use of that space usually was ceded to tenants, but only temporarily, since the gangs would return.

The more novel interactions between gang member and tenant stemmed from the gang's newly formed role as a commercial force in the housing development's hidden economies, which translated foremost into an increased presence in public space. Only a small part of the gang's public activities before 1990 was tied to extended periods of violence, in which the gangs traded gunfire in full view and prolonged, large-scale gang wars led tenants to reduce their public interaction dramatically.[30] Shootings between gangs, even if economically motivated, tended to be directed by one gang member at another. The public was certainly threatened, but tenants make a clear distinction between these drive-bys and the large-scale wars after 1990 or so, when the norm became members driving through enemy territory shooting almost indiscriminately at crowds.[31]

A more deep-seated concern regarding safe public passage stemmed from the pervasive gang-controlled drug trafficking and the high levels of use within the tenant body. The nearly continuous traffic of casual tenant users and addicts—as well as their counterparts who came to Robert Taylor from surrounding areas—meant that some tenants interacted routinely with the gang as customers and others were forced to pass through sales areas. In some buildings, Black Kings factions may have broken into a vacated apartment to peddle their wares, but this did not occur in all buildings, and it usually lasted only for several weeks, until tenants successfully lobbied the CHA to board up the apartment. More common were drug transactions day and night in lobbies, store fronts, park areas, and parking lots. Teams of gang members made tenants uncomfortable, but so too did the constant presence of severely addicted customers who curried the favor of salespersons, who pleaded for free samples, and whose cries might escalate into desperate acts as their need for crack and heroin took over.

The sale of drugs was part of the gang's overall use of public space for business, loitering, meetings, and surveillance of police traffic and enemy gang members. An average day saw the leaders survey the gang's narcotics sales "spots," discuss citywide gang developments with their superiors in the parking lots, initiate gambling or basketball games outside, visit with family members, and otherwise pass their time walking about the housing development. The general BK rank-and-file membership was also noticeable to tenants because they tended to congregate near buildings and would periodically stop passers-by—including tenants living in the high-rises—to frisk them and question them about their whereabouts. At times, the gang forcibly prevented people from entering the buildings.

A smaller number of tenants came into direct contact with members as a result of the gang's extortion from local entrepreneurs who made money off the books, a practice that was fully expected by tenants after 1990. The gang confronted purveyors of goods and services directly in public or semiprivate areas within buildings, often with little attempt to hide their calls for payoffs. BK leaders "taxed" people for the right to earn income on "BK turf," a practice they defended in terms of their commitment to "our people." Typically, they charged hawkers in their area a monthly fee. Gypsy cab drivers, car mechanics, prostitutes, and others subjected to the new rule of law were incensed because "hustles," "fixes," and other hidden-work schemes were crucial for their sustenance. Many were already paying off LAC officers and believed that a second such disbursement to the gang was unfair. Kenny Davenport, who paid Grady in order to distribute marijuana in a parking lot, interpreted the "payoff" primarily as a means for the BKs to "signify" their authority:

> They always be signifying, that's what gangs do. That's why niggers hated these fools. [BK leaders] walked around like they were kings or something, like it was their land or something. Man, people were struggling, you know, trying to get their hustle on and you got these young cats selling drugs and making that money. I think if folks wouldn't have had to pay [Black Kings an extortionary fee], they [would've] got along better from jumpstreet. But that's how BKs is. They started signifying and never stopped.

Davenport believed that the BKs chose underground activity to showcase their control because it was so common in the development: "Everyone hustles, so you hassle lots of folks, that means everyone got to respect you, you dig?" The BKs had their reasons for taxing people, but Kenny's explanation attributes too much forethought and strategizing to the leaders, who instead see the practice as a way of "keeping the peace" so that everyone could benefit from hustling.

The BKs performed a number of "positive functions" in the housing development that buttressed the leaders' belief that they were helping "our people"—by which they meant the tenant body.[32] Tenants admitted that some of the BKs' services were helpful, but these were highly irregular and no one relied on them. The most common assistance that BK members provided was a disbursement of cash or an offer of escort, typically for a tenant needing to run an errand or traverse gang boundaries during a period of gang-related conflict. Black Kings members admitted offering such services, but usually only to their relatives, friends, and those who promised them a favor in return, such as silence during a police investigation. Several times a year, the BKs would come to the aid of tenants in crisis. For example, when the Housing Authority placed turnstiles in the lobbies to restrict the flow of traffic and limit loitering, BK leaders removed them, much to the happiness of tenants, who protested that they were fire hazards in a sixteen-story high-rise with only one exit. Black Kings leaders also answered the call of tenants who wanted to physically punish a storeowner accused of abusing young women or giving them small disbursements of groceries in exchange for sexual favors; tenants' cries to police were perceived as ineffective, so many came to the BKs, who would summarily beat up the storeowner.

Such BK assistance did not win over a majority of the population; nor did it produce an identifiable contingent among the tenant body that favored the street gang's presence and activities. Instead, through these actions, the BKs reproduced a support base of individuals in the population who would defend the gang against accusations by the media, law enforcement and CHA officials, or other tenants that the BKs were a wholly destructive force. These individuals could be parents, friends, or relatives of the Black Kings. Some tenants, such as Ottie Davis, did believe that gangs possessed "a good and bad side," but the BKs had few outright supporters.

The provision of escorts and theatrics such as beatings and pulling out turnstiles were relatively rare happenings. The majority of the gang's positive functions were actually activities that BK members and tenants interpreted differently. For example, BK members who stood outside lobby areas and on street corners to observe passers-by defended these actions as part of their security provision for the community. Few tenants accepted this explanation and understood the surveillance instead as disruptive of their free use of public space.

They perceived these actions as ostensibly "signifying" power ("they're just signifying, just trying to boss us around") and as part of the gang members' overall task of safeguarding their trade ("they just don't want other folks selling drugs in the buildings"). Similarly, while acknowledging the meager monetary yield, Prince suggested that street taxation was a means for tenants to acknowledge the BKs' charitable activities: "Folks got to realize what we do around here. Shit, we watching out for 'em, keeping the peace, and they bitching about giving up a little something for that. How can you get something by having us around, but you don't want to pay your share?" Tenants regarded such arguments skeptically. One man who came to the Twenty-ninth St. parking lot to sell men's clothing asked Prince Williams from whom he needed protection: "You all [the gang] or the police?" Prince replied with caustic wit, "That's on you, nigger. Depends. Look around, you see any police up in here? You pay and we don't whup your ass." The majority of tenants did not accept the philanthropic arguments advanced by Prince Williams and his colleagues, and most were adamant that the BK leaders were simply interested in amassing power and generating revenue.

With such a cynical attitude on the part of tenants toward the BK's putative protection, it was impossible for the gang to regulate all informal economic activity locally. Tenants realized that the gang could not offer them many practical benefits. Unlike LAC officers, BK leaders claimed no influence with law enforcement agencies, and so their promises of "protection" for entrepreneurs was rightly interpreted by tenants as little more than a form of intimidation and a guarantee only against punishment by the gang itself. Their belief was confirmed by BK leaders who harassed customers. In so doing, they decreased an entrepreneur's revenue base. Sometimes, if the negotiation failed, the leaders sent Daniel, their "enforcer," whose diplomacy ("beat the shit out of them first, and then listen to what they got to say") might produce a settlement but might also end a business.

In fact, despite its promises to the contrary, the gang could not really ensure that merchants would be protected against the tax imposed by the LAC. These tenant-management representatives historically regulated underground trading by advertising their capacity to help people avoid detection from the state, which some still managed to do. Consequently, the gang leaders had to challenge LAC officers continuously for a share of street taxes. Most tenants preferred to pay off the LAC and suffer any consequences if the gang chose to retaliate—which could take the form of either indifference or physical abuse. The Black Kings never embraced all underground activity; nor did they successfully wrest complete regulatory control from the LAC. (In 1992, for example, Edith Huddle counted twenty-six entrepreneurs operating in the 210 building who were not regulated by her or by the BK leader Mason, who had jurisdiction in that high-rise.) For the BK leaders, the symbolic effect of taxation—signifying a protective role in the community—plainly outweighed the economic benefit. Ultimately, BK leaders were most successful when taxing larger, visible, off-the-books ventures, such as Tom and Jake's car-repair service, which was located in the parking lot, as well as storeowners who sold goods under the table or who paid fifty cents on the dollar for food stamps.

After 1988, when the BK leaders began to speak publicly about their desire to provide assistance to the community, it was not evident that they understood what kind of help they could provide, nor that any good they could do might be negated by their own deleterious activities. Each of the BK leaders could articulate with pride, but in a vague manner, that he felt an obligation to "black people" and wanted to "better the community," but the leaders' everyday dealings with the public often belied a concern or a devotion to "our people." Very rarely did they allocate time in their meetings for discussion of gang-tenant relations. Nor did they admit to putting into practice the group's tenets stipulating "harmonious" treatment of other blacks. And although Prince instructed younger members to understand "where they came from" and to "respect older folk," it was usually in a moment of crisis that attention would be shown to the non-gang public. News of a police investigation into the gang's activities, for example, prompted Prince to summarily dispatch his officers to help tenants run errands and buy groceries. In fact, notwithstanding their lofty ambitions to assist the housing development, by 1990 the leaders were surprised at the high level of engagement with the public that their entrepreneurial shift had effected, and only later did they come to perceive the possible role that they could have in the community's affairs.

The BK leaders did not agree among themselves on the appropriate ways to become involved in the housing development. Practical situations often brought into relief their own discordant views. In 1990, Prince and Jamie had different opinions of Carlton—the treasurer for the four BK sets—who assaulted a tenant for refusing to pay off the gang ($100) when he sold car parts in the Twenty-ninth St. parking lot:

> "Nigger didn't pay [$100]!" yelled Jamie. "Carlton was right. We ain't gonna let that cat sell no more around here."
>
> "No, just make sure he pay what he owes us," said Prince. "Folks got to make their money, you can't be beating up every nigger, man."
>
> "Fuck that," said Jamie. "Ain't like we didn't tell him [that] he got to pay us."
>
> "No, nigger," said Prince. "Look, you got hundred people ain't paying us shit. We'll get it back. Just let him go. People got to get their hustle on, just like you. Carlton gave the nigger his ass-whupping, that's straight. You ain't got to do nothing else."
>
> "You crazy?" quipped Jamie. "We're BKs! These fools can't be playing with us."

Prince Williams and Anthony Kline stood at one extreme by advocating an approach to gang leadership that eschewed confrontation and provided tenants with direct assistance; both regularly helped residents catch burglars or find domestic abusers. Jamie, by contrast, was schooled by the former BK leader Jon Lenard, who had stricter rules. Jamie supported the BK's community-based ethos but favored a bare-bones, prudent charity because he did not want tenants to expect kindness from the gang. Help, in his view, should be an indirect by-product of the BK's self-interested pursuits—for example, a legitimate derivative might be the gang's drive-by patrols, which were ostensibly directed at locating enemy gang members, but which also deterred car theft. His model of the benevolent dictator was shared by Mason and Grady, each of whom distributed money to needy families in their building but matched their largesse with physical abuse of people who refused to honor their extortion—specifically, when BKs asked individuals to use apartments to store their drugs and weapons or to remain noncompliant in police investigations.

The BK leaders' desire to assist the community was partly mitigated by their unflattering perception of those tenants who purchased narcotics from them. The leaders often proclaimed that their sale of illicit goods appeared harmful, but according to Prince, in fact, the organization was "just taking money from folks who don't care and giving it back to the community." When asked to point to specific customers "who don't give a shit about the community," the leaders usually singled out the most hardened, who hardly represented the majority of users, but who were convenient and defenseless scapegoats who allowed the BK leaders to affirm their own perceived role as Robin Hood figures.

Different BK leaders cultivated different relationships with the tenants in their territories. In some high-rises (such as those controlled by Prince and the Twenty-seventh St. BKs), leaders curried tenant favor, which usually led to less vocal tenant complaints against members (though residents' silence might have been motivated by fear of reprisal). Leaders elsewhere failed to do so, resulting in more frequent outcries and direct altercations between gang members and tenants. Some gang leaders routinely gave money to households, whereas others were far more miserly and needed prodding by their colleagues to help tenants in need. Consequently, in 1990, one could identify three typical tenant-gang relations, their relative occurrence weighted differently in each building: a small percentage of tenants accepted gang payoffs; some tenants debated with the gang leaders directly or complained to LAC and CHA staff; most household members avoided gang members altogether by shutting their doors and adjusting their schedules.

With their attempts at taxation and their occasional gift-giving to tenants, BK leaders had infringed on the once exclusive domain of the LAC. Public arguments erupted from time to time between gang leaders and LAC representatives. Judy Harris claimed that the arguments did not turn violent, but that "[gangs] was just creating a nuisance and people was getting fed up because all this yelling and shit was bringing in more police around the area and then *nobody* was making no money!" However, Kenny Davenport recalls that, on occasion, BKs broke the windows of people who were sympathetic to the LAC or refused entry to those visiting the LAC office. Their threats of force enabled them to get away with such acts.

Gang members had always interacted with the LAC, but historically their collaborations had been minimal because gangs could offer little to LAC officers. But when the BK's main business became drug trafficking, argues LAC Officer Kelly Davis, the gangs solicited the help of the LAC: "That's when [gangs] was all over us, because they needed us to help them hide from police." Grady Lenard paid an LAC floor captain to package drugs in an abandoned apartment, and LAC President Kim Walton admitted receiving "a few dollars a week" from Anthony Kline to remain quiet about gang activity. In return, Kline agreed to keep Twenty-seventh St. BK activity away from children living in Walton's high-rise. Moreover, whereas it had been common for *any* BK member—leader or rank-and-file—to offer a bribe to LAC officers, after 1990 the BK leaders monopolized this practice in the hope of making it more effective and excoriated members who met with these brokers. This executive decision to centralize extortion reduced the discretionary payoffs between rank-and-file members and LAC officers but did not eliminate them outright.

Prince and the other leaders did not consider payoffs to LAC leaders or CHA staff to be a means to gain local legitimacy. Instead, payoffs were a practical means to procure assistance in the BKs' efforts to protect their drug-trafficking enterprise. Years later, the LAC building presidents Kim Walton and Edna Baxter admitted to the continued receipt of BK bribes. They recalled standing their ground in the face of criticism from the LAC and tenants. Baxter stated that people were largely hypocritical given that they rarely protested when the backdoor gang-LAC collaborations led to minimized gang recruitment, or to reductions in gang loitering and gunfire. She stated flatly that criticism of her own dealings with the gangs came from farther south—near the buildings south of Twenty-ninth St., which had more disruptive gang activity. She claimed that tenants there were jealous of her successful handling of the BKs, as well as the success of other LAC officers north of that historic dividing line:

> In my building, shit, it was safe, folks don't ask how you do this, they don't meddle in what I do because they're safe. It's only people down there [south of Twenty-ninth St.] that always complain about us working with gangs, taking their money. Shit! These niggers want to give it to us, fine, shit, they *taking* it from us, why not *give* it to us.

Kim Walton was also candid in defending the compromises she had made with Anthony Kline and Prince. She felt that "the gangs are here to stay"; thus her acceptance of their money was the only realistic option available to help tenants buy groceries or pay their rent.

The arrangements between the LAC leadership and the BK leaders did not escape the notice of tenants. Many did not agree with the LAC that the benefits of secretive negotiations with gang leaders would trickle down to the constituents in the buildings. They felt that their leaders' receipt of the gang's money did little for most of the residents in a high-rise. In public gatherings, they questioned their LAC leaders and demanded to know how they would benefit from LAC-gang collaborations. One tenant interrupted an LAC meeting, screaming, "How come you all be working with [the gangs] and taking their money, but you can't get them to stop shooting outside?" Others commonly complained that households experienced little advantage from these payoffs. Louisa Lenard, a tenant living in 218, was critical of LAC leaders who accepted extortionary payments, but she readily conceded the difficult plight of some officers who had few other places to turn for resources: "You see, you really couldn't get no help if you was on LAC. CHA was, well, it seemed like they was always doing something corrupt. You see, you didn't have no choice. Gangs was going to deal dope. I know, *my son* [Jon Lenard] used to run the whole thing. So [an LAC leader] just had to say to [the gangs] where and when they could do it, keep it away from the children."

LAC leaders defended their behavior in ways that echoed Louisa Lenard's observations. They had few resources in the wider community to which they could turn for assistance either for protection against gang harassment and resolution of gang-related conflicts, or for social services that might provide alternative programs and opportunities for youth. This assessment may have been accurate, but it did not minimize the anger brewing among tenants. Most LAC officers actually admitted that negotiations with the gangs did little to stop drug trafficking. Instead, they emphasized the small reductions in the gang's harassment of tenants that collaboration could afford.

With the tenants and their leadership growing less unified after 1990, it was the Black Kings who experienced the greatest benefits. The decision by several LAC leaders to accept the gang's payoffs made it difficult for tenants to focus their anger at the gangs—for example, by collectively lobbying law enforcement for protection. Those LAC officers who eschewed the receipt of the gang's largesse were equally handicapped. They found it difficult to bring together the LAC leadership in a unified effort to improve their security. Meanwhile, much to the dismay of tenant leaders, the CHA and Chicago police bureaus showed no intention of directing their resources away from "suppression" tactics to more mundane, everyday forms of protection that might prevent or mitigate the effects of gang-related violence.

From 1988 until 1991, it was not altogether difficult to argue that the street gang's actions had clearly worsened the conditions in Robert Taylor, not only in the obvious and most visible ways (through public violence, harassment, and drug trafficking), but also in the less well documented manner by which the gangs had disrupted the trust between tenants and their leadership. As the Black Kings moved about and conducted their business, which included bribing and winning the influence of various tenant constituencies, they left in their wake the charred remains of solid tenant relations.

None of this internal realignment could be divorced from tenants' perceptions of the limitations of formal agents of social control. Viewing the police as a nonresource would be catastrophic for residents of any American community, and for a community like Robert Taylor, this tragedy was exacerbated by tenants' own lack of resources. By the start of the 1990s, tenants had few expectations that law enforcement, as currently organized, could help them cope with gangs. Even those police officers who once were empathetic to the plight of ghetto youth no longer saw any redeemable qualities in people like Prince Williams, who they felt had a chance to leave the ghetto behind and who chose drug trafficking instead. Tenants began admitting to themselves that law enforcement services, and their own existing modes of dealing with conflict, would have to be supplemented by other methods of conflict resolution, gang-tenant mediation, and even preventative policies.

The tenant leaders, of course, cannot be absolved for colluding with the gang, even though they were right to suggest that assistance from other sources was lacking. As they had done in the past, tenant leaders sought to consolidate their own power, and some thought that establishing partnerships with the gang might be the most productive course of action. This logic, as one tenant leader explained, was premised on the notion that "the gangs are here to stay"; thus, the sooner tenants intervened and tried to establish a beachhead by working with the BKs, the better their chances would be to create safety in the long run. This view undergirded the belief of those leaders who accepted the inevitability of the corporate gang and framed the receipt of the gang's largesse as the best of all possible worlds, that is, the optimal strategy to retain some semblance of control in the face of a powerful new community actor. Not everyone shared this belief, however, and tenants knew that they stood at a crossroads. They had just been given a glimpse of how the corporate gang would erode their own capacity to ensure the well-being of their constituents. They now needed to figure out for themselves whether the gang could be a legitimate actor in the affairs of the community and what type of intervention might work to help control some of the outlaw organization's behavior. Thus far, the signs were not promising.

As they neared the thirtieth anniversary of the Robert Taylor Homes in 1992, the tenants of the housing development were coming to terms with the changing face of gang activity. In the largest inner cities, the neighborhood gang was now like an economic franchise, one member of a larger underground supergang family that was not always successful as an entrepreneur, but that was certainly dogged in its staying power. Local gang leaders had a perceptibly different type of symbolic and material power than in the past, grounded in their ability to amass revenue, to sway the aspirations of younger generations who faced few mobility paths, and to entertain the notion that their own "shady" status might actually benefit their families and their community. All such attributes meant that the gang and its leaders would have a much more pernicious effect than ever before on the social fabric of the community.

Prince Williams, Anthony Kline, and the other BK leaders were selling drugs, taxing and intimidating entrepreneurs, paying off the LAC and security guards, and otherwise trying to enlist household support for their activities. But though they had burrowed deeply into the social fabric of the housing development, they lacked their predecessors' wanton disregard for the community. To be sure, BK leaders' statements of philanthropic intent were hypocritical: using drug sales as a means to take money from "people who don't give a shit about the community" to give to those who needed it amounted to stealing from the poor to give to the poor. They were more interested in monetary pursuits and conspicuous consumption than in community affairs, but they did seem willing to consider the effects of their actions on others around them, even if only to protect their own mercantilism.

Moreover, their biographies suggest that they had several opportunities to take a different path, one that would have led them out of the Black Kings. Their eventual climb up the ladder of gangland was partly a product of their own aspirations, based on a dissatisfaction with what they perceived to be dead-end jobs. Unlike many young people in America, they lacked intermediary institutions to which their families and community could turn in order to deter them from lives of crime. As the BK leaders experimented with different paths, they had little guidance apart from their families, who tried as best they could in the face of overwhelming odds to redirect the leaders' energies. With the exception of Prince Williams, the BK leaders had few opportunities for mainstream career development, and in Prince's case, perhaps his lack of excitement and inability to feel appreciated at his corporate-sector job would have been redressed if he worked for a longer period—though this is not guaranteed. It is clear, however, that the terrain of gangland fitted well with the leaders' understandings of the proper role of an American male: they had a visible and measurable authority over others, to some degree they had the freedom to evade "strict supervision" and control their daily routine, they experienced mobility in the underground career ladder, and they had income with which they could help to support their families. Giving this up for available service-sector work may have been to "do the right thing," but it also meant confronting weakness and impotence.

Instead, they labored in the gang and worked to carve out a niche in the housing development community that would support their sense of themselves as leaders, providers, men, and family members. Their gifts to residents and the occasional provision of services confused some tenants, particularly tenant leaders who were struggling to work with this supposedly philanthropic energy in productive ways. However, the popular consensus seemed to be moving toward a largely critical perception of the gang leader as a force that could help the community. Some tenants still held out hope that the intentions of Prince Williams and his colleagues might provide a basis to turn the gang away from trafficking, but as harassment and violence grew, this view was looking more dreamlike than real.

In fact, Prince, Anthony, C-Note, Mason, Grady, and Jamie had yet to be seriously challenged to prove their commitment to the rest of the housing development. BK leaders had not demonstrated to tenants that they understood their widespread concerns over safety and welfare, and they had not worked alongside tenants in any common initiative. In 1991, when a war between the Black Kings and the Sharks erupted, resulting in the death of several people and a halt to local traffic and commerce, the leaders' claims of benevolence were put to the test. Residents began to hold them accountable for their deleterious actions, and some offered the gang leaders concrete ways to show their concern for the housing development. From the perspective of tenants, the coming months would reveal whether the Black Kings and their charismatic leaders had the mettle to live up to their word to "better the community."

5 | Street-Gang Diplomacy

"If you really want to get some peace around here, you're going to have to play their game," said Will Jackson, the director of the Grace Center, at the end of 1991. Sitting around a large table at the center, the six tenant leaders on the Local Advisory Council, looking for a strategy to combat gang activity, listened attentively. Will Jackson had called the tenants to the meeting to end some of the contention that had characterized the relationship between residents and their leaders for the past few years. The lack of trust between the two parties stemmed from the gang's illicit activities and noncriminal intrusions into the community's affairs. As the differences of opinion moved beyond debates to in-fighting and minimal cooperation, the discordance among tenants threatened to be as debilitating for the quality of life in Robert Taylor as the gang's own behavior.

The Black Kings were in the second month of an extremely violent conflict with the Sharks gang, a state of affairs that had dramatically decreased public safety. Will Jackson brought the tenant leaders together to air differences and consider possible responses to the violence. They agreed on three important points: they could not stop gangs from selling drugs and having a public presence; tenants and passersby would continue to buy their illicit wares; and tenants were too fearful to challenge the gangs directly. Gang prevention was unrealistic at this point, they conceded, so they settled on two more modest objectives: resolve conflicts and, in peaceful periods, force BK leaders to live up to their stated desire to "better the community." "You got to take them at their word," said Jackson. "When they say they want to help the community, [we] want to see if they mean it." He hoped to redirect the gang's energies away from underground economic regulation and toward "community clean ups," "escorts for the elderly," and limited "hanging out" in public space.

To initiate such changes, Jackson made a proposal that caught everyone by surprise. "You have to go to prison and meet with their leaders, get their support for what you're trying to do. Anyway, you don't have much choice because they control everything." This suggestion broke the silence and caused shouts of "You're crazy!" "Prison? We trying to get *out* of prison," and "Go ahead, we'll be waiting right here for you!" Only Edith Huddle, the tenant leader in the 210 high-rise, nodded in ascent. "He's right. These people just doing what their bosses telling them to do. Maybe we got to go to prison and talk to the *real* [Sharks and BK] leaders." For the remainder of the meeting, Huddle and Jackson defended the proposal by arguing not only that local conflicts spanned neighborhoods—for example, the Sharks in a southern community (Englewood) came to shoot at Robert Taylor gangs—but also that the local gangs were fighting in battles they neither instigated nor wished to join. "You know Prince and them," said Edith Huddle, referring to the local Black Kings leaders, with a hint of sarcasm as she tried to make her point. "They ain't like that, [Prince] never killed nobody. All of them, they fight, but it's out of their control, they just following orders." Huddle knew the local leaders were responsible for their behavior, but she also understood that gang leaders from many neighborhoods would need to be involved in efforts to curb gang warfare and violence. Others dissented, wanting to keep conflict resolution local, although they recognized that gang violence had roots outside the housing development.

The LAC officers walked out into a cold November afternoon unsure of their next steps and uncertain how nonlocalized conflict resolution and gang-LAC cooperation might be achieved. As 1991 ended, they wondered, along with their constituents, if the rhythms of "project living" now included extended periods of violent gang warfare. Episodes of sustained street-gang conflict were occurring with greater regularity, marked by sudden gunfire and then a return to relative quiet. Some feared that this cycle was now ingrained in their lives, alongside household hardships, general disrepair, and inadequate security. They lobbied for police resources, but they felt that their abandonment by law enforcement and CHA security was not going to be rectified soon. They expected no help from either party, at least in the immediate future. Few if any among them allowed the gang's sporadic offers of assistance to the community to sway their belief that the overriding interest of the group was to maintain a lucrative drug trade. They may have welcomed the token generosity of the Black Kings leaders, whether this meant escorts or occasional funds for their own programs, but they reasoned that these offerings were motivated primarily by the BK leaders' economic imperatives.

The cold of an approaching Chicago winter was not without some promise, however. As Cathy Blanchard said, with Will Jackson in mind, "It's been a long time since you had somebody around here caring about us, really trying to help kids around here." The Grace Center sat in the middle of the Robert Taylor development, and when its director reached out to both gangs and tenants, the center sat in the middle of their lives. Will Jackson's actions demonstrated that tenants would have to be as resourceful and innovative as the gangs they battled. In this case, they would have to confront the reality that gangs are local entities with broader roots. Jackson anticipated that this road would be steep, but he did not foresee the obstacles along the way, many of which stemmed from other individuals and organizations in and around the housing development who, long ago, had abandoned the difficult task of working with troubled youth, and who were hesitant to intervene in the pressing problems that public housing tenants faced.

On the Margins, in the Ghetto

The large Chicago community in which Robert Taylor sits, sometimes referred to as Greater Grand Boulevard, is an extremely poor area with double-digit unemployment, in which 60 percent of households live in poverty (1990), and with little new housing and commercial development during the 1980s. For nearly every good or service, including employment training, medical and psychological care, laundry, clothes and housewares, and entertainment, residents of Robert Taylor must cross State Street and travel east into Greater Grand Boulevard—an area that has lacked sufficient resources for its own population since the First World War. When the 1991 gang wars erupted in Robert Taylor, tenants looked expectantly to organizations in Greater Grand Boulevard, as well as to the CHA and Chicago police, for help in resolving conflicts and restoring a secure climate. Their quest brought into sharp relief the "social isolation" of the housing development, not only from the wider world but also from the impoverished inner city.[1] That is, their attempts to procure help showed that they suffered not only a dearth of resources but also a stigmatized identity among local organizations that made acquiring existing services an uphill battle. When they attempted to procure assistance for gang-related conflicts, the "elite," well-funded social-service providers in the surrounding community did not come to their aid, citing a hesitation to intervene in "political issues" in public housing.[2] As they had done in the past when abandoned by the majority of mainstream organizations, tenants welcomed assistance from grassroots providers but relied primarily on their own networks to combat the gang and drug problem.[3]

After the mid-1980s, large gang families in Chicago's poor African-American communities—Kings, Disciples, El Rukn, Vicelord—became invested in crack economies. Their underground commerce generated more pernicious forms of conflict than ever before, including shootings, weapons use, and visible sales traffic. The government's response, namely, "gang suppression" wherein police agencies worked without the support of other community institutions, had few positive results. Thus at the start of the 1990s, community leaders in Robert Taylor began looking elsewhere for help. They knew that the tenant body would probably develop some indigenous techniques to fight gangs and control youth. They were hopeful, given their tradition of cooperation and self-enforcement, but they also expressed dismay in the face of high levels of destructive activities among tenants as well as neglect from organizations in the city.

Tenants' need for a two-pronged approach, that is, seeking any available outside help while creating indigenous mechanisms, took on a greater sense of urgency once the 1991 gang wars commenced. Takeover attempts of several Black Kings–controlled high-rises by the local Sharks gang came as little surprise. Sets of Black Kings and Sharks in other parts of the city had been fighting since 1990, and in the summer of 1991, the war had spread to the disputed Black Kings–Shark turf boundary—Twenty-third St. One spur to the city-wide war was economic: adding buildings to their "turf" increased the gang's customer base for drugs and recruits. The other precipitate of the war was rooted in adolescent rivalry, specifically in the fights of Sharks and BK members during and after school.

The 1991 outbreak also witnessed a marked escalation in the duration and level of gang-related violence. The citywide BK leaders were distraught at the heightened gunfire in Robert Taylor, which was threatening their drug revenues. Jamie Caldwell was the "chief" of the BKs, the highest ranking of four leaders, each of whom commanded a BK set in the housing development. But his leadership showed signs of ineffectiveness. Caldwell and older BK members were actively executing drive-by raids on Sharks gang members, thereby adding more fuel to the BK-Sharks conflict. To restore the integrity of their economic venture, Caldwell's superiors, Latrell and Darell Watkins, responded to his ineffective leadership with physical reprimand—they took Jamie to an alley and beat him severely.

The Watkins brothers lived in a working-class black neighborhood to the southeast of the housing development, and they had "rank" over at least three thousand other BKs living in the South Side communities in and around Robert Taylor. Their ostensible role was that of high-ranking gang leaders, but they conceived of themselves as managers of BK drug trafficking: "I guess you could call me a drug boss," said Latrell. "You know, like the Mafia, but yeah, I deal with a lot of different things in the organization." As "drug bosses," the Watkins brothers were upset that a police presence and tenant complaints in Robert Taylor had risen steadily under Jamie's command.

To secure his "rank," Jamie tried to reduce some of the raids, but his assertiveness amounted to too little, too late. Latrell Watkins determined that Jamie was incapable of handling the "community side of [gangbanging]," including the management of effective relations with police, residents, and storeowners. In the middle of the citywide gang war, Latrell promptly revoked Jamie's title as chief, explaining that "we took him out because the nigger couldn't keep up, he was making money . . . he ain't understood about the community side of what we do. Gangbanging is not just about making money, see, you got to keep a low profile, keep lot of people quiet, and you can't always just go around beating the shit out of niggers."

After 1991, the BKs in Robert Taylor had a new organizational structure. Latrell and Darrell Watkins named C-Note chief over half of the Robert Taylor Black Kings, that is, the "Twenty-seventh St. BKs," who operated between Twenty-third St. and Twenty-ninth St. They allowed Jamie to remain chief over the BKs south of Twenty-ninth St., which included his own set ("The End"), the "210 BKs," led by Mason Watson, and the "218 BKs," led by Grady Lenard.

The imposed restructuring by the Watkins brothers signaled quite plainly that the city's Black Kings gang was trying to mimic an organized criminal enterprise, with petty accumulation as the driving motive behind their decision making, internal organization, and external relations. This did not mean that all gangs were well-oiled machines in the underground economy—nor that the majority of members of each gang traded actively—but rather that revenue generation had become an organizational imperative. More accurately, it was an obsession of the higher-ranking citywide leaders that motivated their guidance of the neighborhood factions under their wing.

If the intent of such actions was to buttress drug trading, the effects did not always follow in predictable fashion. The executive decision to revamp the Robert Taylor Black Kings actually led to increased gang-related conflict as well as heightened instability for the entire tenant body, thereby threatening revenue generation. With the division of the BKs along Twenty-ninth St., the four sets busily fought their enemy, the Sharks, but internal antagonisms also surfaced as each tried to exert control of the local drug market and claim the status of the commercially superlative BK set. Moreover, internal BK fighting was more of a hindrance to the quality of life of residents than were formal gang wars; members saw one another daily and a conflict could erupt at any time, with little provocation and with friends and families in close proximity.

By 1991, tenants had exhausted two traditional mechanisms for controlling gang behavior. Direct interaction with gang members had been useful when a gang was based in a building and its members were not completely beholden to other leaders. For example, a tenant might ask a gang member to curb drug selling, or LAC officers might join together with police to pressure a gang leader. But with a more diffuse leadership structure, pressuring the gang leader of one building, say, Mason Watson in the 210 high-rise, might not be effective. Mason now had to consult with other leaders and get them to agree. In addition, the entrepreneurial thrust of gang activity meant a premium was placed on sales. Mason would be less likely to concede to tenant demands if they diminished his sales revenue or his stature in the eyes of watchful superiors. Whereas tenants had once worked together to monitor gang activity, as in the case of tenant patrols, they were now much more fearful in the face of an entrepreneurial gang that would readily use violence and intimidation to guarantee its profits from drug sales.

Similarly, tenants had previously used relationships with empathetic police officers to help control a gang's public activities. Now the gang's common use of weapons made police and tenants less likely to approach gang members informally. Michael Reedy, a Chicago police officer who had grown up in Robert Taylor and who had become a member of the tactical unit assigned specifically to gang activity, admitted that his colleagues spent less time than before "calling in on folks just to say hello." His own disdain for backroom dialogue with Prince, Jamie, and other leaders stems from the gang's "obsess[ion] with money" as opposed to community support:

When I was growing up [in Robert Taylor], gangs was good *and* bad, but they always knew where they came from. These cats talk a lot about helping the community, but if people start complaining and they can't sell the drugs, they beat them up . . . Me and Edith Huddle, we used to work with all these guys. We didn't stop them from dealing or nothing, but we could talk with them, get information, or get them to stop doing things. See, it's like you said, you don't see us doing that no more. Folks are scared, and police, we just can't take that chance, because these guys kill cops. So yeah, we usually go in together, use what some call "mob action," but it's just a pressure tactic we use.

With less frequent contact and cooperation and greater apprehension of gun-toting gangs, the gulf between tenants and the law enforcement community widened, affecting not only the control of gang-related activities, but also police response to domestic violence, medical emergencies, and property crime. Police officers who once engaged in brokerage relations with tenants expressed clear hesitation when entering the housing development to meet with residents, and when they did, their attention was overwhelmingly directed at gangs and drugs, leaving little energy for other pressing matters.

These police-tenant relations reflected a shift in law enforcement's gang and drug interdiction efforts within Chicago's public housing complexes, what has been commonly referred to in the national context as the move to "gang suppression." The broad components of suppression included low priority for prevention and treatment, high priority for assault, robbery, and other "street crime," and "heavy surveillance, along with rapid, certain and serious sanctioning."[4] The "mob action" referred to by the officer was one such suppression tactic in which police dispersed gang members who occupied public spaces. This was part of an overall preference on the part of CHA Chairman Lane and the Chicago Police Department for suppression approaches, also called "emergency procedures." Another practice was Operation Clean Sweep, unannounced searches of apartments, and "stop and frisk actions," which had been formally outlawed. At the same time, neither the CHA nor the Chicago police

were adequately incorporating preventive policing in which the police patrolled on foot to interact and become familiar with residents,
street-corner dwellers, and storeowners. When foot patrols *were* incorporated, as in the 1994 Building Interdiction Team Effort (BITE)
program, they were used in a largely token manner, in the form of occasional discussions by law enforcement officers with tenants who
happened to be nearby.[5]

In Robert Taylor, tougher law enforcement strategies produced
growing distrust between the police and a tenant body that in various
eras had feared law enforcement as much as the corporate gang.[6]
Sweeps of apartments in search of drugs led to debates regarding the
suspension of constitutional search-and-seizure protections for public housing tenants. Such tactics split the tenant body by dividing
those who favored "state of emergency" latitude for police from dissenters who could not support such an abuse of civil rights. Tenants
also complained that police were using the mob action aimed at gang
members to arrest non-gang-affiliated youth, from whom they hoped
to obtain information on criminal activities. In "townhall" meetings,
demonstrations, and marches, tenants criticized Chicago police, tactical unit personnel, and CHA security guards and police. Conversely, at all of these events and in the media, law enforcement
agents stood their ground by rebuffing the accusations and issuing
their own reprisals that tenants should "stop helping the gangs and
start helping the police." Because gangs had well-stocked caches of
weapons—for example, the Twenty-seventh St. Black Kings stored
guns, knives, and bullets in an abandoned apartment—and the physical environment placed officers at great risk of sniper fire when approaching buildings, police were justified when asserting that Robert
Taylor was a difficult community to protect.

Chicago Police Officer Michael Reedy admitted spending much of
his time convincing tenants and police to work together: "Lot of cops,
they had no idea what it's like living in public housing, so I'm always
busy educating them . . . You got tenants who think we [in the police
force] the Ku Klux Klan or something, and I know they got to get their

hustles on, make their money. I know when to look the other way, I'm not stupid. But you got to give me something back, like the good old days when I was growing up. One hand washed the other." Notwithstanding Reedy's efforts, tenants expected little help from police in gang-related matters—and they were not pleased with the law enforcement response to other transgressions.

The police could not be expected to address the complex needs of at-risk youth in Robert Taylor, as a formal evaluation of social services in Greater Grand Boulevard stated: "In too many instances, the community is relying on law enforcement agencies to control [problems associated with juvenile delinquency]."[7] Policing would prove successful only if other service providers, such as youth centers and schools, played a more productive role in the lives of at-risk youth. At the turn of the decade, however, this was wishful thinking. The authors who claimed that police should have a limited role in youth development also concluded that providers in and around Robert Taylor were not vigorously addressing the social problems faced by young people, either alone or with the police.[8]

Tenants in Robert Taylor had difficulties getting provider agencies to address their needs adequately. Historically, the housing development had never been sufficiently served, but the numbers tell only part of the story. In 1992, fifty-two organizations provided Robert Taylor and its immediately surrounding neighbors in private-market housing with social, educational, spiritual, psychological, and medical assistance—perhaps an adequate number if the population was largely employed, but not for one that was jobless, impoverished, and reliant on public welfare support. An official evaluation of agencies specifically designed to serve the housing development concluded that, "despite the apparent availability of services near the project area, limitations on these services impede their accessibility to project area residents."[9] The report cited poor community relations, inconvenient hours of operation, and a lack of understanding of the tenants' needs. It also pointed to social and economic barriers—which would probably hold true for *any* poor constituency—including "absence of patient resources including child care, transportation, lack of finances, long waiting times, [and] fear of being tested for drugs."[10]

Some services, such as prenatal care, were unnecessarily duplicated while others, such as gang intervention, were not being offered. Although providers in and around Robert Taylor distributed much-needed medical and social services to hundreds of its families, the majority offered quite specific programs such as prenatal or dental care, pregnancy counseling, abuse and addiction services, and job training. A more holistic, collaborative approach to service delivery might have been more effective, but most agencies were loath to integrate into the daily life of the housing development in a way that overstepped their defined area of expertise or that broadened their reach to include the criminally active or gang-affiliated youth. Discussions with staff at nearly two-thirds of the facilities confirmed this shared reluctance to become involved in local affairs.[11]

The agencies' hesitation derived in part from the perception that the "troubled youth" in Robert Taylor required resources beyond what they could provide. In the words of a director of a teenage counseling center, "We can't be expected to help everybody. We just try and do what we can, and a lot of times, the needs of the troubled youth are more than we can handle. We have to focus our resources on some of the better-performing children and youth. We're sorry about that, but we all make choices." A principal of a nearby high school stated, "Yeah, you can criticize us for doing nothing, but you probably don't see all that we do *inside* the school. We face the same problems here, in the building, as [residents of Robert Taylor] do inside their buildings. And frankly, we just don't have the resources to solve *all* the problems." Only three agencies saw the need to intervene on behalf of Robert Taylor's tenants in politicized matters, such as housing maintenance, adequate police services, city-service provision, and gang-conflict mediation, as part of their purview—namely, the Grace Center, the Boys and Girls Club, and 100 Black Men, a group of ex–public housing tenants affiliated with a small church.[12]

The rest shared a common approach: "We stay out of political issues. We focus on helping people."

It would be unfair to judge these agencies solely on the basis of their choice to stay "out of political issues." For many service providers, in Robert Taylor and elsewhere in Chicago's poorest areas, the client pool of poor and needy households has grown steadily. Given that most organizations have suffered reductions in funding and staffing, it makes sense that they would temper public expectations with modest assessments of their helping role.[13]

Whether unintentional or unavoidable, however, the depoliticized posture of these agencies has meant that many government, public nonprofit, and private-sector organizations have actively distanced themselves from the needs of Robert Taylor. Tenants did not necessarily expect each and every local agency to help fight gangs, march with them at Housing Authority headquarters, or otherwise address the most difficult quality-of-life issues such as security and services. However, they were disappointed when their calls for such assistance met with flat refusals for material and symbolic support. During a 1991 tenant campaign to raise police awareness of gang activity, LAC President Kim Walton and several tenants solicited support from local organizations but were despondent when they received very little. "They all just say they got to protect themselves," said Walton. "Against what? . . . They ain't victims of police brutality. Why can't they stand next to us? They don't even say, 'We're there with you.' Nothing." Another long-time resident echoed Walton's sentiments, but with specific reference to four of the largest churches that ministered to Robert Taylor: "Churches just kind of, you know, stopped being involved with what was going on. They just kept to themselves, and well, I still go to church, but it ain't like I think they are going to help do anything around here." Given the historically prominent role of churches in improving life for black urban Americans, it was noteworthy to hear that tenants had few relationships to local churches and that they expected them to provide little ballast in their struggle to address community needs; in general, churches entered into community affairs timidly, if at all, and usually in ways that did not broach the most sensitive issues, such as youth development and maintenance of the high-rises.

It was apparent that tenants would have to rely on their own Local Advisory Council for help. Since 1971, the LAC had been their primary advocate, either acting alone or in concert with those entities open to intimate collaboration with residents over "political issues." In the spring of 1990, for example, fifteen of the twenty-eight buildings in Robert Taylor had an LAC-sponsored tenant initiative to address gang-related conflicts, and in only two high-rises did the LAC acquire support from another organization when a local pastor led a vigil for "troubled youth." The strength of the LAC was in devising casual, non-institutionally based methods to secure a range of services. Tenants did not necessarily prefer informal support over bureaucratically based service delivery, but their experience over three decades left little reason for them to patronize local organizations. Thus, tenants' own active patronization of informal assistance networks helped to increase their social distance from local service providers.

Relying on their own creativity and whatever resources they could muster was certainly nothing new for tenants. But when they faced the challenges of gang intervention, they felt abandoned. Somewhat to their surprise, they met few organizations in the surrounding Greater Grand Boulevard community that would offer help. They could recall an earlier period—usually the 1960s—when organizations were less bureaucratic, less specialized, and more organically tied to the black community, which meant that the organizations were willing to involve themselves in "messy shit and fight right next to us, for anything." They did not expect their struggles with gangs to include lobbying for legitimacy and resources from other community actors.

Their work put to the test the pervading wisdom of social observers who, at the end of the 1980s, could only remark that the poor were living in "socially disorganized" communities where individuals were not working actively to address their needs. Ironically, those who used this language tended to pay little attention to the ways in which poor residents tried to perform functions such as gang intervention or social control. Quite often, "what appear[ed] to outside observers as social disorganization 'often turn[ed] out to be simply a different form of social organization if one takes the trouble to look closely.'"[14] Typically, observers assumed that a high percentage of single-parent families or low levels of formal organization indicated tenant apathy and little community involvement. They often conflated high levels of social problems with pathologies in thought and action among poor residents. To be sure, the Robert Taylor community was not coping adequately with gang activity and other deleterious tenant practices, but this was not necessarily a result of a lack of effort, or worse, a behavioral pathology. Yet these were the explanations advanced by adherents of the social-disorganization perspective, who at the same time often failed to mention the "changing activities of dominant institutions [that contributed] to organizing the social space of the ghetto in particularly destabilizing ways."[15] Agencies in the wider community, ranging from schools to hospitals to service providers, had grown tentative in the "political" issues of public housing, as had philanthropies and foundations, which were equally conservative in their outlook. Nor was the city, state, or federal government adding to its police "gang suppression" programs a concomitant focus on counseling, education, and other integral services.

Those drawing on the social-disorganization explanation had effectively written struggle, contest, and negotiation out of the equation when it came to understanding the predicament of the American urban poor. Yet this was precisely the state of affairs that characterized a tenant body in Robert Taylor that was fighting received wisdom on gang intervention in the wider world as well as "social predators" at home who destabilized everyday life.[16] Ensuring the viability of their communities was one long, continuous struggle in which tenants sought to come together to change and improve their communities.

The impact of their social isolation both from the mainstream and within their own ghetto neighborhoods was to make the road ahead even tougher.

Will Jackson's "Band-Aid" Diplomacy

"My father was a preacher, did you know that?" said Will Jackson. "It's hard for me not to think of my work as what they call ministry. Lot of people see real hard kids, gangbangers. I see sheep wandering, babies." Will often spoke in metaphors when he described his background and his reasons for taking the position as director of the Grace Center. Started in 1989 by a large church in a community to the east of the housing development, the center was one of only two large social-service organizations in Robert Taylor—the other being the Boys and Girls Club. The center offered programs for people of all ages, and Will Jackson wanted to reach out to gangs and "highly troubled youth." Jackson's strategy to offer services to these marginal constituencies had not been seen in the housing development for decades: instead of a law enforcement–based approach, he favored using the "gang structure" to transform the values of gang members.[17] As this tall, lanky fifty-year-old walked around the community shaking hands with gang-affiliated youths and asking them to join the center, tenants stood in disbelief, waiting with mixed feelings while observing the man they would call "the craziest nigger in Robert Taylor."

It is understandable that tenants in Robert Taylor were circumspect when the Grace Center entered into some of the most politicized aspects of community life.[18] Many received the center's programmatic innovations with skepticism, and residents were slow to join the center.[19] Their tentative reception stemmed from their exposure over the past decade to a litany of "suppression" programs in which law enforcement made few attempts to solicit their opinions and involvement. By the end of the 1980s, tenants had grown accustomed to police busts, sweeps, tactical units, mob action, mass search and seizures, fingerprinting, raids, and other paramilitary techniques.

They did not expect to see an unarmed man developing relationships with gang leaders.

Tenants' ambivalence stemmed from Jackson's intimate relationship with gang members, which in their minds harked back to earlier such efforts to co-opt the gang. Tenants were aware of past initiatives in which Chicago street gangs received large sums of money from government and philanthropic agencies. These programs used the so-called gang-structure approach by succoring gang leaders who had some enterprising qualities, hiring them as staff members and outreach workers, and then hoping that they would redirect the energies of their underlings away from crime and into mainstream employment.[20] Formal evaluations of gang-structure programs were mixed, citing both reductions in some criminal activities and increases in others.[21]

Tenant opinions of the gang structure also vary. Residents agree, however, that the approach is dangerous and can lead to co-optation by the gang. This was on their minds when they heard that Will Jackson wanted to bring gang members into the center. Ottie Davis warned, "That nigger best be careful, playing with fire. Man ain't from around here, don't know what gangs is like. This ain't Minnesota."

Raised in the hinterlands of Minnesota, Will Jackson had worked close to home for twenty years managing a network of social-service agencies. Then a Chicago pastor recruited him to run the Grace Center, and after being assured that he could service all segments of the community, including "highly troubled youth," Jackson accepted the offer. He divided the center's activities into educational, social, and recreational divisions. He had four staff members and hired Christie Woodson and Kenny Davenport as outreach workers because of their knowledge of local gang dynamics. Jackson, Woodson, and Davenport spent the first year advertising the facility, replete with computers, photocopying machines, and telephones, to the tenant body. With few other such agencies nearby, the center became a popular meeting place.

Jackson noticed an immediate drop in the center's attendance when any hint of gang-related antagonism surfaced, whether between rival gangs or between gangs and tenants. To instill a sense of security, he first restored tenant confidence in the power of the LAC leaders, whose capacity to dole out services had been diminished by federal cuts to public housing and the CHA's prioritization of security over maintenance. To do this, he let LAC officers open a snack bar at the center, all proceeds from which went to assist Robert Taylor households. He also lobbied local stores to donate food each week, which was turned over to LAC leaders so that they could form packages for their needy constituents. Thus, LAC leaders once again became trusted providers.

Jackson spent time meeting privately with gang leaders, advertising the center and recruiting their participation for social and educational programs. He never instructed them to eliminate deleterious activities, such as drug distribution. Instead, he gauged their willingness to compromise, alter their use of public space, and resolve conflicts through dialogue. His efforts showed early signs of promise. In one incident, tenant leaders were furious that the Twenty-seventh St. BK members took advantage of "check day"—when public-assistance money was distributed in the form of AFDC and General Assistance payments—by reducing crack cocaine prices and selling near the stores where tenants bought groceries and other supplies. Jackson successfully persuaded C-Note to restrict sales activities to noncommercial areas. As he explained, "Folks got money in their hands, they want to feel good, just like you and me, and Twenty-seventh St. [BKs] was taking advantage of them. That ain't right. These people are vulnerable, they can't always turn that down."

Jackson viewed gang members as children who simply needed positive feedback and encouragement. His belief may have been wellintentioned, but he did not seem attuned to the gang's significant adult base, those in their twenties and thirties who joined the gang for income as well as peer support. The BK leader Jamie Caldwell did not hide the gang's self-interested economic motives in using the center as a cover from the law: "We wanted to use the center, shit, that's it. We're tired of meeting outside. [Jackson] knows that, he knows we meet to do our [business] in there." Jackson was aware of this, but he felt that the BKs would be closely monitored in the center and would be too busy in structured programs to conduct their business. In his view, gang meetings were still preferable to "these kids just hanging out on the streets. The more they're in [the center], the less they doing drugs and harassing folks."

Jackson's third push was to sponsor discreet meetings between LAC officers and gang leaders. This approach was grounded in a particular principle of conflict resolution that he followed, namely, to have parties engage in dialogue during times of relative peace as well as during crisis periods. But, says Kenny Davenport, it was also motivated by the BK leader Prince Williams, who told Jackson that "BKs [are] interested in helping their community." To push Prince and the other leaders along, the Grace Center staff devised relatively straightforward collaborations between the Black Kings and LAC leaders. Trash pickups, hallway cleaning, removing gang members who conducted business in parks, and limiting the public drinking of younger members were some of the ways Jackson arranged to allow tenants and gangs to work together.

Initially, only Prince, who had some authority over the Twenty-seventh St. BKs, received Will Jackson's proposals warmly. He convinced the Twenty-seventh St. BK leader, C-Note, to ensure that his younger members participated in the proposed activities. The Twenty-seventh St. BKs worked with LAC Building President Kim Walton—the most powerful LAC figure in their territory—to pick up trash around Twenty-ninth St., and Prince promised to initiate stiffer penalties for the younger members who were truant or who dropped out of school for extended periods. The other BK leaders—Mason, Grady, and Jamie—begrudgingly followed the lead of the Twenty-seventh St. BKs and worked with Grace Center staff and tenant leaders. However, their participation in collaborative activities quickly diminished, and they agreed only to limit drinking and truancy among their membership.

Near the end of 1992, Will Jackson, Christie Woodson, and Kenny Davenport communicated with gang and tenant leaders in every building from Twenty-third St. to Thirty-first St.—although not every building had a cooperative program, such as trash pickup, or formal deliberations between the two parties. In most high-rises, the three Grace Center staff members would make covert phone calls or visit BK and LAC leaders in order to make note of gang-related conflicts and suggest possible settlement tactics. The fruit of their labor was evident in the familiarity they enjoyed with the gang and tenant leaders. In a typical week at the Grace Center, the staff heard reports of a dozen gang-related conflicts, most within an hour or two of their occurrence. They immediately dispatched a courier to bring the aggrieved, injured, or violated parties to the Grace Center, phoned a police officer for medical assistance if necessary, and made visits to the local gang leader and LAC officer to begin the conflict-resolution process.

Jackson did not enjoy monopolizing the conflict-mediation process, so he and Kenny Davenport actively recruited other community-based organizations, asking that they "adopt" a building and work closely with the tenant body. He encountered several reactions. Grassroots providers, such as storefront churches or nearby block clubs, expressed interest but themselves lacked resources and manpower. The larger, well-established social-service agencies were afraid of hurting their public reputation by working too closely with street gangs. Another set of larger organizations agreed to help him, but they wanted him to obtain assurance that gang leaders would cease drug distribution first, which he felt would jeopardize his trust with the gang.

The organizations that eventually helped Jackson were small, grassroots groups, like the Washington Area Confederation, that had few staff and minimal resources, but that were in close contact with troubled youth. They had little outside funding, and many were alienated from the larger, established providers that served poor areas. They went in and out of existence depending on funding, but they tried to dedicate resources to the most marginal constituencies. None, however, had ever worked collaboratively in an effort to combat gang activity: "These were all good, decent folks that just didn't get no attention from the big boys," said Ottie Davis. "They work alone, man, they work late at night."

Will Jackson's success with this "lower tier" of community organizations was offset by rising tenant antipathy for his work style. The gang's sale of drugs and its intimate ties to tenant leadership were the primary and unresolvable points of contention. Many tenants visited the Grace Center to complain that gang members were paying LAC officers and CHA security guards for protection during drug sales. They blamed Jackson for laying the groundwork for this covert scheme by legitimizing the gang as a partially positive force in the housing development. Although Jackson could not be held completely accountable for the gang's trafficking, it was clear that his approach had deleterious, perhaps unintended, consequences for the housing development. Jackson had allowed Robert Taylor BK leaders and others across the city, whom the local leaders invited, to come to the center for billiard games or to socialize. Jackson allowed these leaders to meet without center staff present, although in public he would tell residents otherwise. Jackson acknowledged the gang's use of the center for business begrudgingly and argued that such allowances were necessary to build trust with the local gangs. Tenants were angry when they heard rumors of unsupervised gang meetings. They wanted Jackson to require gang members to eliminate drug trafficking, and when he refused, they said the local gangs were "running the show." In the buildings north of Twenty-ninth St., tenants organized a small protest of the Grace Center, threatening to take their children away if Jackson persisted in his approach.

Tenants accused their own leadership of receiving personal gifts from the gang, such as money and cars, in exchange for small concessions from gang members, such as reduced trafficking in certain areas. Tenants were not simply speculating about the exchange of money between the gang and the center and the LAC. They were drawing logical inferences based on Jackson's own statements in which he boasted of accepting gang "donations" to purchase new play equipment for the center. Jackson's own staff was upset at the intimate contact between the center and local gangs. Two of his initial hires quit, citing not only Jackson's use of "dirty money" from the gang to pay center personnel, but also the gang's intimidating presence and use of drugs in the center hallways, which they said Jackson was ignoring. Jackson defended some of these practices as necessary for the gang to feel a sense of ownership in the center.

There soon emerged the hints of an ideological divide between, on the one hand, Jackson, the LAC leaders, and those who favored his use of the gang-structure approach, and, on the other, those tenants who could not support any concessions to the gangs. At the heart of the disagreement was a sharply contrasting conception of the gang and its role in the housing development. Jackson portrayed the gang as youths who were interested in the Black Kings for social purposes, that is, for camaraderie and a sense of belonging; drug trafficking was only a secondary motivation, he thought. He would argue that if young people would begin to use the Black Kings in noncriminal ways—"like a college fraternity," he said, "where they do fun things together"—they would eventually forget about drug dealing. There was strong resonance between his philosophy and the reform programs in vogue in the 1950s and 1960s that sought to "change gang members' values, attitudes, and perceptions. Behavioral change would follow."[22]

Jackson had misperceived the makeup of the gang and the extent to which the gang members were entrepreneurially motivated. He operated with an antiquated mid-twentieth-century model of youth gangs, made up of adolescents who were engaged in petty delinquency and truancy. He failed to realize that drug-based revenue was a motive for many members, if only to help their households make ends meet. His reform-oriented approach did not seem adequately tailored to a corporate gang whose members were invested in drug economies, whether out of thrill-seeking or necessity. He ignored the pleas of his own staff, who said that BKs were really only interested in drug trafficking and who wanted to confront this practice directly. In fact, Jackson provided the local gangs with more center resources, opening the center in the evenings and placing gang leaders on the payroll as part-time outreach workers.

Families grew indignant and some pulled their children out of the center because they feared a strong gang presence. Their frustration with Will Jackson spilled over at times, and they directed their anger at him for events in which he may have had no direct role. When a BK was shot by Sharks in a drive-by shooting, people said Jackson's intervention strategy was to blame. Some asked that he discontinue conflict mediation unless he received promises from gangs to elimi- nate public drug trafficking. Jackson replied, "I just can't [tell them to stop trafficking drugs in the buildings]. They're going to sell that stuff somewhere, and they don't have apartments. I know these guys will never stop selling outside, and [I] think you lose more if you keep asking them to do that. They won't do nothing for you."

With the Grace Center's assistance, gang-related disputes were be- ing resolved more quickly, but there was no indication that they were being prevented. Will Jackson understood the limits of his self-de- scribed "Band-Aid" diplomacy and was not oblivious to accusations that the center was reinforcing the drug trade. It did not appear, how- ever, that he would change his position on the drug-trafficking issue. Instead, he adhered to the gang-structure approach and continued to seek out opportunities to work with the gang's leaders and within its organization to effect change. As he said in one meeting with LAC leaders, "We have to figure out how to get them to stop dealing out in the open. That's what's causing the fuss around here." He reintro- duced an earlier idea, all but forgotten by the others, namely, "to go to prison and meet with their leaders."

Indeed, one pressure point for the corporate gang was the city- wide command structure in which local BK leaders followed orders from on high. Jackson believed that to lessen gang-related conflicts, Robert Taylor had to respond to the gang's local and citywide makeup. He did not want to ask the higher-ranking leaders to reduce the BK's involvement in the narcotics trade. In fact, he wanted to use their own desire to stabilize the drug trade by reducing gang conflicts, and thereby police activity. He asked them to pressure Robert Taylor BKs to participate in center programs and to reduce their harassment of tenants.

Jackson's perspective was not shared by all of the LAC leaders around the table. His form of intervention was quite risky, and the leaders remained hesitant to lend support, some positing that the status quo, however intolerable, might still be better than "going to bed with the Devil," in the words of one tenant. But most were not yet willing to withdraw their involvement with Jackson and relinquish one of their only sources of organizational support in the housing development. As LAC Building President Edith Huddle suggested in a tenant meeting called to create support for the new intervention, the community was socially isolated, and "[we] need to stick by [Jackson and the Grace] Center because they're all we got right now."

The Robert Taylor community did benefit in some respects from Will Jackson's gang-structure approach. On many occasions, he had persuaded gang leaders to use dialogue as opposed to violence to settle their disputes, and he had opened the lines of communication with gang leaders, which showed some promise in minimizing conflict escalation. Given that law enforcement, the CHA, and service providers in the wider community offered little help, it was difficult for tenants to withdraw their full support for the Grace Center's brand of conflict resolution. Thus, although tenants protested Jackson's work style, they wanted him to continue his mediation efforts, and early in 1992, the Grace Center worked busily to conduct conflict mediation in nearly two-thirds of the high-rises.

The question remained, however, whether the long-term outcomes of the Grace Center's mediation would ultimately be destructive for the residents of Robert Taylor. There were signs that the gang was co-opting the center for its own purposes. Some of the gang's violence may have decreased, but members' presence in public areas and their trafficking were more noticeable, and their drug trade had actually shown signs of greater stability. Moreover, it was not clear that Jackson was going to request that the gang reduce its narcotics trafficking. As important, the gang had clearly disrupted the tenants' relationship with the LAC, an organization that may not have been fully responsive to tenants' needs, but one that nevertheless had been their best advocate during the last three decades. As families began withdrawing their children from center activities, the facility appeared more like a gang clubhouse than a mainstream social-service provider. The benefits of intimate collaboration with the gang were offset by these developments.

Jackson and the tenant leadership realized that they needed to act quickly and decisively to forestall the gang's ascent. However, Jackson was operating with an anachronistic model of the gang that did not match the activities of the Black Kings. Moreover, his belief that interactions with imprisoned and citywide leaders could occur without demands to reduce drug trafficking appeared naive in the face of the gang's immersion in local underground economies. It began to seem that he was unresponsive to the community. Yet despite their own withdrawal from the center, many tenants actually remained cautiously optimistic, as Jackson began driving downstate, into the farmlands and out to the Illinois penitentiary and the imprisoned Black Kings leaders, that change might still be on the horizon.

Community Justice

Into 1992, Will Jackson and staff members of the Grace Center were persuading grassroots organizations to "adopt" a building in Robert Taylor and help them to mediate gang-tenant disputes. Jackson learned that Latrell and Darrell Watkins (the BKs who supervised Robert Taylor's gang leaders) had been meeting with BK leaders in the development to discuss the Grace Center's mediation campaign. The Watkins brothers did not want Robert Taylor BKs to "waste time" helping the community if drug revenue began falling. As Darrell said, "You could tell [the BK leaders in Robert Taylor] liked walking around, helping folks. Their heads got real big, thinking they was the mayor or something." When asked if that didn't make people happy and thus increase sales, Darrell replied, "Yeah, but don't waste time with that shit. That's what we said because, back then, it was about the money."

If the behavior of the Black Kings was dictated by city-level gang leaders, then intervention and mediation efforts by the LAC, the Grace Center, and other stakeholders might need readjustment. To modify their efforts, in 1992 Will Jackson enlisted the assistance of ex–gang members and No More Wars, an organization with ties to the Watkins brothers and other citywide Black Kings leaders. A social worker and several ex–gang members had formed No More Wars back in 1988 in order to resolve disputes in the poor black neighborhoods of southern Chicago. By 1991, the group was known in Chicago's social-service community for a strategy that used the authority of the gang's highest-ranking imprisoned leaders to pressure the rank-and-file membership to reduce in-school fighting, limit their use of weapons, and form peace treaties with enemy groups. The Grace Center's attempts to enlist No More Wars and intervene on two fronts—at the local level and citywide—made clear the difficulty of gang intervention when a gang has a local and a metropolitan identity. For the Black Kings in Robert Taylor, addressing the gang's vast organizational structure opened a Pandora's box. By working intimately with citywide superiors, members could reduce violence and limit escalation of gang conflicts, but they would also risk disparaging treatment from their peers for their creative, nontraditional efforts. Moreover, early efforts on the part of the Grace Center to work from within the gang structure had revealed that if the local and citywide intervention strategy sought violence reduction and peace treaties but did not seek an immediate end to drug trafficking, it might exacerbate, rather than restore, the community's failing sense of security.

The dynamics in Robert Taylor beg reconsideration of a nearly sacred tenet in gang studies, namely, that gangs and neighborhoods are synonymous.[23] The first large study of American street gangs—

Frederic Thrasher's *The Gang*—championed the community rooted-
ness of gang activity by showing that gangs are local peer groups that
will remain active in a geographically circumscribed area unless their
families relocate.[24] According to Thrasher, in "interstitial" areas of
working-class and poor residents, gangs provide local youth with an
identity and social support. Their deep-seated connection to their immediate neighborhood is born from everyday practices including
naming systems, interactions with local residents and organizations,
and intergang rivalries. Subsequent research in the postwar era and
the 1960s affirmed the gang's strong local identity.[25] Relatively recent
studies suggest, however, that the connection to a neighborhood is
not important for all gangs and that cross-neighborhood patterns may
be as noteworthy—for example, a gang may have members who live
in different geographic areas.[26]

Contemporary researchers generally look askance at supra-neighborhood gang dynamics.[27] Many are justifiably leery of reports of
multi-neighborhood gang alliances given that these claims buttressed the 1980s specter, promulgated by media and law enforcement agencies, of a regional and national street-gang criminal
enterprise.[28] In Chicago, available data do not suggest the existence
of well-coordinated "supergangs." However, research does indicate
that the relationship of a gang to its neighborhood no longer con-
forms to the street-corner group engaged in petty delinquency on
their turf. Especially among the city's black and Latino gangs, some
local factions have joined "coalitions, confederations, 'supergangs'
and nations—presumably creating or developing even more sophisticated structures on the basis of prison experience."[29]

These changes are not always solely the intention of gang leaders
who rationally plan their groups' expansion. In Chicago, they followed from incidental contacts in prison and juvenile-detention facilities,[30] non-neighborhood-based recruitment, family movement,
and seasonal residence patterns.[31] The earliest signs of supergang formation could be detected in the 1970s and had their roots in attempts
by prison officials early in the decade to use gangs as vehicles for

maintaining order inside penitentiaries.[32] Groups of inmates, each typically taking on the name of a gang family, banded together in prison. Toward the end of the 1970s, as individuals left jails and prisons, the alliances of gangs, different families, and nations remained, although their purpose was not clear. Neither were the motives for continued supergang associations on the streets quite evident since the gangs were not heavily invested in underground economies and were not interacting socially. However, it is important to note that the gang's reach over a large metropolitan landscape, via the ties of different gang families, occurred well before the onset of crack cocaine or even any serious immersion by sets in street-based underground economies; indeed, "the corporate gang . . . predated crack," writes the sociologist Malcolm Klein.[33] Thus, it cannot be argued that supergangs were a direct or inevitable outcome of heightened drug trafficking, and in fact, their metropolitan networks may have provided some of the infrastructure through which a coordinated crack economy could subsequently flourish.

By 1992, the Robert Taylor Black Kings had ties to a federation of neighborhood-based gangs called "Black Kings Nation." Members spoke of a deep bond to the Nation, but their sense of belonging was not framed by much actual intercourse with other Chicago BK members, and most of the sets had little engagement with one another. Instead, members were integrated practically into BK Nation by interaction with two superiors, Darrell and Latrell Watkins, who visited the housing development to instruct, and pass news to, local BK leaders. The Watkins brothers rarely coordinated the activities of the BK sets they controlled with others outside their region, and they had great latitude to demand monetary tributes and otherwise dictate the behavior of the sets under their command. If the brothers made regular payments to their own superiors and reduced police "busts" of BK drug operations, they were free to use their power with considerable discretion.

In the early 1990s, although law enforcement frightened the public with reports that Vicelord, El Rukn, Disciples, Black Kings, and other Chicago gang families were marching in a disciplined manner, neighborhood gang sets in the Robert Taylor Homes had minimal involvement in the citywide movement.[34] They were only rarely ordered by their superiors to change their behavior, help affiliates, plan wars, and so on. Instead, a neighborhood-based set remained in contact with a superior primarily to turn over drug revenue, to report on attempted takeovers by rivals, and for general camaraderie. Indeed, higher-ranking superiors, such as the Watkins brothers, contacted one another far more frequently—to direct the drug trade or to launder revenue—than members and leaders of individual factions, such as Jamie Caldwell or Prince Williams, contacted one another. Locally, the gang was a social and economic base for its members; regionally, it was an organized criminal enterprise, not always adeptly managed, but one whose leaders paid little attention to non-economic and non-criminal gang activities.

This relation between neighborhood gangs and their "family" or "nation" effectively rewrote the rules for localized conflict mediation given that the gang's actions could originate elsewhere.[35] In general, neither community- nor government-led initiatives in large urban cities have successfully handled the modern gang's dual identity—either that of a group divided into local and citywide factions or that of a group tied together by social and entrepreneurial activities. Most authorities work from the premise that the gang has a self-evident, quasi-sacred relationship to its neighborhood and that its broader makeup is not necessarily relevant. To be sure, a gang that spans neighborhoods is not an easy force to control, especially if its members are willing to use violence and can mobilize other resources to defend their entrepreneurial commitments. It is understandable that fear and unfamiliarity may dissuade communities from working with gangs' citywide and imprisoned leaders or from constructing cross-neighborhood gang mediation. Nevertheless, strategies that are not "broad based," with various actors in multiple sites working together, may have only limited gains when the gangs are partially supra-neighborhood entities at "all segments and all levels of society."[36]

Will Jackson and Edith Huddle were adamant that poor communities must end their social isolation from the larger society and from local organizations if they were to curb gang conflict. Their efforts to tie Robert Taylor to other communities commenced when they asked the No More Wars organization—which was busy resolving gang disputes on Chicago's West Side—to forge a peace treaty between the gangs in Robert Taylor. For a month, Huddle and Jackson met with Jeremy Coals, the leader of No More Wars, and their discussions produced a threefold strategy. No More Wars would settle BK-Shark disputes at the Grace Center, Coals and Huddle would conduct public-relations meetings to publicize the new resolution techniques, and all three would visit the highest-ranking Sharks and BK leaders in prison to win their support. The higher-ranking leaders participated because they saw an opportunity to create a climate in Robert Taylor favorable for drug distribution, and, faced with threats of punishment from their superiors or removal from office, the local set leaders had little choice but to become involved as well.

At the outset, Coals, Jackson, and gang leaders in Robert Taylor visited the state penitentiary, and together with jailed BK and Sharks leaders, they worked out resolutions of disputes in the housing development. Coals said that part of his success with the jailed leaders derived from his willingness to grant the gang a legitimate status in the community. Like Jackson, he said that these early dialogues did not broach the subject of drug trafficking—Coals and Jackson consciously avoided the drug trade because they feared that gang leaders would withhold their blessing and involvement if they thought that their economic ventures were being threatened. After a working relationship was established, Coals, Jackson, and the gang leaders in Robert Taylor tried to resolve most of the local disputes at the Grace Center itself, returning to the penitentiary primarily to update jailed leaders. Twice monthly, in a center conference room or in Jackson's office, they discussed incidents of fighting between school-aged members, "turf" violations wherein BKs sold drugs in Sharks territory, and other conflicts. Until April 1992, as wars between Sharks and Black Kings factions continued across the city, the Grace Center and No More Wars prevented conflict escalation in the housing development. Few were celebrating, however, for they expected antagonisms to rekindle after May, when the school year ended.

Having created a temporary détente between the two local gangs, No More Wars turned its attention to the Robert Taylor tenant body and campaigned for its cooperation and broad-based support. Some LAC leaders assisted Jeremy Coals by organizing formal meetings between residents and his staff, and in the spring of 1992, Coals and Edith Huddle met with tenants in seven buildings in the Black Kings territory and three Sharks-controlled buildings; other buildings showed low tenant interest or low-level gang activity. Tenants voiced two opinions. One vocal body supported No More Wars and applauded its efforts to reduce gang violence; some asked that No More Wars also organize demonstrations to demand increased police protection. Another constituency flatly refused to legitimate direct negotiation with gangs, and they pressed for complete involvement of law enforcement agencies in order not to alienate police, the Housing Authority, and other organizations in the surrounding community. The following vituperative exchange in a February 1992 meeting in the 230 high-rise exemplified the difference of opinion:

> "This is worse than you all taking gangs' money," yelled Amy Madison. "Now, you just helping them to sell drugs whenever they want."
>
> "Let them tell you what they doing," a tenant interrupted Amy. "All they doing is getting these folks to sit down at a table, solve their problems without shooting all the time."
>
> "No," said Jeremy Coals, in response to Amy Madison's accusation. "[No More Wars] ain't gonna help [gangs] sell drugs in your building."
>
> "Are you telling them to stop?" asked Madison.
>
> "No, we ain't working that way. We trying to get them to stop warring," replied Coals.
>
> "Ain't working that way?!" yelled LAC Building President Kelly Davis. "Looks to me like you working any way you want. I ain't gonna let them sell drugs up in my building. People gonna feel safe in here."

"That's what we trying to do," said Coals. "Let you all feel safe. Let you use the area again."

"Listen to the man, Ms. Davis," yelled someone from the back of the room. "You ain't done nothing and gang's still selling that shit. So why can't we let [No More Wars] work with them? Shit, if [No More Wars is] that crazy, let these niggers do their thing. I want to go outside, shit, I ain't been outside for the longest."

Gatherings in other buildings followed this script. A vocal tenant constituency challenged No More Wars staff on their refusal to address the gang's drug trafficking. However, tenants also appreciated that No More Wars was involved in local affairs, and they tempered their criticisms with suggestions that the organization pay more attention to failing building maintenance. In nearly every audience, irrespective of the level of support for No More Wars, there was general agreement that the CHA benefited from attention to street-gang activity because it drew scrutiny away from the agency's own negligence. Both Jeremy Coals and Edith Huddle promised to use any demonstrable reduction in gang violence as leverage to convince the CHA to transfer money from security to maintenance provision.

For its part, the Housing Authority had settled into a security posture that relied on paramilitary raids, sweeps, and mob action procedures—all costly efforts, but ones that allowed the municipal administration to make dramatic shows of opposition to the gangs. The CHA had clearly moved away from its historic use of brokerage diplomacy, whereby CHA staff gave promises of services to LAC leaders, who then distributed them to tenants at their discretion. In separate interviews, two CHA managers who worked in several different high-rise developments voiced their disagreement with the agency's decision to switch its priorities in recent years from daily maintenance and upkeep to anti-gang activity. And they lamented the reduced use of "friendly policies" that enabled them to remain in contact with tenants through constant attention to maintenance:

If you can get an LAC president to listen to you, you're going to have more success managing these large developments. You can't just go in all the time with dogs, police, and that kind of thing. Not everyone [in CHA] supports the sweeps and all the police activity. I like the friendly policies we used to have. Give LAC a few work orders, let them give them to the households as they wanted, people were happy, you didn't see lots of protests like you do now.

It's simple, really. If the relationship between me [a CHA manager] and the LAC breaks down, forget it. Tenants don't get what they want. If a tenant can't call the LAC president, say, "I want my door fixed," and LAC can't call me and then I call and get someone to fix it, then you're screwed. [CHA Chairman] Vince Lane has been against us [managers], but he don't understand the wash-your-back policy. You know? We do a little favor for LAC, they do something for us. It's easy, really, but it just doesn't seem to work, because we don't have that power no more. We can't work with LAC like that, and I think everyone's doing worse for it.

LAC leaders expressed similar disappointment at their inability to offer Housing Authority services to their constituents. Because they could not ensure the physical upkeep of their buildings and had only mixed success in gang intervention, LAC leaders such as Kelly Davis believed their own positions to be in danger. Hearing reports that her constituents sought new leadership, Davis said in the spring of 1992, "I know what they're saying. They think I ain't got no more power, can't do nothing for them. Fine, get me out, shit, I don't need this hassle. They don't pay me enough to deal with them gangs."

In the middle of May 1992, when gang hostilities between the Sharks and the Black Kings began to escalate in Robert Taylor, No More Wars staffers and their colleagues at the Grace Center (Kenny Davenport, Christie Woodson, and Will Jackson) looked closely for any breakdown in the BK-Sharks peace treaty. They called on high school counselors and security guards to make note of gang-related altercations. They spoke with men on the street corner, prostitutes, and other gang-employed "lookouts" in order to discern whether the Black Kings had moved all sales locations inside buildings—a clear sign of war readiness in that the members were trying to reduce their chances of being injured in drive-by shootings. They searched for minor altercations among neighboring BK and Sharks street-level dealers—a typical spark for a gang war—and they called imprisoned leaders in order to update themselves on citywide tensions. They also made preparations for tenants to transport schoolchildren, asking men who belonged to several storefront churches that supported No More Wars to volunteer their time by walking children to and from school. They expanded the Grace Center's hours of operation and asked Sharks and BK leaders to meet at the center once a week to keep the lines of communication open.

When shots were fired outside a local high school in early June, and a small girl playing in the development died after being caught in gang crossfire, it seemed as though their efforts were for naught. Fearing a public image of weakness if they did not respond to the Sharks' actions, BK leaders declared war on the rival gang, and gunfire ensued for several days. Tenants kept children inside hot apartments and limited their own public movement. The visible, public reaction of tenants was manifest in their strong showings at townhall discussions, where they angrily charged CHA representatives and police spokespersons with ineffective enforcement. Some participated in nightly vigils and "take-back-the-night" marches, and they gathered around television reporters to express their frustration.

Behind the scenes, people watched intently as Will Jackson, Edith Huddle, and Jeremy Coals met with gang leaders at the Grace Center. The cause of the warfare, which had become public knowledge, was the BK takeover of two buildings that had formerly been part of the Sharks' territory. At a Grace Center meeting, Mickey, the Sharks leader, said he believed that the BKs were trying to expand their market, but Jamie and Prince retorted that the Sharks in the two buildings had defected to BK Nation by voluntarily switching their allegiance. Because voluntary transfers could engender retaliatory punishment, Coals and Jackson visited imprisoned Sharks leaders to prevent a revenge attack. The leaders' own interest in minimizing any threats to their economic ventures probably motivated the quick issuance of a reprieve and instructions to the factions at Robert Taylor that the war was over. Prince and Mickey had no choice but to end their fighting. The four-day shooting between Sharks and BK members culminated in a "peace walk," whereby Prince and Jamie led one thousand Black Kings members into Sharks territory. Jeremy Coals clasped the hands of the Sharks leader Mickey and the BK leader Prince, and then proclaimed, "No more wars, that's our name, that's the game we playing. You all must now walk in peace." The Black Kings turned and walked back into their own territory.

The novel negotiation made both supporters and critics of the Grace Center excitably nervous. This unprecedented reach into the depths of the gang structure appeared to some as a warning that gangs had successfully co-opted community leaders in order to boost their drug operations. However, even those tenants and LAC leaders who were not initially supportive now applauded No More Wars and Grace Center staffers for pursuing a diplomatic solution. The LAC leaders Kelly Davis and Cathy Blanchard, two of the harshest critics, did not become outright supporters, but they acknowledged that their constituents were impressed that outreach was occurring during wars and not months afterward.

In public conversations, the successful mediation became fodder for summerlong debates among supporters of non-law-enforcement-based mediation and others who preferred a more conservative approach that incorporated Chicago police. Tenants who did not endorse the No More Wars strategy—namely, negotiation with no demands that gangs discontinue drug trafficking—offered a cautious commendation: "I'm happy I can go outside, enjoy myself. I ain't saying that ain't no big thing. Let's see if Will and them can stop all the drugs and the shooting. That's when I'll say they're doing right around here."

As tenants debated the merits of the new gang-intervention schemes, some of their leaders worked with Will Jackson and Jeremy Coals to redress the isolation of the housing development. News of the successful diplomacy had spread to surrounding neighborhoods as No More Wars advertised its services to churches, school principals, block clubs, and residents. Jackson suggested that Jeremy Coals invite community stakeholders to the Grace Center, where they could meet their counterparts in Robert Taylor. Promoting cross-neighborhood intercourse was one of Jackson's two stated motives for supporting mediation outside the housing development, the second being a perceived failure of "elite" social-service agencies in those areas to "reach out to troubled kids" and reduce the isolation of gang-affiliated youths.

Jackson's actions were not fully altruistic, however. His conflict mediation had thrust him into the limelight of ghetto politics, and he began acting in ways that showed a clear interest in self-aggrandizement. The cross-neighborhood interactions presented him with opportunities for personal advancement, and he capitalized on them by successfully catapulting himself into the role of one of several recognized spokespersons for the non-elite providers and organizations in these ghetto neighborhoods. His stature in the surrounding communities increased to the point that more conservative providers, themselves unwilling to conduct outreach to gangs, opened dialogues with him and recruited him to serve on their committees and commissions. He recognized that his presence provided the elite actors with an easy way to show their own funders that they were cognizant of the local grassroots sector and troubled youth. However, he thought this was a small price to pay for the possible access to resources that mainstreaming might bring him.

The cross-neighborhood involvement—either with other providers or with other gangs—had only minimal benefits for Robert Taylor as a whole; however, it did help to line the pockets of Jackson and his friends. Jackson accepted increased funding from citywide Black Kings gang leaders who now came to the center, which he continued to defend as necessary to cultivate a sense of ownership for the center among the gangs. He was less willing to reveal the ultimate use of the funds, but the inclusion of Jeremy Coals, directors of grassroots organizations in other neighborhoods, and various citywide Black Kings leaders on the center's payroll only fueled tenants' speculation that the center was a "gang clubhouse" and that the gang's funds were benefiting a fortunate few. Jackson was not managing public dissension by explicitly indicating how the accumulated funds were being spent to help the broader community.

By the autumn of 1992, No More Wars was holding ongoing meetings at the center for residents and community-based organizations in nearly one dozen Chicago communities, including Washington Park, Englewood, Chatham, Grand Crossing, and Roseland. Staff members summoned residents, organizations, and gang leaders to meet with one another. By late 1992, leaders of three black Chicago street-gang families were coming to hear speeches from No More Wars on diverse topics, ranging from the benefits of mandatory school attendance to planning for future entry into the legitimate labor force. These workshops, which No More Wars advertised as conflict-reduction sessions, were unmistakably helping to increase the gang's organizational cohesion. Tenant leaders were furious, and they demanded that Jackson and Coals restrict instruction to voter education.

The multisite intervention underwritten by the Grace Center affected the struggles of Robert Taylor's tenants to combat their own gangs. After observing the gang-resident mediation designed by No More Wars for private residential communities (in which residents and gang members confronted one another), LAC Officer Edith Huddle asked Jeremy Coals to replicate the forums in Robert Taylor. Together, they devised a relatively informal community court that convened several times each month at the Grace Center. Tenants could report a gang member's behavior and demand punishment and restitution. They enlisted three ex–gang leaders from other communities—who they felt would be neutral—to join them on a "jury" that determined fault and ascertained proper redress. In a second-floor classroom, the gang leaders punished guilty parties themselves—typically the gang's reprimands were physical punishment whereas the jury secured apologies, monetary payments, and the return of stolen goods. Tenants did not participate in droves; for example, in the third month, only seven people used the court's services, but there were some benefits. Although gang-tenant conflicts continued (and increased in some areas, such as "The End," the three buildings that Jamie controlled), bringing parties to appear in front of the court reduced the number of antagonisms that evolved into physical altercations. As important, two pernicious problems that plagued tenants—BK sexual harassment and extortion of underground entrepreneurs—were now heard in front of the six "justices."

Edith Huddle and Jeremy Coals increased their cross-neighborhood collaborations, organizing "youth rallies" at the center with representatives of nearly every community in which No More Wars was active. Minority political leaders on the City Council and in the state legislature attended to voice their support for the citywide "peace treaty" between warring gangs. In addition, Coals showed signs that he might make maintenance and upkeep of the housing development part of the No More Wars political platform. He used gang members to conduct door-to-door surveys of Robert Taylor high-rises, documenting with photographs and signed testimonies any physical hazard or sign of disrepair (Cathy Blanchard and Kelly Davis, who opposed Coals's methods, asked tenants not to speak to the surveyors). Will Jackson then called the media and held "public information days" for journalists to view exhibits of the photographs and meet with tenants who reported holes in their walls and unfulfilled work orders, and who displayed infants with "rat and roach bites."

Tenants overwhelmingly supported the use of No More Wars to publicize physical distress, but they wanted such issues to assume even greater priority in the organization's campaigns. However, neither Coals, Jackson, nor others involved in this initiative had moved beyond the occasional press release to help tenants form a sustained, unified front that could work toward more responsive CHA maintenance provision. Tenants were justified in their fears that these publicity drives were primarily serving as self-interested ways for No More Wars staffers—and Jackson and the tenant leaders who joined their stage—to better their public image by demonstrating a commitment to the needs of the housing development.

At the dawn of 1993, the vibrant atmosphere at the Grace Center, with nightly activities bringing in individuals from surrounding neighborhoods, gave the impression that Robert Taylor had responded to its social isolation from mainstream social-service organizations. Tenants had formed new relationships with smaller agencies, grassroots providers, and committed individuals who had a history of informal gang intervention in their own communities. Edith Huddle and Kim Walton traveled to workshops and rallies to share their experiences with other communities, and they joined neighboring Washington Park residents to protest the placement of power lines in and around Robert Taylor. Community-based organizations brought rival gang members to the Grace Center, where they met one another and participated in youth voter-registration drives. The gains for Robert Taylor included actual resources, in the form of manpower and access to programs in the wider community, as well as continuous contact with gang leaders for rapid dispute resolution.

Working so closely with gangs and organizations that did not publicly question the gangs' entrepreneurial interests had noticeable drawbacks, however, for ensuring the viability of the housing development. Reductions in gang wars did not necessarily make the tenant body feel more comfortable when sharing public space with gang members. They still had to pass by youths who dealt drugs openly. The Grace Center was complicit in the gang's actions, many believed, because the mediators still refused to challenge BK drug distribution. Moreover, the center was itself dedicating greater resources to events co-sponsored with No More Wars, which left reduced program offerings for children in Robert Taylor. At an LAC meeting in 210, Louisa Lenard admonished Will Jackson for turning the center into a "gang clubhouse":

> You keep wondering why no kids come around to the center no more. It's because you turned the place into a gang clubhouse, that's why. They up in there, dealing drugs, having those parties, doing all sorts of nasty things all night long. I know. If you don't stop, it's going to get out of control. Ain't none of us will feel safe coming there, and you know it.

Lenard's allegations, which were being repeated by a growing number of disgruntled tenants, were affirmed by the center's own budgetary and programming priorities. Staffers such as Kenny Davenport and Christie Woodson spoke out against Jackson's plan to target nearly three-quarters of the center's programs to gang-affiliated youth by eliminating some after-school programs and field trips for children—instead, Jackson wanted to organize a midnight basketball league in which gangs could compete with one another. Woodson, who had been handling the center's accounting, warned Jackson that the use of gang proceeds might not be fiscally prudent, but Jackson ignored these and other cautions from staff members. Tenants saw themselves facing the loss of one of the few community-based organizations left in Robert Taylor.

With greater frequency, tenants complained to their LAC officers about those developments, many of which had circulated widely in the rumor mill. Even the building "block club" meetings, usually sedate occasions marked by card games and the exchange of food, grew contentious as tenants used examples of new apartment purchases to accuse leaseholders of accepting the gang's largesse. The community court, the household surveys, gang-sponsored recreational programs, and the purchase of playground equipment by gang leaders may have been helpful, but to some the price appeared to be high, that is, acceptance of drug trafficking and the presence of powerful citywide gang leaders in their community.

The center's move to accommodate gang members over other youth signaled that gang activity had commanded an increased share of community energy and resources. The attention to gang activity by tenant leaders and local organizations effectively detracted from their ability to tackle the deterioration of the housing development and the many other pressing problems they faced. Tenants who once made casual comments to their leadership regarding the overemphasis on gang-related problems now expressed their concerns more forcefully. This loose-knit constituency was led by the LAC leader Cathy Blanchard, who busily lobbied her colleagues on the LAC to return to traditional issues facing public housing tenants, such as apartment repair and unemployment. She tried to convince other LAC officers that improving maintenance would actually help promote the use of public space among tenants, and thereby possibly have a deterrent effect on gangs. However, in 1992, the powerful tenant leaders were deeply involved with No More Wars and its citywide grassroots activities. Blanchard's pleas did not fall on deaf ears—no tenant leader could fully ignore the dilapidated conditions of apartments and public grounds—but the LAC members had limited resources, and with gang violence posing such a serious threat to habitability, turning their gaze elsewhere did not seem appropriate. Blanchard continued her campaign to make service provision more central, hoping that in the coming months she would win greater support for her efforts.

Debates over the community court and the use of gang members for security purposes had created a rift in the tenant body. On one side, LAC officers and tenant-patrol leaders from three high-rises formed a pro–No More Wars constituency that favored the organization's gang-mediation services. By working with Will Jackson and Jeremy Coals, they had abandoned their dialogues with CHA and Chicago police spokespersons. In effect, they had moved to a position outside the formal institutional apparatus. LAC Building President Edna Baxter said after attending a No More Wars rally, "Look how alive we are. You just feel alive yelling and shouting. I don't want to talk with them fools at CHA no more, all the time promising you stuff, making you happy you got a new doorknob or a stove. That's our right! We shouldn't be begging." On the other side, Edith Huddle was the most vocal proponent of those who favored conflict-oriented strategies. Huddle's longtime friend in the 218 high-rise, LAC Building President Cathy Blanchard, emerged as the spokesperson for those calling for a return to more conservative brokerage-style diplomacy. She advocated the continued use of the LAC as a political broker that secured resources by deal-making. Her supporters were fearful of returning to the pre-1971 era, when they had no elected tenant-management representation. They wanted to refocus gang-intervention efforts on campaigns for greater police protection.

As the two sides debated, they began to differentiate among gang-related activities that compromised their security. They distinguished threats to safety from gang wars, which were relatively infrequent, from the daily insecurity that stemmed from the gang's drug distribution and use of public space. They argued that the Grace Center's efforts may have helped with the former, but at the expense of the latter. In a community meeting with Will Jackson, a twenty-two-year-old mother of two, Martha Simmell, expressed this sentiment: "Ain't saying we're ungrateful for your help, but as long as these niggers selling dope every day, we still ain't gonna send our children outside. Tell them folks no drug dealing. You got to start doing that or you ain't doing nothing for us." Some suggested, once again, that the Grace Center either demand an end to drug distribution or rescind its intimate relationship with gangs altogether.

Tenants' distinction between gang wars and the gang's daily public presence was an accurate one, and it was not being addressed by the Grace Center and No More Wars in their mediation efforts—most of which were useful for responding to the more visible and perilous conflicts, such as wars and drive-by shootings. This was unfortunate because the gang's daily habitation of public and semi-private spaces in and around the high-rises was a more persistent security threat than the gang wars. In fact, even with the intervention of Jeremy Coals and Will Jackson, gang wars still erupted; the primary (and no doubt valuable) service of the two mediators was to limit their duration. The Grace Center's inability to restrict the gang's use of public space was ironic given that Jackson's original interest was to ensure safe passage for inhabitants by moving gangs off the streets and into the center. Jackson and Coals's rejoinder that the gangs' public loitering had become less violent did not satisfy tenants. The Grace Center's posture was ultimately tragic and instructive: gang members who stood in public, selling drugs and harassing passers-by with little resistance from tenants (who justifiably feared them) and with minimal challenge from the LAC (who were fighting one another over whether to support No More Wars), showed the limits of an approach that worked within the gang structure but did not directly challenge the gang's drug trafficking.

From the perspective of Ottie Davis, the situation also indicated the pitfalls of a community that relied on "poverty pimps," his less-than-affectionate name for Jackson and Coals. By this, he meant those community spokespersons whose rising stature led to their inability to understand the actual needs of their constituents, in this case, tenants who had to see local gangs daily:

> You have this man [Will Jackson] who's getting lot of attention, lot of money, not just gang money but now he's got government money too I hear. His head is real big. Now, he hires Coals, puts [LAC Officer] Huddle on his payroll, he got some church pastors, a school principal, they all getting money. So they all ain't stopping to see what they doing. Just too busy with the attention and the money. They been making things worse, I ain't afraid to say it.

The Black Kings leadership in Robert Taylor was similarly affected by the new developments. Mason, Grady, and Jamie had shown disdain for the new intimate contact with tenants and those in the surrounding communities. They attended the rallies and cross-neighborhood gatherings at the Grace Center reluctantly, often failing to appear at community clean-ups and other collaborations with tenants. Prince Williams, however, seemed to revel in the glory of a prominent community profile and promptly dispatched his members to work with tenants. He helped the Grace Center staffer Kenny Davenport to create an after-school tutoring program that school-aged BKs had to attend. He accompanied No More Wars staffers to other neighborhoods to resolve gang-related conflicts. Not surprisingly, Prince had less contentious relations with those tenants who favored working with No More Wars. In recognition of the increasing profitability of the drug trade in Robert Taylor, in the spring of 1993, Prince's superiors named him "chief" of all BKs in the housing development, demoting C-Note as leader of the Twenty-seventh

St. BK set and giving Prince "rank" over that set as well as the three controlled by Jamie, Mason, and Grady. Prince now had full control of the drug and extortion revenues of his own set—the Twenty-seventh St. BKs—and he could extract underground revenue from the other three. He was, in Kenny Davenport's words, "the top dog in Robert Taylor."

With Prince Williams as the "top dog" of all Robert Taylor BKs, the implications for the overall community were clear. The Black Kings were not likely to continue doing favors for tenants and assisting tenant leaders unless they believed that such actions would help maintain a climate favorable to their entrepreneurial activities. Two years earlier, tenants had spoken of the gang's desire to "better the community" as a potential lever to move the Black Kings into a more positive direction; there were few who would now portray the BK leaders as anything other than businessmen for whom community betterment was a side affair. The staunchest critics of the gangs remained grateful for the BK leaders' willingness to provide assistance and monetary contributions. After all, these were extremely poor tenants, most of whom lived below the poverty line. Yet there were few who offered empathy to Prince and his peers by depicting them primarily as wayward youth who could be turned away from drugs. There was deep resentment in the public discourse toward the Black Kings, whom tenants saw as crass hustlers. The Black Kings had not ruined their hope that youth would once again be the vanguard of change in the community, but they were steadfast in their belief that such change would be premised on the elimination of organized criminal activity, which in this case happened to be drug dealing by a supergang.

———

In 1993, activity in the Robert Taylor Homes unfolded at a feverish pace. The close-knit relations among street gangs, residents, and community organizations on Chicago's South Side had gained popularity. No More Wars staff members used their influence with the street gangs to move from conflict mediation to grassroots advocacy and community organizing. They sponsored tenant marches, publicized CHA neglect in several high-rise complexes throughout the city, sponsored boycotts of irresponsible stores that overcharged or harassed customers, and promoted interaction at the Grace Center between Robert Taylor and other public and private residential communities. In tenant meetings, press conferences, and everyday discussions with tenants, they spoke of the reduction in gang violence and the availability of full-time conflict mediators for a resource-depleted community. Robert Taylor's social isolation from larger institutions and local service providers seemed ameliorated through increased contact with smaller organizations, city politicians, religious leaders, and other grassroots actors who had moved into the No More Wars camp.

In the shadow of these small but significant victories, other developments pointed to a marked decrease in the quality of life in the housing development. Local Black Kings gang members were conducting their entrepreneurial activities with abandon—selling narcotics and extorting businesses and underground merchants—and BK leaders flaunted their riches with conspicuous displays of consumer goods, large outdoor parties, and token disbursements to the tenants. As a small but active tenant constituency fought over collaborations with gangs, little energy was left to wage a cohesive campaign against other concerns, such as addiction, drug use, tenant apathy, and household hardships.

Notwithstanding its problems and challenges, it would be unfair to characterize the housing development as a socially disorganized community. When observers used this phrase in the late 1980s and early 1990s in documenting the plight of the urban poor, they did so at the cost of ignoring the ongoing work of residents to build livable communities. They failed to provide a perspective from which to see how daily needs were being met, if ever so tenuously and imperfectly, through negotiation, struggle, and cooperation. Concepts such as disorganization become akin to an "urban orientalism," writes the sociologist Loic Wacquant, removing accountability from those in the wider world who affect the lives of the poor in important ways. "Understanding the ghetto as an institutional form of mechanisms of ethno-racial closure and control allows one to recognize that it does not suffer from 'social disorganization' . . . the ghetto is organized according to different principles, in response to a unique set of structural and strategic constraints that bear on the racialized enclaves of the city as on no other segment of America's territory."[37]

Robert Taylor was struggling with problems that had a local texture but that were shaped by larger social forces. The formal agents of social control, the ones that most Americans would expect to play a central role in the prevention and resolution of social problems, were ineffective in responding to disruptions and almost wholly absent in preventing their occurrence. The police presence consisted largely of crude suppression efforts designed to break up gangs that had little documented effect on reducing gang violence or drug trafficking. Tenants were not surprised at this law enforcement posture, but they fought spiritedly alongside their leadership, attending townhall meetings and calling police commanders, to demand more protection and responsive police practices. Given the infighting that plagued their own leadership, these battles were not part of any systematic protest; nevertheless, tenants kept the policing issue alive through their individual dissension. In 1993, there appeared to be a small turnaround as some tenants demanded that law enforcement not single out gang activity as the premiere social problem, but address domestic abuse, theft, and property crimes as well. A groundswell of support formed for tenant mobilization around these problems, as well as CHA upkeep and city-service allocation, all of which had been overshadowed by the gang's practices.[38]

Conspicuously absent from these struggles were social-service providers in the broader community—schools, social workers, community advocates and philanthropic foundations, churches, youth agencies, counseling centers, and so on. For a population hovering around twenty thousand, it was striking to see the dearth of providers at tenants' side. There were many agencies servicing Robert Taylor, but they did so on an individual or family basis. On numerous occasions, tenants and staff members at the Grace Center asked local service providers to help them address collective issues, but they declined to intervene in the contentious "political issues" in the housing development. One can only speculate whether their acceptance of the tenants' entreaties would have created more effective interventions against local gangs. Perhaps if Coals and Jackson had worked alongside other agencies, their refusal to confront the gang's drug trafficking would have been challenged and would not have become the basis of local gang mediation. The absence of such peers does not excuse the center's posture with respect to the gangs, or the self-interested practices of its director and his colleagues, but it did remove valuable resources and guidance, thereby decreasing the number of choices available to the tenants of Robert Taylor to enhance their security and welfare. Given the absence of a wider base of moral and material support, it was unrealistic to expect that Robert Taylor would have much success in combating the gangs.

The few successes of Coals, Jackson, and others stemmed from a strategy that was ill suited to the presence of a corporate street gang. Their work resembled the reform and social work programs of the 1960s that placed emphasis on transforming gang members' behavior from within the gang. These initiatives typically incorporated social workers and community residents to mediate gang conflicts and assumed that reformed gang leaders could encourage more productive behavior among their members. The gang-structure approach did not always work; indeed, it was most successful in improving the lives of youth and their communities when it included a job-placement component that offered gang members opportunities if they exited the gang.

In modern-day Chicago, with few avenues of employment and mobility open to poor young blacks, and with gangs becoming an important source of employment, the conflict resolution initiated by Will Jackson and Jeremy Coals could have only limited success. The

Black Kings were too entrepreneurial in their outlook and members were far too pessimistic about finding employment to quit the gang's drug trade. Although some tenants may have preferred the reformist effort to Chicago law enforcement's "gang suppression," this preference did not necessarily translate into actual, widespread tenant support for the center and its "Band-Aid" diplomacy. While Jackson, Coals, and their backers in the tenant body continued to cite their modest gains, others in the tenant body grew unwilling to see their accomplishments as justification for stabilizing the gang's narcotics trade. The Grace Center's new status as a hub for historically alienated African-American constituencies in Chicago could not be divorced from its other identity as a hub for Black Kings gangs throughout the city to conduct their illicit affairs under the cloak of relative security.

As 1993 moved forward, many tenants made their feelings known by looking for new community leaders and new methods to combat gang activity and ensure their well-being. In this manner, while one voice in Robert Taylor construed the new movement of gangs, tenants, and grassroots organizations as empowering, another labeled it as regressive and dangerous. The discordance spoke to longstanding differences of opinion regarding the role of the street gang in the African-American urban community and the strategies that were most appropriate for controlling the deleterious effects of gang activity. Yet because gang activity was wrapped up in related issues such as procurement of city services and relations between public housing and organizations in the surrounding ghetto, the differences that were manifesting themselves spoke to broader issues concerning the means by which the black community should organize on its own behalf and the role that its leadership should play in this process. This was a battle that had some resemblance to those fought in the 1960s; indeed, nearly three decades later, many of the same philosophical issues were surfacing again. As with all periods of political struggle for change, no one knew what the future would hold.

The Beginning of the
End of a Modern Ghetto

"The men, they beat us," Grace Center staff member Christie Wood-son proclaimed to an assembled body of tenant and community leaders at the center. A resident of Robert Taylor for all of her thirty-five years, Woodson in 1993 mobilized several hundred young female parents and heads-of-households to call attention to needs that ranged from day care to companionship. Physical abuse and sexual harassment were their top priorities. Woodson did not want to air her grievances in front of the "community court," the newly devised forum at the Grace Center to resolve conflicts stemming from local gang activity. The gang's harassment of young women in Robert Taylor had become so pervasive that she requested a separate meeting with Grace Center Director Will Jackson, the LAC leader Edith Huddle, and gang-conflict mediator Jeremy Coals, one that would be devoted entirely to her concerns.

Woodson's testimony featured the allegations of nearly one dozen women who, in a four-week period, had all reported suffering abuse at the hands of youths in the Black Kings street gang. The domestic and public harassment of women had been a concern of community leaders for decades, but Will Jackson feared that he was partially responsible for the recent rise in incidents. He wondered if the mobilization of gang members in "peace summits," neighborhood rallies, and collaborative activities with tenants had mistakenly given the gang members a sense of legitimacy. This outreach was not providing an impetus for the Black Kings to behave themselves, feared Jackson. "We're trying to right their ways, that's the long-run hope we have. But these cats think they can do what they want. Maybe, they think they can beat up women, show they're powerful. We have to stop that."

For nearly three years, Jackson, Huddle, and other local leaders had labored to convince residents that the habitability of Robert Taylor would improve if they worked with gang members. Capitalize on the BK leaders' desire to "better the community" and offer them chances to work with tenants, argued Jackson, and it would be possible to redirect gang members away from criminal activities. Jackson and Huddle still had support from tenants for their strategy, but the gang's recent abuse of young women seemed to have mobilized collective opposition. People had grown increasingly skeptical of the benefits of cooperation and compromise with the gangs. Gang violence and wars may have declined, but the day-to-day public presence of gang members had increased. The latest reports of sexual harassment by BK members further aggrieved tenants and did not help to win their continued support for non–law enforcement approaches to gang intervention. The most furious tenants seemed intent on disrupting the mechanisms that Jackson, Huddle, and others had devised.

Tenants in Robert Taylor could hardly recall a time when there was no active community debate regarding how to improve the quality of life in the housing development. However, the recent difference of opinion felt unique to many. People not only fought with one another about the approach to gang activity, but they were also raising more abstract, deep-seated concerns regarding community, politics, and personhood. Some suggested that tenants exclude gang members from legitimate community membership, even if the BKs were children, kin, and neighbors. Others questioned whether the LAC had overstepped its bounds by working so intimately with gangs; perhaps the tenant advocate should seek more modest goals. Moreover, a growing number of tenants were leaving Robert Taylor altogether, taking advantage of the Housing Authority's family programs that subsidized private-market rent. In a community that had only known struggle, and that had embraced it courageously, there were whispers of futility, voices that questioned whether the black community could suffer the challenge of "project living" any longer. Those in the wider world were also addressing the current state as well as the future of public housing more seriously than in the past. "Should public housing be blown up? Is solution by dynamite . . . our best option?" asked a *Washington Post* reporter in 1991. Among those who inhabited the high-rise apartments in Robert Taylor, the only consensus seemed to be that the housing development was on the verge of another fundamental period of change, one in which the old rules and relationships would be cast aside once again.

Reform or Rebellion?

Since the late 1960s, when the roots of protest and empowerment took hold in Robert Taylor, every few years a band of tenants would publicly criticize the quality of tenant leadership and open up debate to address the best strategy to meet community needs. In 1989, for example, tenants formed the Chicago Housing Authority Residents Taking Action (CHARTA), a small organization that provided an alternative to the Local Advisory Council and its two decades of unquestioned reign as the recognized voice of Chicago's public housing tenants. CHARTA's workshops educated tenants on the use of municipal bureaucracies and lobbied the state of Illinois to recognize its five hundred members as a representative tenant body. Ultimately, it suffered the fate of every other movement that opposed the LAC, namely, a quiet dissolution.

In this historical context of episodic challenges to existing tenant representation, the energy of the 1993 debates regarding the new conflict-resolution forum in Robert Taylor made people take notice. Tenants were not simply accusing leaders of patronage, graft, co-optation, and ineffectiveness; they were criticizing one another as well as their leadership, and the battle was animated by the ghost of an earlier struggle regarding political strategy that had been waged in public housing in the early 1970s. At that time, the creation of the LAC had ushered in a shift in *realpolitik* from direct protest on city streets to consensus-building in boardrooms. In 1993, the issue at hand was gang activity, but the dispute was also touching on whether to use collective protest or a less confrontational posture to address quality-of-life concerns.

As they debated which strategy would best make Robert Taylor a livable community, tenants invoked previous struggles that had brought households together to improve their lives.[1] In doing so, they effectively reconstructed a history of the Robert Taylor community.

At times, this history of political activity and cooperation offered guidance, dissuading tenants from repeating unsuccessful efforts or prompting them to reconsider an initiative that had worked at an earlier time. In other cases, they spoke of their remembrances in a highly biographical manner, sprinkling them with anecdotes. Their debates over how they had worked in the past were as animated as their contemporary struggles, and this investment in their own history seemed as important to them as locating a resource or service. Did the street gang continue to have the potential for helping the black community, as it had in the past? Was the LAC a tenant advocate, as in the early 1970s; did it simply need new blood to work more effectively, or had it outgrown its usefulness altogether? The answers to these questions were critical for the production of their identity and bore great weight on how they would cope with the present threats to the community's well-being.

This "collective memory . . . is an active process of sense-making through time," writes the sociologist Jeffrey Olick, and it is subject to the vicissitudes and uncertainties of history.[2] In 1993, as tenants in Robert Taylor sought to address the rising harassment of young women by members of the Black Kings street gang, they often focused their discussions on the "public memory" of the LAC. This elected representative body became the vehicle, the symbol of "tradition invented and reinvented in everyday life," with which individuals advanced one or the other perspective regarding the best approach to ensuring their collective welfare.[3] Some tenants defended the contemporary efforts of Jackson and Huddle—that is, working with gangs—by depicting the LAC as a courageous elected body that had always used nontraditional methods to assist households. Others saw this history differently, pointing instead to the LAC's unique stature as an organization respected by municipal agencies—this respect being the basis of its capacity to garner resources and assist tenants. Gang intervention was anathema to them.

Another voice that could be heard in these debates argued that the LAC was becoming a "senior citizens group" and needed to redis-cover its identity by connecting with a constituency that it had ig-nored, namely, predominantly single female teenage and twenty-something parents and heads-of-households. Sustained allegations that the LAC was ignoring the concerns of younger women came as a surprise to tenant leaders and local activists because this constitu-ency had not been very vocal in past years and had relatively weak connections with many of the traditional organizations in the com-munity. Church pastors who readily admitted that tenants had mini-mal interest in their weekly ministry would report even less success in their efforts to recruit young women. Social-service agencies that offered prenatal care or family medical services spoke of intermittent contact with these young women. Job-placement centers, high schools offering after-school G.E.D. and skills training, and various social-service providers waged nearly continuous campaigns to in-crease their outreach to the younger households in Robert Taylor. A young-adult female presence at LAC meetings was extremely rare, and even in the most active buildings, such as the group of three near Kim Walton's 205 high-rise, only a handful of young women re-mained committed to working alongside the LAC.

Although their patronization of local organizations was minimal and their political voice was not loud, young women in the housing development had a strong presence in part because of the changing demographics of the Robert Taylor population. There had been a gradual drop in the development's population from 1962 to 1992; in the 1970s, nearly 25,000 documented tenants inhabited Robert Tay-lor's 4,300 apartments, but by 1992, only 12,300 lived there legally. Part of the decline reflected the heightened vacancy rates and the slow pace with which the Housing Authority rehabbed apartments for newcomers. Moreover, at the start of the 1990s, there was a nearly complete saturation of local demography with leaseholders who reported no "wage or salary." In 1980, this figure was 85 percent, and by 1992, it had risen to 95.7 percent. Nearly 95 percent of households claimed government social welfare as their sole source of income.[4] The number of individuals within each household, on average, dropped from 4.7 in 1980 to 3.5 in 1992, and so too did the average number of minors (from 4.0 in 1980 to 2.2 in 1992). Year by year, the average age of households moving into Robert Taylor decreased. Perhaps most alarming in light of the overall decline in population, 67 percent of the households entering the housing development after 1990 were headed by individuals under thirty years of age. In sum, then, in a declining population, the small household headed by a single mother was prominent.

These younger residents began to "split off" from the older leaseholders, argues Judy Harris, contending that something other than purely generational differences were at root:

> It wasn't like it was before, because Sally, Mary, and them, they just split off from Ms. Huddle, my momma, and all those older folk. They all mommas themselves, you know, but they act like their mommas can't teach them nothing. You know, [Sally and Mary] was in them gangs and that's how they got what they needed. But before, you know, you had to march, march up and down the street, protest, fight, all that good stuff! These women, they expect their [welfare] checks each month and they happy. They wasn't working with us no more.

For Harris and her friend Christie Woodson, what was significant about the new, younger tenants was their use of alternate (that is, non-LAC-based) social networks to meet their basic needs—most had reached maturity in the mid- and late 1980s, when the LAC was already declining as a guarantor of safety and welfare. Harris and Woodson, whose daughters were involved in peer groups that included young mothers, grew increasingly familiar with these younger women, and after 1990, the two organized events, such as baby showers, and located services, such as day care and job training, for them. Once the Grace Center opened, Woodson encouraged the women to participate in its programs, to look for jobs and educational opportunities posted at the center's library, or to leave their children and find a respite from nurturing duties. By the autumn of 1992, several hundred young women were coming to the center each week. On occasion, a guest speaker would attend, such as a beauty salon owner who gave styling lessons or a nurse who offered advice to expectant mothers, but usually the women moved about the center, using computer facilities, recreational equipment, or watching television and talking with one another.

When in 1993 there were weekly reports of physical abuse of young women at the hands of Black Kings gang members, many women stopped attending programs at the Grace Center for fear of meeting BKs. In most of the reported incidents, gang members between eighteen and twenty-one were the perpetrators. The most common incidents were groping and lewd comments, but women also reported assaults on dates, and some said they had sexual relations with BKs out of fear of physical beatings. There were several accusations of rape that received much attention. The abuses were themselves troubling, but so too was the fact that they occurred in public. Sometimes the harassment or assault took place at a planned event such as a basketball game or a picnic, but women were also attacked while "hanging out" on housing development grounds or even within the Grace Center. Tenants were further upset at the openly defiant attitude that the younger men displayed when confronted by their accusers. As one young woman stated, "They proud of what they doing. Shit. Ain't like they sorry or nothing. Like they don't even, you know . . . Like they don't feel nothing when they hurting us." From Christie Woodson's perspective, locating immediate medical assistance and shelter for victims would provide only a partial solution given that the root cause was male bravado. In other words, in order to preclude an act of harassment or abuse, intervention would need to occur at an earlier stage and involve the gang as a whole.

Christie Woodson and Judy Harris's initial efforts to locate support services bypassed the LAC completely. "I never even thought of asking them old ladies," says Woodson, who believed that the generational divide was too great to bridge. They first approached social-ser-vice agencies in the wider area who specialized in women's health issues. The response they received was not unlike what Will Jackson had heard when informed that the agencies did not want to address gang-related activities. Once they found out that the gangs were in-volved to such a great degree, said Harris, the agencies flatly stated that they feared the safety of their own staff and so could not enter the community. Besides, the closest agency was located a mile away from the housing development, and young women either were unwilling to travel there on a regular basis to receive treatment and counseling, citing unfamiliarity with the territory, or lacked the funds to make the trip each week. Although Harris understood the women's material hardships, she was disappointed at their lack of involvement. She was also frustrated at the lack of help she was receiving from the agencies themselves, though she was not particularly surprised:

> I worked at one of them health clinics. You got hundreds of women com-ing in, you don't got no time to be dealing with all the problems women [in Robert Taylor] have. You just do what you can. And lot of these peo-ple, they scared to come around here, so you can't really ask them to do much.

Woodson and Harris asked Will Jackson to make the Grace Center into a "safe space." The center was "playing favorite, doing all this shit for the mens but ain't doing nothing for the women," argued Woodson. "We wanted a safe space where women could be together, not worry about the men." Will Jackson offered the women extended hours at the center, but he did not address any of their harassment-related concerns directly by agreeing to negotiate with gang members or pressuring them to curb their abusive practices. By this point, Jackson was work-ing intimately with many of the citywide gang leaders to bring gang members into the center, and he was often nonresponsive when a ten-ant constituency asked him to criticize gang members.

Woodson and Harris then called on the services of a friend, Yolanda Trachsel, a citywide leader of the Black Sisters United

(BSU)—a federation of neighborhood-based "girl gangs."[5] Organized in the late 1970s, the BSU was an informal coalition of peer groups that met in much the same manner as the young women attending the Grace Center, that is, sporadically, and primarily for social activities and sharing of resources. Trachsel decided that BSU would issue a collective response to the problems of gang-member-initiated sexual abuse in Robert Taylor by opening a dialogue between BSU and BK gang leaders. Together with Woodson and Harris, she formed a delegation to meet with citywide and imprisoned Black Kings gang leaders to seek their help in constraining BKs in the housing development. Trachsel thought it was essential to be "going so high [in the BK hierarchy]" in order to leverage enough pressure on male gang members, who otherwise paid women little heed:

> Because, you see, these [Black Kings members in Robert Taylor] ain't gonna listen to nobody right now. They all about making money, they fighting each other for control around here . . . I seen these folks get their ass-whupped by [their superiors]. And if I tell [the superiors] that BKs around here is beating up women and leaders ain't doing nothing, shit! There's gonna be another ass-whupping. And I want to be there for that!

Latrell and Darell Watkins, two regional BK officers with authority over the Robert Taylor BKs, were sympathetic to the women's requests because Yolanda Trachsel and girl gang members were part of their larger network that sold narcotics with BK members throughout the city. As a result, they told their subordinates in Robert Taylor—that is, the five BK leaders, C-Note, Prince, Mason, Jamie, and Grady—to "control their troops." It was not surprising that Prince Williams acted quickly with promises to punish members of his "Twenty-seventh St. BKs" if they harassed women; he had already shown signs of responsiveness to tenants out of a desire not only to help them but also to keep a "low profile," by which he usually meant a climate free of disturbances to the BK drug trade. Christie Woodson sought the cooperation of other BK leaders, but with less success. She confronted Mason outside the 210 high-rise:

"You all better stop that shit!" Woodson cried out, pushing Mason in the chest. "[Your superiors] told you all you can't be doing that shit no more."

"Fuck that. We do what we want 'round here. You all start giving us shit, we gonna take care of you!" Mason said, punching his palm with a clenched fist and looking out of the corner of his eye to see who else was listening.

Christie started getting upset and moved directly in front of Mason: "C'mon nigger, take care of me now, nigger!" She swung and hit Mason in the side of the head and then jumped on him.

"Get off me, bitch!" said Mason. "I ain't 'bout to fight you, you better get the fuck off of me!"

Judy Harris ran over to help and began hitting Mason over the head with her purse.

"You all ain't gonna beat us no more," yelled Harris. "Get up so I can beat your ass."

When they heard about the incident, Latrell and Darrell Watkins punished and severely beat Mason for his inaction and verbally reprimanded Grady and Jamie, fining them each several thousand dollars for their insubordination. Concerned that continued acts of sexual abuse might bring outside agencies, such as police and social services, into Robert Taylor, the Watkins brothers were willing to intervene to keep others outside the area of their drug trafficking.

Woodson and Trachsel devised a method by which the male gang members could assist victims of harassment, and with Prince's assent, the Twenty-seventh St. BK "security" patrols would add to their duties the punishment of gang members who abused women. Hearing of this plan, the LAC leaders Edith Huddle and Kim Walton asked the Black Kings security force to apprehend non-gang-affiliated harassers as well. Their requests would provide them with an opportunity both to serve tenants and to defend themselves against their critics who said that the BKs' practices had little utility for the community. The use of the BK posse was relatively rare, but even sporadic assistance was helpful, argues Shadie Sanders, a tenant in the 205 building who helped found tenant patrols and who had lobbied since the 1970s for battered women's shelters and related support services. For her, assistance from the gang was not ideal, but with few other alternatives, it could not be turned down:

> It wasn't easy. I don't care much for [the gangs], but I care a lot about the women around here, and we had to do something. We had to do something . . . The first time I saw Twenty-seventh [St. BK gang members] chase a man down, I couldn't believe it. This guy was beating up Ms. Elvers on the ninth floor, and we had to watch this go on for some time. She was too scared to do anything, and we tried calling the police and getting her help. But we couldn't find nothing close by. Prince and them ran after him, right over there [pointing to the grass next to the 210 building]. They beat him and beat him and beat him and then they took him back to Ms. Elvers and they made him apologize. Lord, have mercy! That man didn't come around causing no fuss no more!

When asked if she was pleased with what the gang was doing, she replied: "Well . . . now don't get me wrong, I wasn't happy that the gangs was doing what the police should've been doing. But I was happy that these mens wasn't coming around so much anymore [and] beating up my friends."

This indigenous policing was not used frequently. BK members punished a perpetrator only five times in 1993, a tiny percentage of the incidents of sexual harassment in the housing development. Neither tenants nor their leaders felt fully comfortable working with gangs, and they knew that the BK's generosity in security matters was motivated by the gang's interest in securing its turf boundaries and enhancing its commerce. By 1994, the collaboration of BK security personnel with tenants had ended, although tenants reported that the incidents of abuse by gang members did decline. A more lasting effect of the short-lived policing mechanism was the debate it sparked among tenants regarding the overall strategy by LAC members to work closely with gangs in various security initiatives, including in the pursuit of sexual harassers, but also in the bodily search of people walking into high-rises and in the provision of safety escorts for residents around the housing development. Shadie Sanders's resigned acceptance of gang members' assistance proved to be one of two contrasting, publicly voiced opinions, the other being outright disgust that tenants were using the Black Kings for their personal security.

Through the summer and autumn of 1993, two distinct constituencies formed within the tenant body around these issues, and both fought for the right to determine how the Robert Taylor community would act to ensure the viability of life in public housing. Given their work with No More Wars and the Grace Center, few were surprised that Edith Huddle and Kim Walton emerged as the leading proponents for the use of gang members and No More Wars to meet household needs. In Huddle's building (210) and among seven buildings north of Twenty-seventh St., where Walton presided, the BK leader Prince doled out cash to LAC officers to buy school supplies for children and to purchase food for tenants; he told hundreds of younger members to join the No More Wars street demonstrations against local storeowners perceived to be mistreating residents; and he gave several thousand dollars to the Grace Center to refurbish its gymnasium and update its computer facilities. Huddle and Walton were opposed by Cathy Blanchard and Paulina Collins, two tenant leaders who not only wanted to end collaboration with gangs, but also were campaigning to unseat Walton, Huddle, and their colleagues who advocated it. Blanchard and Collins adopted a straightforward strategy: in meetings and casual conversations with tenants, they referred to incidents of LAC–gang member cooperation and argued that the CHA would abandon its willingness to cooperate with the LAC if LAC officials and tenants grew too friendly with gangs. There had been numerous vituperative exchanges in the public meetings of CHA personnel and tenants wherein the agency accused tenants of conspiring to assist the gangs; agency spokespersons suggested that they could not justify increasing security if their own clients would not demonstrate an equal commitment to controlling youth behavior.

The divide between the two camps widened considerably as tenants debated the new LAC posture. At the heart of their battle was control over the type of leadership that the LAC would provide. As tenants debated, it was clear that their differences were part of an older, deeply entrenched disagreement regarding how best to mobilize blacks for political action. Their feuds over the proper posture for the LAC to adopt fitted the ideological split in African-American urban politics over the relative merits of protest and conflict versus working with the powers that be as a guide for collective political action.[6] Cathy Blanchard, Paulina Collins, and other tenants promised to use the elected tenant-management body as a vehicle for consensus building with administrative agencies. Blanchard suggested that the LAC should not seek short-term benefits—especially by working with gang members—since this would engender increased alienation from the larger community. "We ain't going back to them days when we couldn't get nothing," said Blanchard. "We fought to get a voice inside CHA, and we ain't gonna lose it." Blanchard wanted the LAC to retain its historic role as broker between tenants and the outside world.

By contrast, Edith Huddle and her supporters argued that the LAC's charter mandated the use of any and all strategies, that is, both confrontation and compromise. Their memory of the LAC stressed conflict; according to the LAC officer Edna Baxter, "You got to fight if you're poor, that's why we started the council long time ago. People forgot that." They argued that the use of imprisoned and ex-gang members to settle disputes, the reliance on local gangs as manpower, and the need to seek grassroots organizational support from other communities were the "only choice[s]" left for them to ensure the security of tenants.

In their public debates—whether in meetings or casually, in hallways and galleries—could be heard the echoes of earlier heated exchanges regarding the most appropriate means by which to ensure the viability of ghetto communities such as Robert Taylor. But the critical role played by the gangs had now transformed this version of grassroots political action. Previously, the fights to make Robert Taylor viable had centered on those wishing to work within the system and those seeking change from outside. In the postwar era, an "accommodationist" camp of black leaders spoke from within the cogs of the political machine and favored working with the ruling white ethnics to improve the Black Belt; an opposing voice had few dealings with the city's power brokers and little tolerance for secretive negotiation. The basic dichotomy was revived in the late 1960s, when a tenant rebellion throughout Chicago's public housing complexes resulted in the ouster of an "accommodationist" class of tenants who personally benefited from their close relations with CHA leadership. Forty years later, the residues of this political lineage could be heard in the debates on tenants' opportunities to act together most effectively not only with the CHA, but also with the local gangs and organizations in the wider community.

The tables were now slightly turned, however, for the actions of those working outside the system, that is, those using street gangs as an ally, were being opposed by those who wished to preserve a place for blacks within existing structures. Huddle, Walton, and their followers may have been justified in their protest of CHA neglect and in their desire to use the LAC as an organizational base from which to garner support and services for the community. But the inclusion of street-gang members (and the use of funds derived from drug dealing that they received via the Grace Center) compromised the value for Robert Taylor of the grassroots coalition to which they belonged. At best, it appeared that they could offer some funds to tenants, an occasional security-related service with gangs as manpower, or a small group of residents around the city who would protest with them in public housing matters. But the drawbacks associated with strengthening the gangs and increasing their presence seemed to outweigh these gains.

Blanchard and Collins may have appeared somewhat conservative in their pleas to preserve the LAC's established position as a broker and continue to accommodate the CHA in order to win services. However, given the gang's dominant position in the Grace Center–No More Wars movement to bring African-American poor communities together, they were justified in their belief that Huddle and Walton might not be providing a viable means for Robert Taylor to help tenants. Blanchard and Collins actually favored youth involvement in protests and voter-registration drives, but they had legitimate reasons to ensure that tenants remain autonomous from the gangs and particularly from their drug revenue. Their emphasis on the LAC as a broker stemmed from their belief that many tenants had worked courageously for three decades to ensure that such a democratically elected entity existed in public housing. If the LAC became aligned with the gangs, its image would be tainted. They speculated that this might give the CHA justification to withdraw funding and support for the organization. Although the CHA gave no public indication that this would occur, many tenants were moving out of the development and the Housing Authority was not lowering its vacancy rates.[7] Thus these leaders did not want to give fodder to a city agency—and to HUD, its manager—that was showing interest in decreasing the local population and rescinding its commitment to public housing.

The significance of this battle could not be gauged by the level of tenant involvement. Among young heads-of-households, especially the several hundred women who came to the Grace Center and met with Christie Woodson and Judy Harris, few said they had been attending the open meetings or deliberating with others about the fate of the LAC. Those who did voice an opinion regarding the LAC's use of brokerage or confrontational techniques generally deferred the choice, prioritizing instead the LAC's need to move beyond its traditional arena—apartment maintenance—and attend to the myriad needs of younger tenants. Mattie Wilkins, a single head-of-household in her mid-twenties, expressed this view: "[The LAC is] a group of mommas who just try and control you. All they do is take money from the gangs, and fight with each other." When asked if the LAC wasn't supposed to make sure apartment repairs were made, she replied:

> Yeah, but that's all they do! I want to work, I don't want to sit around all day, doing nothing. We keep telling them to help us get jobs, 'cause I know people in other projects doing that . . . I don't want [to be an LAC

officer] anyway. It don't pay nothing and you just hear people complain all day!

For Mattie and her peers, personal networks and the Grace Center proved far more useful to meet their needs than the LAC. They looked also to Judy Harris and Christie Woodson, who at the end of 1993 had developed nightly programs at the center including counseling and computer training, domestic-abuse assistance, and social activities such as dances and food sales. While many younger women framed the LAC as anachronistic, the political body was nevertheless the primary reference point for their own mobilization. Although critical of the LAC, Woodson also liked to say, "We're the new LAC around here, it ain't the gangs, it's us ladies that's helping folks."

Middle-aged and senior segments of the population were more attuned to the dissension within LAC ranks, but their actual involvement in the movement to reconfigure the representative body varied. Only a small percentage showed their partisanship through participation in the activities sponsored by No More Wars and Edith Huddle—or, if they shared the opposing view, attendance at the meetings that Cathy Blanchard organized.[8] Throughout 1993, casual conversation evidenced vigorous debates concerning tenant politics and the role of the LAC, but tenants' active participation grew irregular. A meeting called by either the Huddle or the Blanchard camp could attract as few as five people or as many as fifty. Althea Jefferson exemplified the most common attitude among tenants: she was concerned about the fate of the LAC, but she monitored the debates from the comfort of her home. After admitting that "we all need to stay together and the LAC is the only group that can help us," Jefferson stated that "people around here just don't really trust [LAC] no more, they ain't got no faith in 'em. We all seen them take money and not do anything. Most are just like CHA, and so that's why you don't see people coming out and working with [LAC] like they used to." Others shared her belief that the LAC was, in theory, the best advocate for tenants. However, this was countered by the perception that the organization had grown out of touch with tenants. The consequence was a general lack of tenant involvement in LAC activities.

If the use of gang members had fueled the polarization of tenant opinion, then the CHA's use of paramilitary law enforcement tactics would bring the conflict between the two constituencies to a head. By 1993, there was little question that the Housing Authority had redirected its resources to the use of tactical, surprise "emergency" policing and away from preventive enforcement and the use of everyday security inside the buildings. The most politically charged procedure was Operation Clean Sweep, wherein the Chicago police would surround a public housing building, usually in the early morning, while the Housing Authority's security force moved through each apartment to find gang members, drugs, and weapons. In theory, restrictions were in place to protect tenants against the potential infringement of their Fourth Amendment rights. However, in practice, tenants reported numerous violations to the press and to the American Civil Liberties Union (ACLU), which had been providing them with legal counsel. For example, Cathy Blanchard cited instances of Chicago police officers' accompanying the CHA force, a practice that was illegal, and Louisa Lenard complained that officers searched through her dressers "and even through my cookie jar," when the rules of engagement prescribed only the search of publicly visible spaces. The Chicago police admitted that the sweeps were conducted illegally.[9]

The CHA sweeps were terribly ineffective. Indeed, they did little to deter gang activity and drug distribution. Given that they were netting only minor arrests, mostly for drug possession, their supporters at the Housing Authority were forced to defend their utility as a surprise anti-gang strategy. One newspaper reporter published an embarrassing appraisal of the sweeps that showed that the agency was not planning its security measures carefully:

> Geniuses at the Chicago Housing Authority and the Police Department keep wondering if perhaps the locations of their "raids" at public housing

projects are getting leaked—seeing as how a sweep of an entire building is yielding just a pistol or two. You security guys might consider that even the Salvation Army received advance notice of last week's raid at [the] Cabrini Green [housing development]. That's how they knew to have their truck there to pass out cocoa and individually wrapped pound cakes for raiders.[10]

The sweeps pitted resident demands for privacy and legal searches against their need for effective law enforcement and security against gang violence and drugs. Whereas Edith Huddle fought in court and participated in street demonstrations to eliminate the use of sweeps, other tenants voiced approval for sweeps and other "emergency procedures," such as fingerprinting of children and CHA-imposed curfews, in an attempt to regain the public spaces of the housing development. In the autumn of 1993, Huddle and LAC Officer Kim Walton used gang members and No More Wars staffers to gather tenant testimonies of sweeps that had been conducted illegally. Her decision to employ gang members drew protests, and during one meeting of tenants in the 210 high-rise, an elderly leaseholder chastised Huddle: "Some of us want police to come around. Shit, that's what they getting paid for. If they want to search my apartment, go on! I ain't got nothing to hide."

Cathy Blanchard, who campaigned publicly for the greater use of sweeps, argued that tenants did not want BK gang members to punish domestic abusers or conduct bodily searches of individuals entering the high-rises. Edith Huddle offered a reply to her argument in one public meeting of tenants at the Grace Center:

> "You ain't had no shootings go on in your building, did you?" asked Huddle. "Shit, it ain't like I like what they doing you know. But it's safer right now."
>
> "Let the [CHA] guards do that," interrupted Blanchard.
>
> "But they ain't doing it," retorted Huddle. "*That's* the problem. And that's why I'm saying we got to march [against these sweeps], 'cause that's the only thing CHA is going to do for us. They ain't gonna make security guards do nothing for us unless we don't let them come 'round our apartments anytime they want to."

"[The gangs] only making it safer to sell their drugs," said Paulina Collins. "BKs don't care about us, shit they just want to make they money."

"Yeah, you right," said Huddle dejectedly. "Don't know what we can do about that."

Huddle and Walton tried repeatedly during the three-hour meeting to reframe the situation for tenants in order to win support for their platform. They argued that residents could lobby for the eradication of sweeps and demand greater police protection, but that at the same time they should employ street-gang members to police public space and respond to reports of sexual harassment. Huddle and Walton exercised somewhat poor political judgment by arguing that the practice of lobbying law enforcement agents for better service provision was independent from the use of gang members for security. The two women were not considering that the CHA and police were citing examples of tenant collusion with gang members as a defense of their need to use more serious tactics, such as sweeps, to rid the community of the gang presence.

At these meetings, there was no way to separate the decision whether or not to support the emergency law enforcement techniques from the larger question of the appropriate posture that the LAC should adopt to win services from the CHA, police, and other municipal agencies. It was the LAC that had organized the press conferences, tenant meetings, and "townhall" forums with police and CHA representatives. The LAC was also the dominant organ through which the housing development expressed public opinion and mobilized interest and support within the wider world. From one corner of the room there came calls for brokerage and compromise, grounded in statements that the LAC was part of the CHA administrative apparatus, that it should use its "inside" position to leverage change, and that the collaboration with gangs threatened its capacity to do so. From the other side of the room came support for confrontation and rebuttals that provided an alternate history of the LAC. As one tenant cried, "LAC ain't getting nothing no more from CHA, so don't you all be fooling yourselves. LAC is for the people." With the discussion so sharply polarized between proponents of compromise and those wishing to yield no quarter, and with no mediator present to provide rapprochement, it was difficult to see how tenants could move forward together in a practical effort to address their concerns.

It was not altogether surprising that the course Robert Taylor would chart in the coming months would be determined in upcoming LAC elections. Individuals vied for the right to represent tenants of their buildings, and the Huddle-Walton and Blanchard-Collins camps sponsored distinctly different candidates for the office of building president and for LAC president of the entire Robert Taylor development. The campaign for LAC president was a choice between two tenants who had lived in Robert Taylor since the 1960s. Victoria Knight lobbied on a platform of "working with our youth and not running away from problems," and she favored collaborations with gang members as well as the use of protest to bring about change in municipal policies. Cassandra Wilkins promised to restore the LAC's original charter, which was "to be a part of government and not a part of the problem." She decried any patronization of gang members and their sympathizers and favored sweeps as "tough love for a community that's misbehaving."

As the elections neared in 1994, tenant support for the Grace Center and No More Wars had waned. Several newspapers in the black community publicized unfavorable ties between Jeremy Coals and the Black Kings organization, listing Coals's use of gang donations for his own political aspirations. Reports such as these made tenants cautious. The Grace Center was implicated in these developments, and Jackson was routinely asked by tenants and journalists to defend his choice of placing gang members and Coals on the agency's payrolls. Perennial gang wars still occurred with uncanny regularity in May and June and September and October, and now and then Jackson and Coals tried to address the conflicts among gang members. However, by this time, Jackson's preference for gang intervention meant that nearly all of the center's programming was for gang-affiliated youth, and only a small number of children and youth attending the

Grace Center were not members of the BKs. Tenants protested the nearly full-time presence of gang members in and around the center by calling the local police commander, who in turn began to conduct raids at the center several times a month. This would not last for long, however, for No More Wars had clearly lost its base of tenant support in the housing development, and Will Jackson decided to resign from the center. The programs dwindled and the gangs returned to using apartments, parks, and other public areas to meet and conduct their business. While drug trafficking flourished and showed no immediate signs of receding, the Black Kings' harassment of young women had subsided in large part owing to the collective opposition that Christie Woodson and Judy Harris had mounted—although domestic abuse in Robert Taylor overall continued to be reported with frequency to the local police.

Will Jackson appeared to be placing distance between himself and the Grace Center. He cited a lack of tenant interest in his approaches to gang intervention, but he was losing his stature as a spokesperson in the broader Grand Boulevard community, and his involvement with the gangs was endangering any chance he might have had to continue as a social-service professional in that area. Although he remained publicly committed to gang intervention, his private actions suggested that he may have wanted to cut some of his ties to the Black Kings. He was busily meeting with other social-service agencies to explore employment possibilities, and he began prominently firing his staff, on whose shoulders he placed much of the blame for the gang's rowdiness and use of center facilities for drug dealing and business meetings.

Few tenants offered public support for LAC leaders still pressing for a militant posture rooted in alignment with the street gangs. The public mood made it clear that the majority of individuals wanted the LAC to conduct political brokerage as its diplomatic strategy with external agencies. Cassandra Wilson won the election handily, and in most of the buildings, tenants had voted out of office those officials who were known to be in the No More Wars camp.

The support for Wilson and her colleagues was a clear tenant mandate for serious reconsideration of the role of the street gang in the affairs of the housing development. The most immediate outcome may have been to end abruptly any further patronization of the gang's security services—of course, some households continued to receive the gang's payoffs to meet their own needs. However, behind this substantive concern, there was the more fundamental question of the means by which tenants should intervene in gang activity and work to limit the effects of an organized criminal enterprise that was deleteriously impacting the housing development. By 1994, it was difficult to find people who still drew favorable comparisons between the Black Kings and earlier gang incarnations and who were still willing to concede that the gang, as such, was not a completely negative force. People's frustrations with the BKs had risen so high that even the most tolerant tenants, those who were once adamant that the BKs were still children in need of nurturing, now believed that the Black Kings were not really a "gang" but a Mafia interested primarily in illicit revenue generation. One person argued that "they're not even good, they're a bad mob, because they don't help the community in no way."

Despite these negative assessments, tenants still had great faith in the power of youth to resist the temptations of the "bad mob" and the lure of drug dealing. Many felt that the Black Kings were best understood as a group of older members, heavily invested in drug trafficking, who could not be excused for their criminal activity and the pressures they placed on younger members to join their trade. It was this late-twenty and thirty-something cohort of gang members who needed to be targeted first and foremost, although tenants' opinions over how to combat gang recruitment and conduct effective intervention varied from job placement to greater law enforcement.

The developments in Robert Taylor invalidated the pragmatic position, held by well-intentioned people such as Edith Huddle, that the gang's services could be used temporarily, that is, until mainstream resources were procured. Perhaps a gang of petty delinquents whose motives for group membership are social support and identity affirmation can serve as a potential resource for a community. But working with an entrepreneurially minded group rooted in illicit underground economies, no matter how selfless the gang's leaders might conceive their role in the community to be, will inevitably pit the interests of tenants who want safety and reduced drug trafficking against the gang, for whom the latter is paramount. Huddle and her colleagues who thought in such a pragmatic manner about the Kings may not have fully grasped the gang's identity, its motives, or its limit as a collaborator.

Criticism of these leaders' behavior and that of a community that supported them must, however, be offered cautiously. It is difficult for most Americans to grasp what life is like under daily conditions of extreme, concentrated poverty and neglect by the wider world, a circumstance that might legitimately drive a set of community stakeholders to work with a local gang as a means to ensure their safety and welfare. Moreover, these gang members are the children of friends and neighbors whom adults want to steer on the right course. To tenants, even in their worse guise, gang members do not appear as foreign enemies. Instead, they are part of a seemingly endless cycle of disadvantaged youth, fraught with developmental challenges, who have few opportunities and who see the gang as a source of social and economic capital. Edith Huddle's work with the street gangs is best seen as driven by a mix of motives, ranging from compassion for the gang-affiliated youth, intolerance for their criminal activity, a wish to protect households from them, and a self-interested need to ensure her own power in the face of their challenges.

Her own decision to push ahead and involve the gang in the affairs of the community also points to the difficulties of working with gangs in the face of few community intermediaries, such as social-service centers and youth outreach workers, who can provide useful mediation among residents, law enforcement, and street gangs. In many communities these actors exercise a mitigating influence by notifying tenants when certain postures toward the gang might be unworkable. They can provide equally valuable instruction and support to police, who are concerned for their own safety when confronting armed youth. And they can find potential areas of leverage and intervention in the gang that might help bring about the changes demanded by the community, such as increased habitability of public space or reduced drug trafficking. Whether these outreach workers can have much success with a drug-trafficking gang is not clear, but preliminary evidence suggests that if they are part of a holistic initiative, rooted in the community as opposed to law enforcement agencies, places such as Robert Taylor may be able to increase their self-efficacy.[11] The current suppression programs designed and implemented by law enforcement—in which the gang is myopically conceived of as a criminal—clearly will have little benefit to people such as Edith Huddle, for whom the gang holds a number of identities, roles, and relations with tenants.

When tenants elected Cassandra Wilkins, they did not throw the gang out of the community in some dramatic fashion. Instead, they cast out the gang as a potentially legitimate player in any tenant-based coalition working to improve the well-being of households. They did so not as a disorganized community, but in a way that revealed the presence of a healthy, normative foundation amid deeply rooted economic impoverishment. In an almost idealized American manner, they deliberated, debated, reflected on their experiences, and determined that using the gang to meet their own needs was ultimately a poor strategy. They fought for what they believed in and voted to determine the course they would take to rectify their situation.

The gang had developed into an organization that was not going to help make the Robert Taylor Homes a habitable community, and so tenants decided that its involvement in non-criminal activities in the housing development would have to be sharply curtailed. This did not necessarily mean that they wanted their tenant leaders and mediators to stop resolving gang-related conflicts. With poor protection offered by city and CHA law enforcement, social order in Robert Taylor would still be dependent on the informal methods that tenants had devised to control youth activity and the numerous other transgressions that threatened their safety. The strength and effectiveness of these casual systems of enforcement and redress, combined with the distribution of a minimum level of policing, maintenance, and up-keep of public areas by administrative agencies, would continue to be critical ingredients in the recipe for ensuring tenant self-efficacy. In fact, tenants still expected the LAC to engage in mediation with gangs, but the popular mood suggested that few wanted their representatives to work with these youths for any other purposes. Certainly, they did not want the LAC to give up its lobbying for more responsive police services that might help reduce the gang's drug trafficking and occupation of public space.

At the end of 1994, Robert Taylor entered a new phase in its history. Many of the new LAC leaders were in their forties, considerably younger than Edith Huddle, Kim Walton, and Edna Baxter, all of whom were in their sixties and now out of office. The new LAC officials demonstrated a far less contentious posture in their dealings with the Housing Authority than had their predecessors, and they were making promises to their constituents daily that conditions in the housing development would improve. One newly elected leader posted a sign on the door of her apartment that read, "The LAC is back, and we're going to make Robert Taylor a home, like it used to be." The new LAC leaders had few public dealings with gangs, but Blanchard and Cassandra Wilkins worked with other building presidents to intervene in gang disputes. However, they were careful not to publicize their mediation, and to further minimize attention to their work, they did not boast of their successes. Rumors of payoffs between LAC officials and gang members could be heard, albeit sparingly; their rarity may have been an indicator of both the actual decline of such payoffs and the tenants' unwillingness to continue discussing such arrangements.

Optimism was not the prevailing mood, however, even among those who supported the new regime. Tenants were experiencing collective exhaustion, a weariness visible on the faces of those surfacing from prolonged struggle or suffering. Gang wars, in-fighting, reduced maintenance, family hardships, and escalated use of police interdiction were taking their toll. People still took pleasure in family life and in leisurely walks through the grounds when they felt it safe to do so, but they reacted with numbness when questioned about deeply politicized community issues. Some of their apathy stemmed from the discussion they heard in the media concerning the need for a drastic new policy to alleviate the conditions in public housing in Chicago, including the possibility of outright demolition. They saw all around them tenants who were moving out to private apartments, some voluntarily and others after being evicted by the CHA for lease violations or because their apartments were unfit to live in. In their buildings, abandonment of their community was evident in the many vacated apartments that were boarded up with placards. By 1995, there were rumors that the Housing Authority had no intention of refurbishing these apartments as units for prospective poor families, and many tenants felt that they knew what lay ahead. Their premonitions were confirmed by reports that Chicago's high-rise developments would soon be demolished. Tenants' concern for the habitability of Robert Taylor was overshadowed by a collective insecurity regarding the very future of their American project.

A Dream Deferred

In the autumn of 1996, Edith Huddle rested her sore leg on a large cardboard box in the center of her living room and stared out the window of the fourteenth-floor apartment that had been her home for thirty years. Filled with photographs, letters, newspaper clippings, and personal mementos, the box was a record of her days in the Robert Taylor Homes. She had been visiting with neighbors and exchanging her photos for those of her friends. The box was the only remaining item in the apartment that had to be carried away before this chapter in her life could be closed. The walls and cupboards were bare, the closets had been cleaned, and her possessions were now in her daughter's house. Edith Huddle looked down at the box and at the empty space around her, glancing occasionally at her daughter. As she picked up her mementos and walked out the door, a line of well-wishers stood in the hallway, waving goodbye to "Ms. Huddle." "Woman was a fighter," said Kenny Davenport, as Huddle walked by. "The woman *is* a fighter, shit!" said his friend Christie Woodson. In the coming months, the same event would be repeated throughout the buildings in the Robert Taylor Homes as tenants packed their belongings, some departing voluntarily, others evicted by the Housing Authority. The clearance of tenants was the first phase of the eventual "demolition and redevelopment" of the largest public housing development in the world.

The departure of these families would appear to be the penultimate nail in the coffin of the original 1930s notion of public housing, that is, as a viable "waystation" for poor families from which they could climb the American social and economic ladder. This New Deal–era ray of hope for the American working and poor classes now seemed a broken promise, a naive experiment that was doomed to fail. After 1995, as Americans rendered their verdict on public housing with phrases celebrating the end of a "nightmare," a "mistake," and the worst example of government social engineering, residents looked as though they had lost something more than a roof and four walls—perhaps the dream of better days ahead. Public housing, no matter its problems, still signified to tenants that they were not forgotten in the national promise of freedom and mobility for all citizens, black and white, rich and poor. Many were not leaving public housing completely; most were probably moving to a government rent-subsidized apartment in the private market—reports indicated that they could find housing primarily in the poorest, racially segregated areas, farthest from job growth and adequate city services. Of those who left for the more expensive private market, many envisioned their move as temporary, for they hoped to return to a subsidized apartment soon in order to start their journey again. For the moment, anyway, the dream of public housing as guaranteed shelter and waystation to better days ahead had been deferred.

Plans to demolish the Robert Taylor Homes had circulated with greater frequency beginning in 1995. In June of that year, the Department of Housing and Urban Development had declared that the CHA Board of Commissioners was unfit to govern the city's public housing developments. HUD officials placed the municipal agency in receivership and formed a new interim management team, citing mismanagement and the failure to ensure decent living conditions as their ostensible motives. To tenants, the takeover was a sure sign that their community may not be around much longer. "The national system of public housing is on trial in Chicago," declared HUD Secretary Henry Cisneros, making Chicago the guinea pig for the future of American public housing.[12] Tenants' fears were justified, for in the ensuing months Congress passed legislation mandating that local housing authorities across the nation conduct "viability" studies to determine the more prudent long-term course of action for their larger developments: rehabilitation or demolition and the "scattered" relocation of tenants throughout the city. There had always been calls to destroy Robert Taylor because it was crime-ridden, a less-than-optimal use of city land, or simply an eyesore (even before its construction was completed, CHA officials publicly regretted their decision to build the development), but the federal takeover and the congressional mandates lent an air of certainty to tenant speculation regarding demolition. The CHA determined that 17,859 of its public housing units across the city failed viability standards. Thirty-four thousand residents would have to be moved out so that all the high-rises in Robert Taylor "could be toppled, some within five years," the rest within ten.[13]

The reaction in the tenant body was mixed. One segment of the population wanted to move out and participate in the CHA's "Section 8" program, whereby eligible individuals receive federal certificates and vouchers to subsidize private-market rents. Another, equally vocal constituency wanted to remain, preferring modernization and upkeep to resettlement. A third camp notified the CHA of its willingness to leave, contingent on relocation to a new public housing dwelling in the neighboring Greater Grand Boulevard community. Because the city and the Housing Authority had no plans to rebuild much new housing locally, tenants either placed themselves on the Section 8 waiting lists (which had exceeded twenty thousand families) or waited to hear whether their own high-rise would escape the wrecking balls.[14]

The redevelopment decision affected daily life by dissolving social networks and peer associations, and thereby disrupting whatever support systems households depended upon to make ends meet. Some tenants spent their time and energy looking for new housing elsewhere in the city, and others were relocated to a different building within Robert Taylor, where they met new neighbors and some unfamiliar challenges. In this atmosphere of perpetual change, it was difficult to sustain the informal ties of reciprocity through which material resources, emotional support, and protective services had traditionally been exchanged. In addition to the tenant body, groups and organizations suffered the impact of reshuffling and the loss of members. Bible-reading groups, senior citizens' clubs that ran errands together, tenant patrols, and block clubs were either reconstituted or disbanded altogether. Churches and other service providers lost clients, shifted their resources to conduct outreach and recruit new tenants, and made new needs assessments to ensure adequate service delivery within the complex.

The Black Kings street gang also changed its daily activities as redevelopment began. Prince Williams took advantage of a federal indictment that had dismantled the organizational structure of the Sharks gang to expand the Black Kings' presence into Sharks territory. He negotiated with BK leaders to the southeast, who agreed to absorb Black Kings members displaced by the CHA's resettlement. While the exodus of gang members had a dampening effect on the visibility of the local gangs, fights between remaining Sharks members and colonizing BK factions continued. The drug trade, now dominated by both crack cocaine and heroin sales, continued to flourish, with one estimate citing "$45,000 worth of drug business done in the Robert Taylor Homes each day."[15]

The Grace Center was still in operation, but its Board of Directors decided to limit programming to children and adolescents under sixteen years of age. The Board prohibited center staff from servicing Robert Taylor's youth and young-adult population—for whom there was no other such center within one mile of the housing development—and it expressly forbade its staff to have dealings with street gangs. The well-known individuals who could successfully mediate gang-related conflict had also left. Will Jackson had resigned, both Christie Woodson and Kenny Davenport moved their families out of Robert Taylor, and Ottie Davis and his wife left the city altogether. Owing to the gang wars, Prince's relationship with the new LAC officers became stilted, and he did not initiate any formal attempts to mollify them or seek collaboration.

As plans for demolition and redevelopment were under way in 1995, the Housing Authority cleared buildings of tenants and placed large cardboard placards on windows to mark the exodus; the city labored to determine the significance of its high-rise public housing communities, including whether the experiment in modernist urban planning should ever be replicated. In their debates over the relative merits of outright destruction of high-rise complexes versus rehabilitation, some asked whether demolition signaled the end of the nation's commitment to housing the poor. Many wondered what would happen to the households evicted from Robert Taylor and other large Chicago public housing complexes. The talk in the streets and in the press, similar to the discourse after the Second World War, when the high-rises were first conceived and built, was emotional and at times contentious. Those favoring the demolition of Robert Taylor cheered the plans while others proclaimed the initiative to be a "conspiracy to remove blacks from their voting power in the inner city and move them to the suburbs."[16] There were public calls to raze the entire complex so that "the nightmare [could be] ended once and for all."[17]

In the ongoing debate, considerations of the habitability of places like the Robert Taylor Homes have been overshadowed by the concerns of parties interested only in the reconfiguration of public housing land. The motives of governments and real estate firms have invaded public discourse and challenged the tenants' rights to remain in their respective areas. Discussions in the most visible media arenas, such as press conferences, talk shows, and the editorial pages of city newspapers, have become shrouded in political posturing and public accusation. Contention is to be expected. Developers thirst for an opportunity to profit from Robert Taylor's valuable real estate tracts, and the mayoral administration is similarly attracted by new prospects for commercial and residential revenue (and the cost savings on social-service delivery). Moreover, given that its own energies are refocused on low-rise and "scattered site" housing, the CHA has expressed relief at the opportunity to leave high-rises behind.

The need to weigh practical concerns of economic productivity and governance are important; however, their introduction has had the effect of replacing concerted examination of the viability of public housing complexes with a more technocratic dialogue regarding the most effective means to meet the interests of developers, tenants, the surging middle and upper class, and the city government. Public rhetoric now regards each party as having an equal stake in the future use of the ninety-six-acre space on which Robert Taylor sits. To claim that public housing developments are a functional or even plausible mode of urban settlement now seems wrongheaded, and perhaps even ignorant, given that public discourse has moved to considerations of how to redevelop, not whether to redevelop.

Despite its prevalence, this framework is not necessarily the best approach to determining the viability of public housing. By almost any criteria that one could use to measure a functional community, it is possible to identify historical periods when Robert Taylor and much of Chicago's public housing were viable, such as the 1940s through the early 1960s. Crime was largely under control—it was not much greater, if at all, than in other areas of the city; public housing provided decent shelter for families, with many leaving eventually for a private-market unit; and management and screening techniques, as well as support from many community organizations and providers, kept its households integrated into the social life of the wider area. Moreover, even in the contemporary period, there are public housing complexes in the largest cities that continue to embody these traits. There is great variation in the functionality of public housing, and whereas Chicago and Los Angeles have been criticized in recent decades, New York's public housing has been celebrated as viable and well planned.

Beneath the histrionics of public debate and the "theatrical manipulation" over land use in Chicago, the impending demise of Robert Taylor, Cabrini Green, Henry Horner, and other famous high-rise communities has provided an opportunity for self-reflection and evaluation.[18] Chicagoans take great pride in being a "city of neighborhoods," and the elimination of Robert Taylor and its West- and North-Side counterparts has put this self-representation to the test. That high-rise developments will no longer be part of the city's neighborhoods is a moot point. However, the significance of this erasure is still a matter of debate—will it signal the abdication of a local and national commitment to the welfare of the poor, or will it mean that high-rise public housing is ultimately unworkable as a solution to America's low-income housing needs, thus making demolition a painful but necessary circumstance to improve tenants' lives?

The consensus view is that Robert Taylor is an unmistakable failure. This view focuses on two practices, the racism and negligence of mid-twentieth-century participants in the creation and administration of the housing development, and the behavioral pathology of the tenant body itself. That is, Robert Taylor was initially the "victim of racist white politicians and white real estate agents who forced construction in black areas, misguided architects who were captivated by modernist high-rise designs, and an American society unwilling to address the roots of impoverishment."[19] Subsequently, gangs and crime, vandalism, single-parent families, and general disrepair reached intractable levels, well beyond the capacity of tenants and administrative agencies to cope and resteer the housing development toward the mainstream. According to this perspective, then, the first mistake was to build Robert Taylor, the second to allow it to remain when its residents became overwhelmingly destitute and its problems uncontrollable. The lesson in this view is that high-rise public housing is a mistaken means by which to provide for the housing needs of America's urban poor.

To be sure, racism in Chicago and unrest among the tenant body did not enhance the quality of life in Robert Taylor, but these factors do not fully explain the genesis and development of social life in this American project over three decades. It is important to note that the housing development was designed, constructed, and then managed not simply by racist or misguided individuals but by people who had good intentions and who seemed sincere in their efforts to house Chicago's poor and needy. Designers thought that high-rises would free the poor from urban ills, not compound their hardships, and their faith was grounded in the science of urban planning. Black politicians made the difficult choice of ghetto public housing versus no low-income housing at all. Well before racist city officials rejected their proposals to locate low-income housing in white communities, CHA officials had wanted to build public housing in ghettos to address local housing shortages. Later, CHA managers fought for the needs of their constituents while their budgets decreased, and politicians tried to infuse the housing development with law enforcement resources in an effort to increase household security.

The consensus view must be modified to reflect the fact that the fate of Robert Taylor—and the potential of "project living" generally—is inseparable from the housing development's involvement in the ongoing transformations of the larger society. Politicians, designers, CHA officials, and service providers operated in social structures that limited their ability to improve conditions at the complex. Some forces that stymied their efforts were local, such as the law enforcement agencies that refused to police, enforce, and secure the housing development. Others were national in scope, perhaps the most important being the dramatic cuts to the nation's public housing program after the mid-1960s. Moreover, not all developments impacting Robert Taylor were ostensibly related to public housing; these would include the economic disenfranchisement of members of the black working class, who lost jobs and avenues for reemployment, and the government's "redlining" practices that failed to subsidize the homeownership aspirations of working- and middle-class blacks, some of whom were trying to move out of Robert Taylor. This would suggest that decisions by those whose actions shaped life for Robert Taylor's tenant body were motivated not only by their own prejudices, but also by the institutionalized racism embedded in surrounding political and economic structures.

The consensus view of public housing habitability also ignores the fact that many urban communities face continuous challenges owing to declining economic health, lowered public and private institutional resources, and household hardships, but that the outcome is not the same in each. In the postwar era, a massive city conservation and renewal program sought to stem the deterioration of neighborhoods throughout Chicago. At the time, Chicago was a decaying, drab, and graying place, a testament to the writer Nelson Algren's description, "an October sort of city, even in the spring." Not only the black ghetto, but also white-ethnic poor and working-class areas of the city, and even middle-class communities, suffered a decaying physical infrastructure as well as hardships that threatened family economic stability. In these locales, there was a tremendous infusion of city, state, and federal dollars to ensure that "tipping" neighborhoods on the verge of "blight" did not become slums. By using state-funded "community-conservation" initiatives, the city built schools and parks, increased street lighting, and ensured adequate sanitation service, all in an effort to create clean, livable neighborhoods. Mayor Richard J. Daley exclaimed proudly as he guided Chicago's reconstruction, "When I walk down the street where I live, I see every street in the city of Chicago."

Apparently, the mayor had not seen the streets of the city's black ghetto, which at that time was a segregated place, filled with middle and upper classes, all of whom lived in a cramped and deteriorating physical space that the historian Arnold Hirsch has described uncompromisingly as a composite of "rabbit warrens" and "death traps." The black ghetto was almost wholly ignored in the conservation movement and instead given the vertical high-rise as a solution to its misery and the cries of its residents for decent, affordable housing.

In the late 1960s, as industrial outmigration and job loss took their toll, Robert Taylor was one of many neighborhoods, black and white, that were threatened. Whereas the housing development and the surrounding black community became a space of overwhelmingly unemployed residents, this did not occur throughout Chicago because unions, city politicians, and private capitalists all redirected resources in ways that favored the city's white residents (and select, politically resourceful middle-class black constituents).[20] Again, between 1970 and 1983, the entire city faced a sluggish national economy, but corporate investment and the municipal support of neighborhoods were being targeted to regions containing predominantly white communities, ensuring that the predominantly black areas on the city's South and West Sides would receive no support.[21]

The example of Chicago suggests that government, civic, and private-sector support plays a key role in the viability of *any* community, not just that of public housing—the inability to perceive this connection being perhaps the most glaring error of the consensus view. Yet in the popular deliberations on public housing in the mid-1990s, few thought seriously about the many resources available to mainstream communities—wherever they might be—that enabled these spaces to function and that allowed them to address problems with young people as well as with household hardship. These purportedly normative, private-market neighborhoods will not have rates of vandalism and crime to match those of public housing. Even so, it is doubtful that residents there are tackling problems that may include gangs, truancy, and criminality largely on their own; instead, they are relying on police, whom they trust and who are responsive and responsible in their enforcement. It is doubtful that many of these mainstream communities suffer compromised public spaces, overwhelmingly littered and hazardous parks and play areas, and a negligent city government. Instead, residents can call their elected representatives to remedy such issues, and they probably feel that they can rely on local organizations to provide sufficient social, recreational, educational, and other human services. It is doubtful that these areas will ever reach unemployment rates of nearly 90 percent or have to resort to hidden income and creative hustling schemes; working and middle-class households across America are no doubt fragile and have a "fear of falling," but they are usually embedded in social networks and possess the requisite political capital to locate new employment sources and ensure that their basic needs are being met.

This is to imply not that some American communities are free of problems, but that we ask more of the poor, and particularly those in public housing, than we expect from other citizens. Would residents of a suburb, to offer only one example, be expected to work largely on their own to curb gang activity, and, if they failed to do so, would most Americans then ask whether suburbs were no longer viable planned spaces of residence? Certainly, suburban residents may call for families to assume more responsibility in their children's lives, but it goes without saying that they would demand that their government provide the protective services to which they are entitled, that their schools educate and ensure that their children are sheltered from gang activity, and that social-service providers bolster their resource allocation and provide counseling, drug treatment, and diversionary programming.

By contrast, in discussions of public housing communities, the onus is placed on families, and even the most well-intentioned observers project onto the tenants the need for heroic, independent action that they would never expect of themselves and their own communities. In too many instances, the very same struggles by public housing tenants to procure basic services that are available in the mainstream are not cast as a sign that tenants lack basic entitlements and that the institutions servicing the community need restructuring.

Compassionate sentiments turn in the worst case to anger, as in the calls that public housing be ended, that police be allowed to suspend constitutional protections and civil rights, and that tenants stop harboring the gangs. At best, these sentiments express pity for those caught in the middle of the debate over public housing.

This leaves open the question whether Robert Taylor would have been a community capable of responding to its challenges—as it did during the first decade of its existence—if the city's political leaders had devoted adequate resources and attention to the development. It is not difficult to document that leaders at the federal and local level made explicit decisions to rescind resources for public housing, thereby forcing tenants and their management to make do with less. At the least, judgments of its habitability cannot be divorced from this climate of neglect and should not occur without full recognition that, from the middle of the 1960s, Robert Taylor was playing catch-up, never able to garner the resources or commitment necessary for household stability. One of the most important foundations for a sustainable community, namely, the presence of a minimum level of support from the state, was lost, and with few signs that it would be restored, each passing year lent credence to arguments that Robert Taylor was facing problems beyond the capacity of its tenants to manage. Notwithstanding the tenants' destructive behavior, the difficulties faced by residents of Robert Taylor in every period of its existence can be seen as a result not of behavioral pathology but of institutional neglect. How the behavior of administrative agencies and tenants is given weight in any explanation, then, is a matter of debate and is influenced by ideology and politics.

Perhaps the determination of the habitability of public housing—or of any community for that matter—is best sought in the capacity of residents to resolve problems and meet their personal and collective needs. Using this measure, the tenants of the Robert Taylor Homes must be acknowledged for their impressive efforts to cope and make life meaningful amid a dearth of resources. From day-care provision to street-gang intervention, the tenant body devised innovative techniques and fought when necessary to ensure their own safety and welfare. The result was the creation of fairly strong, cohesive networks, wherein individuals worked with one another to respond as best they could to their ever-present challenges. Ultimately, however, the resilience they displayed could never provide a permanent basis to foster habitability. Working outside the law and continually sharing resources were short-term solutions that, for Robert Taylor's poor families, proved to be inadequate as hardships continued and assistance from the broader society withered. If these innovative survival strategies had been buttressed with government resources and adequate economic development in public housing neighborhoods, perhaps tenants' networks and associations could have been strengthened and the capacity of the overall community to meet its needs could have been restored.

The larger lesson is that it may be impossible for a community to create its own law and order. Wherever communities develop a quasi-juridical foundation to cope with extremely dangerous practices such as gang wars and drug trafficking, a rapid, responsible initiative that recreates the presence of mainstream legal institutions may be the best course to chart. Recent community policing efforts have suggested that an approach that embeds the police and the judicial system within the community—often, quite literally, by placing courts and jails there—may be a means by which to staunch outlaw justice and create more effective relationships between the poor and the wider world.

Even as they developed internal procedures to address their needs, the tenants of Robert Taylor did not necessarily live in complete isolation, that is, in a "city within a city," effectively disconnected from the wider world. Throughout their attempts to supplant their lack of mainstream resources with informal support systems, tenants lobbied and demanded their fair share of goods and services from the organizations that were neglecting them. Tenants were "unemployed," but they still participated in the local economy as part-time and hidden workers, consumers, and taxpayers. Police ignored Robert Taylor relative to other neighborhoods, but law enforcement officers were nevertheless part of an informal system of localized policing and redress. Similarly, while service providers and government agencies did not respond to all the needs of households, tenants still asked them to be of assistance and welcomed staff members who could help individual families.

To remember the struggles of Robert Taylor's tenants is important, but not at the price of pitying those who have passed through the 4,500 apartments or, in the final instance, rendering them as victims of an uncaring world. There is no community in which ongoing collective labor is not required to ensure livability, though the resources available to communities will differ. In its first three years, Robert Taylor was a success by any definition, in large part because the CHA and tenants had the freedom and resources to meet household needs. The two parties screened applicants rigorously, mixed working and poor families in the high-rises, and drew on the resources of the wider community to support tenants and decrease their sense of isolation. By the mid-1960s, the deluge of impoverished households that came to the Housing Authority seeking shelter made this conscious planning and social engineering unworkable. Buildings soon became filled with households in poverty, the CHA and organizations in the complex were stretched beyond their capacities, and those in the surrounding communities themselves were coping with a growing population of poor families. The conditions worsened as the years passed, and by the end of the 1980s, few could predict how the community would survive. The rising hardship did not, however, eclipse the spirit of the tenants; nor for that matter did it fully erase the habitability of the housing development. Residents' hopefulness is apparent in their acute awareness of their past, the ways in which they celebrate their collective history, and the meaningful and sometimes deliberate ways they keep this history alive in their current actions.

One of the most difficult challenges of representing tenants' personal and collective histories has been to ensure that their experiences and outlooks make their way onto these pages. This has taken on a greater urgency given that, at the time of this writing, only one-half of the twenty-eight buildings in the Robert Taylor Homes are occupied, and even in those high-rises, families are being evicted, relocated, and displaced so that the development may soon be razed. As the individual buildings come down, one by one, the community should be remembered for the ways in which tenants took sustenance from both the joy and the struggle of "project living."

Author's Note

This study of the Robert Taylor Homes follows a tradition of American sociology that has used ethnographic methods to explicate small-scale life in cities. Ethnography usually refers to the collection of information on the behavior of actors in a particular context over an extended period of time. Ethnographers "hang out." Ethnography is a craft of bringing out the richness of people's lives and analyzing their complexity in some comprehensible way.

This study departs from conventional ethnographies of urban life in two ways. In most studies, participant observation is not typically used as a means to gather recent historical data. Whereas nearly one-half of this book examines change and continuity, most studies of urban life typically devote a chapter or a few paragraphs to the history of the fieldsite. Moreover, the explicit concern with community in this research, specifically the relationship of the Robert Taylor Homes to wider spaces and institutions, is no longer standard practice in sociological research.[1] Only a few ethnographers continue to observe communities *in toto* anymore, most of them preferring to focus instead on the behavior of individual agents and social groups. And while some have made spirited calls for "global ethnography," that is, tying local patterns into broader webs of significance, this is by no means an accepted vision of most researchers.

My approach to this project has been influenced by the work of researchers in various disciplines who have tried to reframe our understanding of history, ethnography, and the articulation of local and global processes. In particular, several prescient themes motivate the use of history and context in this body of work, which reaches back to E. P. Thompson and the social historians of the 1960s, to more recent works by the anthropologists Jean and John Comaroff and Marshall Sahlins.

The critical question is how one can build a framework for understanding patterns at a very local level that themselves may be shaped by forces emanating from the larger society. We live in a global age, so the saying goes, yet this worn phrase remains a challenge for researchers who want to unearth the texture of the people they study, when there may be a complex, non-localized, and not very easily identifiable set of people and institutions shaping their informants' lives. We know that local behavior is shaped by abstract forces, such as shifts in the "market" and the restructuring of "global capitalism," but to study this interaction in a practical way is by no means a straightforward task, especially in an ethnography whose field of observation may be highly circumscribed—for example, peer group or street corner. The challenge may be expressed as one of "[not] reifying and decontextualizing the local communities . . . or denying them any dynamic integrity beyond that wrought by external forces."[2] To translate this caveat into the study of Robert Taylor, the challenge becomes how best to write the experiences of tenants in a way that does not reduce them to passive victims of larger social forces or see them as wholly responsible for their fate and their circumstances, that is, uninfluenced by larger structures.

Anthropologists have recently offered a way to address this challenge.[3] The researcher must distinguish between two types of historical processes. One is internal to a group or community and stems from its own unique belief systems, lifestyles, symbols, and practices; the other is at the level of the broader society. Borrowing the words of Jean and John Comaroff, "All local worlds have their own intrinsic historicity, an internal dialectic of structure and practice that shapes, reproduces, and transforms the character of everyday life within them—and . . . mediates their encounters with the universe beyond." It is the interaction of these local worlds with the structures, agents, and ideologies of the larger world that produces observable social patterns. In this study, life within Robert Taylor is presented through the attitudes and practices of tenants whose lives revolved around the American project, but their experiences are continually shaped by contact with others in the wider world. These "external" factors may be practical, as in the behavior of state agencies that administer the housing development, or they may be ideological, as in the growing conservative mood of the American electorate, which helped to retrench government services for the poor and needy. In either case, learned and accepted ways of living among the tenant body were continually reconstituted as they encountered changing modes of governance, redefined opportunities for livelihood and well-being, and shifting ideologies of personhood and collective responsibility in the larger society.

Consider tenants' use of gang members for security services, in particular, for catching perpetrators of domestic abuse or apartment burglars. This practice was in part an adaptation to the lack of available policing. But it can only really be understood through an awareness of tenants' history of establishing social order and assisting households, a central part of which included residents' expectations of help and protection from agencies in the wider world. Their decision to work alongside gangs and use them in their tradition of indigenous enforcement was partly a product of decades of interacting with agencies, politicians, and bureaucrats who failed to provide them with such security.

Their expectations of police, their views toward gangs, and how they respond to crime are embedded in the community and will influence how people act in the future.[4] They create structures that shape possible behavior, guide individuals to feel, act, and think in certain ways, and filter their receipt of the world around them.[5] These historical structures can include belief systems and ideologies, associations and relationships, and particular practices and symbols through which people create their identities and express themselves, all of which are ingrained in the "collective culture" of the community, to borrow Ruth Horowitz's phrase. The brokerage system that defines tenants' relationships to the police is one such historical structure. Residents' understanding of what the police could do, and would not do, in the interest of maintaining order in the housing development was framed by their past dealings with law enforcement. This manifested itself as a perception of neglect as well as the need to rely on brokers who had influence with law enforcement officers and who could bring about a timely police response.

Pursuing the tenant brokerage example, when the earliest signs of the gang's corporate turn emerged at the dawn of the 1980s, the system of brokerage that was in place helped tenants deal with the changes wrought by the BKs' new identity: namely, the switch to narcotics trafficking and law enforcement's preference for more punitive, suppression-based strategies in inner cities. Tenants coped with these changes not only by lobbying formally for greater protection from gang activity, but also by continuing to rely on tenant brokers who would ask police to speak with the gang leaders. Many tenants were far more certain that the police would continue their use of casual, off-the-books techniques to provide help than they were that law enforcement would redress their historic neglect through greater manpower allocation. However, few officers felt comfortable negotiating informally with an armed gang force, and eventually the brokerage system was destabilized and proved more useful for problems such as property theft and less so for corporate gang activity. In this moment when the old and expected relations between tenants and police no longer held up, and the newer arrangements had yet to be devised—one part of what the anthropologist Marshall Sahlins calls the "structure of conjuncture" to denote the meeting of groups with different value systems—tenants began shifting their own expectations of what the police could do. As a result, they eventually created new means of indigenous enforcement.[6]

In the context of the poor, attentiveness to historical structures can be a means of acknowledging that individuals have some self-efficacy and control over their lives, despite being saddled by hardships and inequity. It respects their established ways of ensuring a high quality of life. In doing so, it enables the researcher to document their interactions with those in the wider world, not as victims or adapters—though they may be oppressed and moved about against their will—but as people with established, ingrained lifestyle practices that may conflict with those of individuals who operate according to different principles. Thus, in "little worlds" such as Robert Taylor, an awareness of history focuses attention away from pathology to "internal politics," thereby enabling one to see that in many disadvantaged communities that lack social and political capital, people nevertheless struggle to ensure habitability.[7]

When I arrived in Robert Taylor, my challenge was to capture the community's history of dealing with collective hardships and to render it in a meaningful way. I was interested in social life from 1962—the year of the development's construction—to the mid-1990s, but unfortunately, few people maintained a detailed mental record of changes in the community during this period. Although there were people willing to share the community's history with me, there was no official community historian who had maintained files of letters, correspondence between tenants and the CHA, newspaper clippings, local newsletters, photographs, and the like. Similarly, CHA records are quite sparse and focus largely on budgets and contracts. Historical records on life in public housing within city archives and local libraries in Chicago were far more useful for 1900 until 1950 or so, well before Robert Taylor was built.

I had initially thought that interviewing people in the community was the best way to learn about historical patterns in Robert Taylor. I would simply ask them to tell me their history. I conducted interviews twice, at the very beginning of the fieldwork, and again toward the end. The first time was experimental: with little understanding of what it means to "hang out" and be an ethnographer, I spent the first six months trying to refine an interview protocol. During this time, I had a chance to observe health-care workers, journalists, and other social scientists conduct interviews in and around the housing development, often with people I knew. Their interviews and mine were often stilted and yielded a stock set of answers, in part because of the confining nature of the interview format, but also because tenants of Robert Taylor are continually being inundated with short, one-time exchanges of information in which a bureaucrat, journalist, or social scientist asks them a battery of questions and then quickly departs. When my own interviews ended, or when the visiting journalist left the room, the conversation would become far more lively, and sometimes tenants would even contradict their answers to the interview questions. This means not that they lied, but rather that interviews do not invite comfortable dialogue.

Eventually I abandoned the use of interviews as a first step toward understanding changes over time. People did not record history in some linear way as a series of mental notes that could be accessed, but in the case of Robert Taylor, the community's ever-changing collective culture generally surfaced in events and behavior. It was clear that my ethnographic study would have to include some type of extended observation.

Ethnography is no less a peculiar mode of engaging with others than is interviewing. It would be naïve to assume that people's conversations with each other were the same in my absence as in my presence. But long-term participant observation affords an opportunity to see a range of human behavior that is otherwise unavailable in a point-in-time interview; conversely, the interview is helpful for forcing individuals to reflect and provide conscious responses to questions that they may never address in everyday conversation. Because I was interested in social interaction, however, and because tenants hide much of their everyday actions from government officials, I could not hope to gather the information I sought without spending time simply observing.

Remaining in the role of observer—and conducting no formal interviews for several years—enabled me to see how the community had changed over time, not only during my tenure, but well before. History was part of social action; specifically, tenants invoked history in their conversations and used it to interpret events in their community, often in very different ways. I made notes of these discordant interpretations; constructed timelines of the past; and tried to identify historical structures, such as the persistence of indigenous enforcement or tenant brokerage, filling in details as best I could. But observation alone would not be sufficient to gain this information, and so I supplemented observational data by returning to casual conversations with individuals. On occasion, I provoked people to consider the history of the housing development. At times, I gathered people together in formal groups and asked them to tell me about a specific time period. Usually, however, I listened for mention of past events in everyday conversations and then intervened with some questions.

I returned to the interview during my final year of fieldwork, typically presenting my charts and timelines to individuals, and then asking them to give me details of their lives during specific periods. I pursued more diligently individuals who had histories of involvement in the political affairs of the community. I spoke with current and past members of the Local Advisory Council, police officers and CHA security guards, and other law enforcement personnel who had lived in Robert Taylor. Where were they in 1971 when the Local Advisory Council was formed? Who has lived in their household since they moved into the housing development? How had they earned income, both legal and underground, since they were young? Because no one could be expected to recall this information immediately, I met with individuals repeatedly. Sometimes they modified the timeline, confirming some dates and events and altering others. What emerged from these interactions was the "collective memory" of the community, not always a consistent record in which all parties agreed on moments of transition, but overlapping narratives of change and continuity that showed discernible patterns.[8] It is this memory, accruing from the various discrete but interrelated historical structures that shape thought, behavior, and engagement with the wider world, that I have tried to present in this study of the Robert Taylor Homes.

Notes

Foreword

1. T. H. Marshall, *Class, Citizenship, and Social Development* (New York: Doubleday, 1964).

2. Barbara Schmitter-Heisler, "A Comparative Perspective on the Underclass," *Theory and Society,* 20: 455–483.

3. Mark Condon, "Public Housing, Crime and the Urban Labor Market: A Study of Black Youths in Chicago," working paper series, Malcolm Wiener Center for Social Policy, John F. Kennedy School of Government, Harvard University, 1991,

4. Ibid., p. 4.

5. Ibid.

Introduction

1. Because I have identified the housing development by its real name, I have taken measures to safeguard the identities of the participants. Names of people and locations have been changed to ensure anonymity, and minor changes have been made to street names and dates to protect the privacy of individuals.

2. The definitive examination of the postwar African-American experience can be found in the writings of William J. Wilson. See *The Declining Significance of Race: Blacks and Changing American Institutions* (Chicago: University of Chicago Press, 1980) and *The Truly Disadvantaged: The Inner City, the Underclass, and Public Policy* (Chicago: University of Chicago Press, 1987).

3. Robert E. Park, Ernest W. Burgess, and Roderick D. McKenzie, *The City* (Chicago: University of Chicago Press, 1925). For an overview, see Craig J. Calhoun, "Community: Toward a Variable Conceptualization for Comparative Research," *Social History,* 5(1) (1980).

4. The concern with community life and the production of social order has waned in the postwar era, having received less value in the face of a growing predilection for scientific and technocratic mastery in the social sciences. Notable postwar studies of urban communities include Herb Gans, *The Urban Villagers: Group and Class in the Life of Italian-Americans* (Glencoe: Free Press, 1962); Elijah Anderson, *Streetwise: Race, Class, and Change in an Urban Community* (Chicago: University of Chicago Press, 1990); Steven Gregory, *Black Corona: Race and the Politics of Place in an Urban Community* (Princeton: Princeton University Press, 1998); Gerald Suttles, *The Social Order of the Slum* (Chicago: University of Chicago Press, 1969); Ruth Horowitz, *Honor and the American Dream: Culture and Identity in a Chicano Community* (New Brunswick: Rutgers University Press, 1983); Mary Patillo, *Black Picket Fences: Privilege and Peril among the Black Middle Class* (Chicago: University of Chicago Press, 1999).

5. "Suburbia and the single-family house became the dominant setting for family life, not only in reality, but in the popular culture as well. Home ownership was literally in the air; it was more than a policy, it was a creed—an idea whose time had come." Barbara Kelly, *Expanding the American Dream: Building and Rebuilding Levittown* (Albany: State University of New York Press, 1993), p. 14. For a critical ethnographic study of the suburban lifestyle, see Herbert J. Gans, *The Levittowners: Ways of Life and Politics in a New Suburban Community* (New York: Pantheon Books, 1967).

6. Social scientists promulgated the distinction between ghetto and mainstream in rigid ways. See, for example, Elliot Liebow, *Tally's Corner: A Study of Negro Streetcorner Men* (Boston: Little, Brown, 1967); Ulf Hannerz, *Soulside: Inquiries into Ghetto Culture and Community* (New York: Columbia University Press, 1969). A critique of this perspective has been offered by Loic J. D. Wacquant, "Three Pernicious Premises in the Study of the American Ghetto," *International Journal of Urban and Regional Research* (July 1997): 341–353.

7. Morris Janowitz, *The Community Press in an Urban Setting: The Social Elements of Urbanism* (Chicago: University of Chicago Press, 1967).

8. The history of Chicago public housing appears in Arnold R. Hirsch, *Making the Second Ghetto: Race and Housing in Chicago, 1940–1960* (Chicago: University of Chicago Press, 1983), and Martin Meyerson and Edward C. Banfield, *Politics, Planning, and the Public Interest: The Case of Public Housing in Chicago* (Glencoe: Free Press, 1955).

9. One of the earliest uses of the term for Chicago's black ghetto is St. Clair Drake and Horace Cayton's masterly ethnography, *Black Metropolis: A Study of Negro Life in a Northern City* (Chicago: University of Chicago Press, 1945). The use of the term would continue after the Second World War but would be supplemented by the contrast of "mainstream" versus "ghetto-specific" behaviors, a distinction that had the same theoretical premise of separateness. See Hannerz, *Soulside;* and Lee Rainwater, *Be-*

hind Ghetto Walls: Black Families in a Federal Slum (Chicago: Aldine, 1970).

10. A historical analysis embodying this perspective is Manning Marable, *Race, Reform, and Rebellion: The Second Reconstruction in Black America, 1945–1982* (Jackson: University of Mississippi Press, 1984).

11. Du Bois combined statistical, historical, and ethnographic observation in a comprehensive study of Philadelphia's Seventh Ward community. See W. E. B. Du Bois, *The Philadelphia Negro* (Millwood, N.Y.: Kraus-Thompson Organization, Ltd., 1973). For a recent discussion of method and narrative in the context of Diasporic Africa, see Paul Gilroy, *The Black Atlantic: Modernity and Double Consciousness* (Cambridge, Mass.: Harvard University Press, 1993).

12. The use of ethnography and historical analysis has received much attention in the last two decades, particularly among anthropologists studying colonial processes. For an inquiry into the methodological problems posed by using participant observation alongside historical research techniques, see John and Jean Comaroff, *Ethnography and the Historical Imagination* (Boulder, Colo.: Westview Press, 1992); and Marshall Sahlins, *Historical Metaphors and Mythical Realities: Structures in the Early Sandwich Islands Kingdom* (Ann Arbor: University of Michigan Press, 1981). For a comparative study of social dynamics similar to this study of tenants and the state, see John L. Comaroff, "Dialectical Systems, History, and Anthropology: Units of Study, Questions of Theory," *Journal of Southern African Studies*, 8 (1982): 143–172.

13. To modify the observation of the historian William Sewell, Jr., written in the context of piecing together the language of French laborers in the post-*ancien* regime, "the key problem becomes the reconstruction of discourse out of fragmentary sources." Thus, like Sewell, I "have endeavored to treat from a single perspective phenomena that are usually thought to be essentially different in kind [as] all meaningful statements, as a set of interrelated texts that demand close reading and careful exegesis." *Work and Revolution in France: The Language of Labor from the Old Regime to 1848* (Cambridge, England: Cambridge University Press, 1980), pp. 9–12. See also Jeffrey K. Olick and Joyce Robbins, "Social Memory Studies: From 'Collective Memory' to the Historical Sociology of Mnemonic Practices," *Annual Review of Sociology*, 25 (1998): 105–140.

1. A Place to Call Home

1. *Chicago Housing Authority Times* (Chicago: Chicago Housing Authority, April 1962).

2. Ibid., October 1962.

3. See Peter Marcuse, "Interpreting 'Public Housing' History," *Journal of Architectural and Planning Research*, 12(3) (Autumn 1995).

4. See Keith Aoki, "Race, Space, and Place: The Relation between Architectural Modernism, Post-Modernism, Urban Planning, and Gentrification," *Fordham Law Journal* 20 (1993). The writings of Le Corbusier can be found in *The Ideas of Le Corbusier on Architecture and Urban Planning,* Jacques Guiton, ed. (New York: George Braziller, 1981).

5. David Brain, "From Public Housing to Private Communities: The Discipline of Design and the Materialization of the Public/Private Distinction in the Built Environment," in Jeff Alan Weintraub and Krishnan Kumar, eds., *Public and Private in Thought and Practice: Perspectives on a Grand Dichotomy* (Chicago: University of Chicago Press, 1997).

6. Ibid.

7. Quote appears in Karen A. Franck and Michael Mostoller, "From Courts to Open Space to Streets: Changes in the Site Design of U.S. Public Housing," *Journal of Architectural and Planning Research* 12:3 (1995): 205.

8. Ibid.

9. Under the direction of Elizabeth Wood in the 1940s, the CHA demonstrated a clear preference for high-rise construction. Nicholas Lemann, *The Promised Land: The Great Black Migration and How It Changed America* (New York: Vintage, 1992), p. 92.

10. Carl Condit, *Chicago, 1930–1970* (Chicago: University of Chicago Press, 1974), p. 159.

11. "The Chicago Wall," *Chicago Tribune,* December 2, 1986.

12. Devereux Bowley, Jr., *The Poorhouse: Subsidized Housing in Chicago* (Carbondale, Ill.: Southern Illinois University Press, 1978).

13. Quote appears in Bowley, *The Poorhouse,* p. 128. For additional commentary on Bauer's decision to critique high-rises, see Franck and Mostoller, "From Courts to Open Space to Streets."

14. Arvarh E. Strickland, *A History of the Chicago Urban League* (Urbana: University of Illinois Press, 1966), p. 168.

15. Bradford D. Hunt, "What Went Wrong with Public Housing?" paper presented at the the Newberry Urban History Group, Chicago, May 16, 1998, p. 3.

16. *Chicago Housing Authority Times* (Chicago: Chicago Housing Authority, April 1962).

17. Ibid., p. 1.

18. "City within a City: Robert R. Taylor Homes," a speech by Robert H. Murphy, appearing in *FREE: A Roosevelt University Magazine,* December 1962. See also *Chicago Housing Authority Statistical Report, 1962–1965* (Chicago: Chicago Housing Authority).

19. "City within a City," p. 6.

20. Dominic A. Pacyga and Ellen Skerrett, *Chicago, City of Neighborhoods: Histories and Tours* (Chicago: Loyola University Press, 1986).

21. See Kenneth E. Hinze, Donald J. Bogue, and Pierre Devise, *Population Projections: Chicago City and Suburban Ring, 1970–2000, by Age, Race, and Sex* (Chicago: Community and Family Study Center, University of Chicago, 1978). In the Grand Boulevard community, nearly 50 percent of the housing was unsound in the 1960s and two-thirds lacked "all plumbing facilities" (the comparable figure for the Washington Park community to the south was 52 percent). In both areas, 95 percent of residents rented their dwellings and less than 7 percent of property owners were non-white. See *Local Community Fact Book,* 1960.

22. The "Robert Taylor" series, *Chicago Tribune,* April 10–15, 1965.

23. "Modern Design for a City Ghetto: Robert R. Taylor Homes," *Look* (29), September 21, 1965.

24. To begin remedying the social and physical decline of the South Side Ghetto, a city needs assessment called for "provision of adequate community facilities, increased open space and improved business clubs," but the Daley administration could do no better than to administer urban renewal "[for] 30 to 50 percent of the area." Pierre Devise, *Chicago's Widening Color Gap* (Chicago: Inter-University Social Research Committee, 1967), p. 79. See also the *Near South Development Area Report* (Chicago: City of Chicago's Department of Development and Planning, 1967).

25. Harry J. Schneider to William L. Bergeron, August 25, 1964. CHA Manager's Reports (Chicago: Chicago Housing Authority Archives).

26. The Housing Authority used two strategies to ameliorate these situations. They leased apartments to outside agencies, such as the school board for temporary classroom space, that wished to deliver services to tenants (see Gus W. Master to William E. Bergeron, July 22, 1969, Chicago Housing Authority Management files [Chicago: Chicago Housing Authority Archives]). Alternatively, they allowed organizations to use the park space or the open areas in the housing development. Both failed, as Hunt ("What Went Wrong?" p. 20) writes, "The CHA leased apartments to numerous social service agencies to provide services, but the level of services provided never matched demand, as most programs were set up on an 'experimental' basis. When the Chicago Public Library opened a single 'Reading and Study Center' in a converted Taylor apartment in early 1969, residents quickly overwhelmed the facility and a second apartment was added."

27. Garth L. Mangum and Stephen F. Seninger, *Coming of Age in the Ghetto: A Dilemma of Youth Unemployment* (Baltimore: Johns Hopkins University Press, 1978); and William K. Tabb, *The Political Economy of the Black Ghetto* (New York: Norton, 1970).

28. Hinze et al., *Population Projections.*

29. Office of the Mayor of the City of Chicago, *Near South Development Area Report, 1967,* p. 16.

30. Outspoken elected and non-elected ghetto leaders waged a continuous battle with the mayor and the School Board for more school funds, but their efforts were largely unsuccessful, as the Board followed the mayor's

pro-segregationist policies by refusing to channel additional resources to black schools. Leaders also struggled, with limited success, to place enterprising black students in training and vocational schools operated by the city and in the white-dominated union apprenticeships. In the Chicago labor market, schools in working and poor communities were one of the primary channels through which young adults entered municipal and private-sector blue-collar jobs (Len O'Connor, *Clout: Mayor Daley and His City* [Chicago: H. Regerney, 1975]).

31. The open external galleries were equally problematic because residents threw appliances and refuse onto the heads of people standing on the ground below, and in one case a child died by falling through the cracks in the railing. In 1972, the CHA began installing floor-to-ceiling mesh wire. See G. W. Lebsock to John L. Waner, April 19, 1972, CHA Management Files (Chicago: Chicago Housing Authority).

32. Lemann, *The Promised Land.*

33. "Design for a City Ghetto," *Look,* vol. 29, September 21, 1965.

34. Gus W. Master, January 17, 1964, CHA Manager's Reports (Chicago: Chicago Housing Authority Archives).

35. "[Half Man's] choice was life in the present tense. School was an investment in a future he didn't believe in: there was little evidence . . . that tomorrow would be any better for young black men, and a lot that it might be worse . . . A lot of his homies . . . were dropping out, too, and for a time the Carters' apartment, 803, became their daytime clubhouse, a place where they could hang out, play cards, and fill the empty time with empty talk (Sylvester Monroe and Peter Goldman, with Vern E. Smith, *Brothers, Black and Poor: A True Story of Courage and Survival* [New York: Morrow, 1988], pp. 93–94).

36. Most of the "baby boomers" with whom I spoke argued that the majority of youths in Robert Taylor did not participate in street gangs in the 1960s.

37. Monroe and Goldman, *Brothers,* p. 34.

38. Sara Evans, "Women's History and Political Theory: Toward a Feminist Approach to Public Life," in Nancy A. Hewitt and Suzanne Lebsock, eds., *Visible Women: New Essays on American Activism* (Urbana: University of Illinois Press, 1993), pp. 120–139.

39. "City within a City," p. 12.

40. Ibid., p. 10.

41. Ulf Hannerz (*Soulside* [New York: Columbia University Press, 1969]) argues that most ghetto dwellers in the 1960s did not participate in organized political activity, but their consciousness about everyday life suggested that the basic aspects of making ends meet were deeply politicized. Most ethnographic studies of the ghetto poor did not see political activity as central in their study; see, for example, Rainwater, *Behind Ghetto Walls* (Chicago: Aldine, 1970); and Elliot Liebow, *Tally's Corner: A Study of Negro Streetcorner Men* (Boston: Little, Brown, 1970).

42. *Chicago Housing Authority Times* (Chicago: Chicago Housing Authority, April 1963).

43. Ibid.

44. Michel de Certeau, *The Practice of Everyday Life* (Berkeley: University of California Press, 1984).

45. For a more complete discussion of the practice of "inhabiting," see Henri Lefebvre, *Writings on Cities* (London: Blackwell, 1996).

46. One study reported in 1964 that the "Bronzeville" community neighboring Robert Taylor had the greatest rate of demolition, slum clearance, and residential and commercial eviction in the city. Jack Meltzer and Associates, *Relocation in Chicago* (Chicago: Community Renewal Program, City of Chicago, 1964), p. 173.

47. *Rehousing Families Displaced by Governmental Action in Chicago* (Chicago: Community Conservation Board, 1961).

48. "In their testimony, CHA officials admitted putting controls on the number of Negro families admitted to the four projects in white neighborhoods . . . [T]he U.S. District Court for the northern district of Illinois took note of the statistics on the racial composition of the four projects and the admission by authority officials that they had, in fact, sought to limit the number of Negro families in the projects [in white neighborhoods]" (Remark on Gautreaux Decision, *Journal of Housing*, 5 [1969]: 249).

49. *Chicago Housing Authority Times* (Chicago: Chicago Housing Authority, April 1962), p. 1.

50. See Hunt, "What Went Wrong?" for an extended discussion based on correspondence between CHA management officials.

51. "In Chicago, most everyone, including the Chairman and board members of CHA, and Mary McGuire, head of the U.S. Public Housing Administration, agreed that some public housing ghettos as Robert Taylor Homes were a mistake and should never have been built" (Devise, *Chicago's Widening Color Gap*, p. 112).

52. "Community culture is not immune to the allure of the culture of the wider society." Horowitz, *Honor and the American Dream*, p. 222.

53. The "Robert Taylor" series, *Chicago Daily News*, April 10, 1965.

54. Curtis Skinner, "Urban Labor Markets and Young Black Men: A Literature Review," *Journal of Economic Issues*, 39 (1995): 47–65, see p. 57; Andrew Brimmer, "Economic Situation of Blacks in the United States," *Review of Black Political Economy*, 2 (1972): 34–52. Manufacturing had been sluggish in the decade and blacks were laid off at disproportionately higher rates than other groups. Similarly, domestic-sector employment for blacks fell by 34 percent; the national figure was 21 percent. "From the mid-1950s through the 1960s, the black unemployment rate was more than double the white rate" (Brimmer, "Economic Situation of Blacks in the United States," p. 44). Jon P. Alston writes that in those rare cases when blacks were able to find employment in the suburbs, it was not

"white collar middle class" jobs, but typically blue-collar work ("The Black Population in Urbanized Areas, 1960," *Journal of Black Studies,* 1970, p. 438).

55. A typical mobility path for ghetto workers nationwide was from blue-collar work to the lower-paying service industries (Mike Davis, *Prisoners of the American Dream* [New York: Verso, 1983]), but many blacks were so "discouraged" by the poor economic field that awaited them that there was an "increasing tendency for [them] not even to look for jobs" (Brimmer, "Economic Situation of Blacks in the United States," p. 37).

56. The effect of the employment shifts on household formation in public housing was mediated by rules determining eligibility for public housing residence. Government legislation stipulated domestic arrangements for recipients of public assistance and for those who received housing subsidies, and in so doing placed constraints on the number of wage-earners in a public housing apartment. Although these regulations were altered after 1967 to permit some additional income supplementation, the public-aid recipient would still have to relinquish part of each dollar earned by a member of the household. These and other such proscriptions remained rigid enough to deter public housing leaseholders and aid recipients throughout the country from disclosing partners, spouses, and household members.

57. "Close cooperation among male and female siblings who share the same household or live near one another has been underestimated by those who have isolated the female household as the most significant domestic unit among the urban poor. A man and his kin contribute positive, valuable resources to his children and enlarge the circle of people both families can count on for help." Colin C. Blaydon and Carol B. Stack, "Income Support Policies and the Family," *Daedalus* (Spring 1977): 147–161.

58. See Joyce Ladner, *Tomorrow's Tomorrow: The Black Woman* (Lincoln: University of Nebraska Press, 1971).

59. Neither the record keeping by the CHA nor that of other administrative agencies permits more in-depth analysis of the forces creating multifamily households; even if such statistics were recorded, one would have to consider them critically owing to the need to hide wage earners from the state.

60. The use of "normal" to define this household arrangement appeared in all CHA statistical reports until the early 1970s. *Chicago Housing Authority Statistical Reports, 1964–1973* (Chicago: Chicago Housing Authority).

61. Lemann, *The Promised Land.*

62. "Dream of Progress Died Quickly at Taylor," *Chicago Tribune,* December 3, 1986.

63. Sixteen-story high-rises with external facing galleries were poor design choices. With only a door to protect them against the elements, apartments remained poorly heated in the winter. Apartments and elevators were both susceptible to direct contact with wind, rain, heat, and snow,

thereby increasing the rate of physical distress. The CHA was aware that such problems might occur. In their initial designs for the high-rise, all hallways were inside buildings, but to meet the $17,000 cost ceiling imposed by the federal government, they switched to external galleries. See "Stages II & III" Correspondence, June 26, 1959, CHA Project Ill 2–37 File, SMA Project 5176 (Chicago: Chicago Housing Authority Archives).

64. "Public Housing Modernization," *Journal of Housing* (April 1971).

65. Personal note, Gus W. Master, October 27, 1964 (Chicago: Chicago Housing Authority Archives).

66. See Paula Giddings, *When and Where I Enter: The Impact of Black Women on Race and Sex in America* (New York: Bantam, 1984).

67. Robert Halpern, *Rebuilding the Inner City: A History of Neighborhood Initiatives to Address Poverty in the United States* (New York: Columbia University Press, 1995).

68. "Public Housing Modernization," *Journal of Housing* (April 1971).

69. "Tenant Management Issues," *Journal of Housing* (October 1970).

70. "Chicago Housing Authority Chairman Expresses His Position on the CHA/Tenant Controversy," *Journal of Housing* (October 1970), p. 541.

71. "Tenants Win Acceptance of Demands during NAHRO National Housing Workshop," *Journal of Housing* (September 1970), pp. 70–72.

72. "CHA's Councils Don't Aid Tenants, Critics Contend," *Chicago Tribune*, October 4, 1987.

73. Ibid.

74. Arnold Hirsch, *Making the Second Ghetto: Race and Housing in Chicago, 1940–1960* (Cambridge, England: Cambridge University Press, 1983); Dempsey Travis, *An Autobiography of Black Politics* (Chicago: Urban Research Institute, 1987).

75. See "Tenant Management Issues" and "Chicago Housing Authority Chairman Expresses His Position on the CHA/Tenant Controversy."

76. Ronald Lawson and Stephen E. Barton, "Sex Roles in Social Movements: A Case Study of the Tenant Movement in New York City," *Signs: Journal of Women in Culture and Society,* 6 (1980): 230–247; Roberta M. Feldman, Susan Stall, and Patricia Wright, "The Community Needs to Be Built by Us: Women Organizing in Chicago Public Housing," in Nancy Naples, ed., *Community Activism and Feminist Politics: Organizing across Race, Class and Gender* (London: Routledge, 1998), pp. 257–274.

77. Kathleen M. Blee, "Introduction: Women on the Left/Women on the Right," in Kathleen M. Blee, ed., *No Middle Ground: Women and Radical Protest* (New York: New York University, 1998), p. 4. See also Patricia Hill Collins, *Black Feminist Thought: Knowledge, Consciousness, and the Politics of Empowerment* (Cambridge, Mass.: Harvard University Press, 1990), p. 47.

78. The concept of "social reproduction" was popularized by feminist scholars in the 1960s and 1970s to raise awareness of the non-valued work that
women performed both at home and in the workplace. See Evelyn
Nakano Glenn, "From Servitude to Service Work: Historical Continuities
in the Racial Division of Labor," *Signs: Journal of Women in Culture and
Society,* 18 (1992): 1–43.

79. Sara M. Evans and Harry C. Boyte, *Free Spaces: The Sources of Democratic
Change in America* (New York: Harper and Row Publishers, 1986).

2. Doing the Hustle

1. The "Robert Taylor" series, *Chicago Daily News,* April 10, 1975.

2. Pierre Devise, *Chicago's Widening Color Gap* (Chicago: Inter University
Social Research Committee, 1967).

3. *Chicago Housing Authority Statistical Report, 1970* (Chicago: Chicago
Housing Authority).

4. They would eventually admit that they were not providing the same protection and law enforcement in Robert Taylor as they were in other city
neighborhoods. "Chicago Project Dwellers Live under Siege," *New York
Times,* August 6, 1980.

5. William Julius Wilson, *The Truly Disadvantaged: The Inner City, the
Underclass, and Public Policy* (Chicago: University of Chicago Press,
1987), ch. 5.

6. Manning Marable, *Race, Reform and Rebellion: The Second Reconstruction in Black America, 1945–1982* (Jackson: University Press of Mississippi, 1984).

7. Eric Foner, "Organized Labor and the Black Worker in the 1970s," *The Insurgent Sociologist,* 8 (1978): 87–89. See also Manning Marable, "The Crisis of the Black Working Class: An Economic and Historical Analysis,"
Science and Society, 46 (Summer 1982).

8. See John McDermott, "Chicago Steps Back from Brink of Race Relations
Disaster," in Dick Simpson, ed., *Chicago's Future: An Agenda for Change*
(Chicago: University of Illinois Press, 1990).

9. For example, the LAC building president Edith Huddle tried unsuccess-
fully to obtain a law enforcement posture in Robert Taylor similar to the
short-lived 1971 experiment in the Cabrini-Green development,
whereby "officers from the Chicago Police Department are on duty inside the CHA development" ("Chicago Police Bring Security, Services in
Cabrini-Green," *Chicago Housing Authority Times,* January 1971). The
Housing Authority did not intend to replicate these schemes in Robert
Taylor or its other larger developments, sometimes preferring that residents police themselves (*Steps into the Seventies: A 1970 CHA Report*
[Chicago: Chicago Housing Authority]).

10. Sylvester Monroe and Peter Goldman, *Brothers, Black and Poor: A True Story of Courage and Survival* (New York: Morrow, 1988), p. 114.

11. St. Clair Drake and Horace Cayton, *Black Metropolis: A Study of Negro Life in a Northern City* (Chicago: University of Chicago Press, 1945).

12. Rufus Schatzberg and Robert J. Kelly, *African-American Organized Crime: A Social History* (New Brunswick, N.J.: Rutgers University Press, 1996).

13. Kevin J. Mumford, *Interzones: Black/White Sex Districts in Chicago and New York in the Early Twentieth Century* (New York: Columbia University Press, 1997).

14. Cyril Robinson, "The Production of Black Violence in Chicago," in David F. Greenberg, ed., *Crime and Capitalism: Readings in Marxist Criminology* (Philadelphia: Temple University Press, 1993).

15. Ramsey Clark and Roy Wilkins, *Search and Destroy: Commission of Inquiry into the Black Panthers and the Police* (New York: Metropolitan Applied Research Center, 1973).

16. D. Bradford Hunt, "What Went Wrong with Public Housing?: The Case of the Robert Taylor Homes," paper delivered at the Newberry Urban History Group, Chicago, May 16, 1998.

17. "'In the past,' [Commander Erskine] Moore said, 'police only responded to calls for help,'" "Metcalfe Outlines Fight on Taylor Homes Crime," *Chicago Sun Times*, June 17, 1974.

18. Similarly, the managers' reports and commissioners' memoranda in the Housing Authority's files do not show any reduced concern among tenants over inadequate police services, or offer any indication that the organization of law enforcement had shifted in any significant manner apart from the additional hiring of several security officers.

19. CHA officials who responded to security matters also included non-law enforcement bureaucrats such as "CHA managers" and "community and tenant relations coordinators."

20. Calvin H. Hall, the general counsel of the CHA, was responsible for responding to tenant complaints and lawsuits alleging that the CHA's failure to provide adequate maintenance was a cause of their insecurity. He often wrote letters of rebuttal to the regional counsel office of the Department of Housing and Urban Development. See HUD Project Files, 2–37 (Chicago: Chicago Housing Authority Archives).

21. See numerous letters written by Gus W. Master, the director of management, to tenants between 1971 and 1976. For example, see letter to Mr. Smith, December 3, 1974, CHA Manager's Reports (Chicago: Chicago Housing Authority Archives).

22. "Chicago Project Dwellers Live under Seige," *New York Times*, August 6, 1980.

23. The disproportionate share of funds supported law enforcement (e.g., hiring additional security guards and establishing additional perimeter pa-

trols), and some funds reached tenant self-enforcement programs (e.g., the twenty-four-hour tenant-patrol organizations). HUD also set aside "modernization" funds to physically secure lobbies with cameras and enclose ground-floor entrances.

24. "House to Probe Crime Woes in Taylor Homes," *Chicago Tribune,* July 28, 1978.

25. Chicago Housing Authority, *Steps into the Seventies.*

26. A classic early 1970s study of the complex interpersonal relationships and identities surrounding the world of hustling is Elijah Anderson, *A Place on the Corner* (Chicago: University of Chicago Press, 1976).

27. Edward Guerrero, *Framing Blackness: The African-American Image in Film* (Philadelphia: Temple University Press, 1993).

28. Bettylou Valentine, *Hustling and Other Hard Work: Life Styles in the Ghetto* (New York: Free Press, 1978), p. 120.

29. The most in-depth study of ghetto hustling in the 1970s is Bettylou Valentine, *Hustling.*

30. Carol Stack, *All Our Kin: Strategies for Survival in a Black Community* (New York: Harper, 1974); Anderson, *Place on the Corner,* 1976.

31. See Jagna Wojcicka Sharff, "The Underground Economy of a Poor Neighborhood," in Leith Mullings, ed., *Cities in the United States* (New York: Columbia University Press, 1987).

32. CHA officials carefully monitored these small entrepreneurial activities by watching over the daily receipts, auditing tenant finances, and conducting surprise inspections of daily receipts. See, for example, letter from Gus W. Master, March 15, 1971, CHA Manager's Reports (Chicago: Chicago Housing Authority Archives).

33. See Drake and Cayton, *Black Metropolis,* for a study of the "shady" in the neighborhoods surrounding Robert Taylor.

34. Francis Ianni has documented the ways in which illicit economies in African-American communities in the 1960s and 1970s relied on the social organization of the community in order to take root and thrive (*Black Mafia: Ethnic Succession Organized in Crime* [New York: Simon and Schuster, 1974], p. 122).

35. Henri Lefebvre, *The Production of Space,* trans. Donald Nicholson-Smith (Oxford: Blackwell, 1976).

36. Rhoda H. Halperin, *Cultural Economies: Past and Present* (Austin: University of Texas Press, 1994).

37. Letter from Ms. Evans to "Area Superintendent," June 10, 1976, CHA Manager's Reports (Chicago: Chicago Housing Authority Archives).

38. Mark Gottdiener, *Postmodern Semiotics: Material Culture and the Forms of Postmodern Life* (Oxford: Blackwell, 1995), p. 84.

39. Matthew Holden, "Black Politicians in the Time of the 'New' Urban Politics," *Review of Black Political Economy,* 2 (1971): 56–71.

40. Adolph Reed, "Black Particularity Reconsidered," *Telos* (Spring 1979), pp. 71–93.

41. Harold M. Baron, *Building Babylon: A Case of Racial Controls in Public Housing* (Evanston, Ill.: Northwestern University Press, 1971), p. 73.

42. See William J. Grimshaw, *Bitter Fruit: Black Politics and the Chicago Machine, 1931–1991* (Chicago: University of Chicago Press, 1992).

43. "Since the wealth of the black bourgeoisie is too inconsequential for this class to wield any political power, the role of Negro politicians has been restricted to attempting to satisfy the demands of Negro voters while acting as the servants of the political machines supported by the propertied classes in the white community." E. Franklin Frazier, *Black Bourgeoisie* (New York: Free Press, 1957), p. 105.

44. Stack, *All Our Kin.*

45. See Theodore L. Cross, *Black Capitalism: Strategy for Business in the Ghetto* (New York: Atheneum, 1970).

46. See Sharff, "Underground Economy"; Valentine, *Hustling;* and Stack, *All Our Kin.*

47. See Timothy Mason Bates, *Black Capitalism: A Quantitative Analysis* (New York: Praeger, 1973).

48. Joseph P. Gaughan and Louis A. Ferman, "Towards an Understanding of the Informal Economy," in *Annals of the American Academy of Political and Social Science,* 493 (1987): 15–25.

49. Ulf Hannerz, *Soulside* (New York: Columbia University Press, 1969), p. 14.

50. In a critique of this research tradition during that era, the anthropologist Richard Fox writes, "Once anthropologists of the ghetto find such heterogeneity [among the lifestyle of excluded and under-privileged populations] to exist, they commonly pursue its content and expression within the boundaries of the excluded populations rather than use it as an insight into the nature of industrial cities in their societies." Richard Fox, *Urban Anthropology: Cities in Their Cultural Settings* (Englewood Cliffs, N.J.: Prentice-Hall, 1977), p. 143.

51. Lee Rainwater offers the most grievous example of the error of separating the quotidian aspects of ghetto life from the ghetto's larger place in society when he writes, "This book, in short, is about intimate personal life in a particular ghetto setting. It does not analyze the larger institutional, social structural, and ideological forces that provide the social, economic, and political context in which lower-class Negro life is lived." See *Behind Ghetto Walls: Black Families in a Federal Slum* (Chicago: Aldine, 1970), p. 3.

3. "What's It Like to Be in Hell?"

1. See Carl Taylor, *Dangerous Society* (East Lansing: Michigan State University Press, 1990). An excellent comparative study of drug dealing by different ethnic groups is Mercer L. Sullivan, *Getting Paid: Youth, Crime, and Work in the Inner City* (Ithaca: Cornell University Press, 1989).

2. The quote appears in D. Garth Taylor, *Minority Housing in Chicago* (Chicago: Chicago Urban League, 1988).

3. William Julius Wilson, *The Truly Disadvantaged: The Inner City, the Underclass, and Public Policy* (Chicago: University of Chicago Press, 1987), p. 21.

4. Richard B. Freeman has concluded that for black youth in the 1980s, crime was driven by the need to earn income, that is, it was "not a deviant behavior on the margin." "Crime and Employment of Disadvantaged Youth," paper presented at the Urban Poverty Workshop, University of Chicago, September 1991.

5. By the late 1980s, 25 percent of young black males would be on parole, probation, or incarcerated, compared with 6 percent of young white males. Clarence Lusane, *Pipe Dream Blues: Racism and the War on Drugs* (Boston, Mass.: South End Press, 1991), p. 23.

6. In Chicago, the Wentworth police district, which housed the Robert Taylor Homes, was considered to be the most violent area in the city: 3.4 percent of Chicago's inhabitants lived in the area, but 11 percent of the city's murders, 9 percent of its rapes, and 13 percent of its aggravated assaults occurred there. Wilson, *Truly Disadvantaged,* pp. 21–26.

7. See Lusane, *Pipe Dream Blues,* for data that dispel the myth that blacks were more prone to crime than whites in the 1980s.

8. Martin Sloane, "The 1983 Housing Act: A Leap Backward," *Journal of Housing* (July/August 1984), pp. 112–113.

9. Of the many ways to measure the effects of Reagan's policies, one statistic is particularly dramatic. In 1980, there were already 500,000 homeless in America; by 1990, there would be 2,000,000.

10. Robert A. Slayton, *The Reagan Approach to Housing: An Examination of Local Impact* (Chicago: Chicago Urban League, 1987), p. 1.

11. Ibid., p. 15.

12. *Community Development Study: Grand Boulevard Washington Park, Target Area* (Chicago: Chicago Urban League, June 1982).

13. Slayton, *Reagan Approach to Housing,* p. 21.

14. Taylor, *Minority Housing in Chicago.*

15. "Chicago Urged to Raze Public Housing Units," *Los Angeles Times,* July 16, 1988.

16. In the mid-1980s, forty-one of fifty-six elevators were dysfunctional, and

Robert Taylor required $62 million in rehabilitation ("Chicago Wall" series, *Chicago Tribune,* December 5, 1986). Vandalism cost the CHA nearly $5,000 per day, but even this was insufficient to keep pace with the vandals' damage to elevators, windows, lighting systems, and public grounds. See also Editorial, *Chicago Tribune,* December 14, 1986.

17. "CHA Fighting a Losing Battle with Maintenance," *Chicago Tribune,* July 17, 1988, and "CHA Establishes Framework for Support from Business Charity," *Chicago Tribune,* December 5, 1988. As an interesting comparison, whereas the CHA was spending about $1,000 per unit for maintenance, at least $2,000 was needed for a comparable low-income private-sector housing unit.

18. See "CHA Establishes Framework for Support from Business Charity," and "CHA Seeks $75.8 Million from HUD for Rehab Work," *Chicago Tribune,* March 23, 1988.

19. *Chicago's Public Housing Crisis: Causes and Solutions* (Chicago: Chicago Urban League, 1988).

20. Ibid., p. 1.

21. In one year alone (1987), the CHA cut its craft and maintenance workforce by 30 percent, while requests for their services were increasing ("CHA Fighting a Losing Battle on Maintenance," *Chicago Tribune,* July 17, 1988). The agency explained this fiscal policy by suggesting that the federal government requires too much paperwork and non-productive accounting. Chicago Urban League, *Chicago's Public Housing Crisis.*

22. Chicago Urban League, *Chicago's Public Housing Crisis.*

23. "There is some evidence that CHA has a policy of emptying buildings in areas where development is taking place." Ibid., p. 13.

24. "New Day for CHA as Bad as the Old One," *Chicago Tribune,* December 12, 1986.

25. Quote appears in "Leadership Battle Keeps CHA in Basement," *Chicago Tribune,* December 11, 1986. In its own evaluation of CHA management from 1984 until 1987, a HUD report stated that "the findings of the review indicate that the CHA Board of Commissioners was ineffective in carrying out its responsibilities." Management Review of the Chicago Housing Authority, Housing and Urban Development (Chicago: Chicago Housing Authority files, HUD Correspondence, April 18, 1999).

26. Compared with those living in "all white areas," public housing residents were involved disproportionately in violent crimes. "[Residents of Chicago public housing] are less likely to be the victims of robbery, burglary or theft. In fact, people who live in all-white areas of Chicago are twice as likely to be theft victims as those who live in CHA high rises. But, those high rise residents are 13 times more likely to be the victims of violent crime." Taylor, "Minority Housing in Chicago."

27. Census data reveal that only 20 percent of the tenant body older than sixteen years of age had a high school diploma.

28. "Chicago Project Dwellers Live under Siege," *New York Times,* August 6, 1980.

29. Chicago Urban League, *Chicago's Public Housing Crisis.*

30. "Tenant Groups Get Big Bucks from CHA," *Chicago Tribune,* March 20, 1988.

31. "CHA Councils Don't Aid Tenants, Critics Contend," *Chicago Tribune,* October 4, 1987. See also "Tenant Management No Public Housing Cure," *Chicago Tribune,* December 10, 1986.

32. For a study of these dynamics in another large Chicago high-rise public housing complex, see Ed Marciniak, *Reclaiming the Inner City: Chicago's Near North Revitalization Confronts Cabrini Green* (Washington, D. C.: National Center for Urban Ethnic Affairs, 1986).

33. The product was *Public Housing Security Manual for the City of Chicago,* Housing Research and Development (Urbana-Champaign: University of Illinois, 1981).

34. Ibid., p. 17.

35. Ibid., p. 14.

36. "Under our Anti-Crime Program . . . we propose to implement a security program at two contiguous high rise developments, Robert Taylor Homes and Stateway Gardens. At Taylor Homes, we propose to provide each of the 28 buildings with enclosed and controlled lobbies and rehabilitated elevators under the PHUIP Targeted Rehabilitation Program. We also propose to install security fencing around the buildings at Taylor Homes." Letter from CHA Chairman Charles R. Swibel to Lawrence B. Simons (Chicago: Chicago Housing Authority Archives, August 22, 1979).

37. See *Chicago Tribune* between December 14 and December 21, 1986.

38. *Chicago Tribune,* July 18, 1987.

39. *Final Report: Urban Initiatives Anti-Crime Program at Robert Taylor Homes and Stateway Gardens* (Chicago: Department of Planning, 1983); *Proposal for Planning Recommendations: Robert Taylor Homes Urban Initiatives Program and Stateway Gardens Anti-Crime Program* (Chicago: James H. Lowry and Associates, 1983).

40. See "Crime Rate up in CHA by 9 Percent," *Chicago Tribune,* June 23, 1988.

41. Chairman Swibel defended the CHA's comprehensive security program for the Robert Taylor Homes by invoking the "natural boundaries" that separated the housing development from surrounding communities, which he felt was an important feature both for facilitating a concentrated security initiative within public housing and for warding off the possible exposure of the surrounding residential communities to high-rise developments. "Displacement [of crime] would not occur [from Robert Taylor and Stateway Gardens] into the surrounding community because of the natural boundaries (train tracks, major commercial streets, expressway

and vacant commercial property), which separate the development from the surrounding community and because of the greater level of security in the design of low-rise buildings which comprise the surrounding community." Letter from CHA Chairman Charles R. Swibel to Lawrence B. Simons, August 22, 1979.

42. Jane Jacobs, *The Death and Life of Great American Cities* (New York: Vintage, 1961), p. 402.

43. "The first thing to understand is that the public peace—the sidewalk and street perch—of cities is not kept primarily by the police, necessary as police are. It is kept primarily by an intricate, almost unconscious network of voluntary controls and standards among the people themselves, and enforced by the people themselves . . . First, there must be a clear demarcation between what is public space and what is private space. Second, there must be eyes upon the street." Quote of Jane Jacobs appears in Philip Kasinitz, *Metropolis: Centre and Symbol of Our Time* (Houndmills: Macmillan, 1995), pp. 113–115.

44. Chicago Urban League, *Chicago's Public Housing Crisis;* "Crime Rate in CHA up by 9 Percent," *Chicago Tribune,* June 23, 1988.

45. See "Tenant Management No Public Housing Cure," *Chicago Tribune,* December 12, 1986; "Leadership Battle Keeps CHA in Basement," *Chicago Tribune,* December 11, 1986; and "CHA's Councils Don't Aid Tenants, Critics Contend," *Chicago Tribune,* October 4, 1987.

46. See "CHA Chief Links Project Managers to Gangs," *Chicago Tribune,* July 2, 1988.

47. Police spokespersons suggest that court prohibitions in the 1970s put an end to the use of the practice, yet officers I spoke with admit to its use in public housing.

48. See John Hagedorn, *People and Folks: Gangs, Crime and the Underclass in a Rustbelt City* (Chicago: Lake View Press, 1988), p. 151, for a comparison with Milwaukee, Wisconsin.

49. Manuel Castells, *From City to Grassroots* (Berkeley, Calif.: University of California Press, 1983).

50. Malcolm Klein refutes the popular misconception that supergang formation arose as a consequence of the crack economy. See *The American Street Gang: Its Nature, Prevalence, and Control* (New York: Oxford University Press, 1995), p. 134.

51. For the written bylaws of most of the well-known Chicago gang families, see Appendix C in George W. Knox, *An Introduction to Gangs* (Bristol, Ind.: Wyndham Hall, 1991).

52. See Irving A. Spergel, "Youth Gangs: Continuity and Change," *Crime and Justice: A Review of Research,* 12 (1990): 202. For general considerations, see Martin Gold and Hans W. Mattick, *Experiment in the Streets: The Chicago Youth Development Project* (Ann Arbor: University of Michigan, Institute for Social Research, 1974).

53. For an overview of this process, see Spergel, "Continuity and Change"; Felix Padilla, *The Gang as an American Enterprise* (New Brunswick, N.J.: Rutgers University Press, 1992); J. Michael Olivero, *Honor, Violence and Upward Mobility: A Case Study of Chicago's Street Gangs during the 1970s and 1980s* (Edinburg, Tex.: Pan American Press).

54. For an insightful analysis of the role of gangs in prison during the 1960s and 1970s, see James B. Jacobs, *Stateville: The Penitentiary in Mass Society* (Chicago: University of Chicago Press, 1977).

55. For a more detailed analysis of the "corporatization" of Chicago's street gangs after 1970, see Sudhir Venkatesh and Steven D. Levitt, "Are We a Family or a Business?": History and Disjuncture in the Urban American Street Gang," *Theory and Society,* 29 (2000).

56. Martin Jankowski argues that modern gangs are best understood as a group of "defiant individuals" who must suspend (to a minimal degree) their non-conformity and disdain for authority—as well as their self-interested pursuits—so that group cohesion can be maintained. Jankowski, *Islands in the Street: Gangs and American Urban Society* (Berkeley: University of California Press, 1991).

57. Ruth Horowitz was one of few observers examining the community's "tolerance" for gang activity. See Horowitz, *Honor and the American Dream: Culture and Identity in a Chicano Community* (New Brunswick, N.J.: Rutgers University Press, 1983).

58. "There is no evidence that large increases in drug trafficking can be significantly attributed to the activities of street gangs . . . But there may be some connections between the drug trade and particular gang members who become at some point employees of criminal adult organizations." Irving Spergel, *The Youth Gang Problem: A Community Approach* (New York: Oxford University Press, 1995).

59. See Ruth Horowitz, "Community Tolerance of Gang Violence," *Social Problems* 34(5) (December 1987), p. 449, and *Honor and the American Dream,* p. 197.

60. I conducted an informal survey of consumers by observing drug purchasing at one of the Black Kings' most lucrative sales spots, near Twenty-ninth Street. With the help of the BK "lookout," whose responsibility was to stand and watch for police officers, I counted the number of consumers who lived in the housing development and those who came from other areas. Roughly 40 percent of the consumers were residents of Robert Taylor, 55 percent were from other neighborhoods, and 5 percent could not be identified with certainty.

61. "CHA Flat Vacancies Soaring," *Chicago Tribune,* June 26, 1988.

62. Two CHA security personnel, along with the commander of the gang tactical unit in Robert Taylor, argue that CHA had handed over responsibility for gang-related activities to Chicago police owing to pressure from Chicago police officials who did not want to yield jurisdiction to another law enforcement body. However, HUD officials, who already had been

cutting their budgets, wanted the CHA to make law enforcement measures a priority. CHA officials were left with few options, one of them being to concentrate on the placement of guards in lobbies and the creation of a separate public housing police force that conducted patrols outside, but that did not disrupt the tactical and gang-intelligence wings of the department that conducted raids inside buildings.

63. In July 1988, as part of his new management philosophy, Chairman Lane admitted that crime and vacancies were related. "The units become vacant and the gang members go up and strip [them]. It doesn't matter if it's nailed down. They take everything. They haul it out and they take it." "CHA Chief Links Projects Managers to Gangs," *Chicago Tribune,* July 2, 1988.

64. These reports became public, but only in 1988, as a result of Chairman Vincent Lane's decision to revamp existing CHA security police. See "CHA Chief Blasts Guards at Projects," *Chicago Tribune,* August 13, 1988; "Managers Challenge CHA Chief over Gang, Drug Accusations," *Chicago Tribune,* July 8, 1988; "CHA Chief Links Project Managers to Gangs," *Chicago Tribune,* July 2, 1988.

65. "Perspective," *Chicago Tribune,* July 27, 1988.

66. See Mike Davis, *Prisoners of the American Dream: Politics and Economy in the History of the U.S. Working Class* (London: Verso, 1986).

67. See Richard A. Cloward and Frances Fox Piven, "The Welfare State in an Age of Industrial Working Class Decline," *Smith College Studies in Social Work* (March 1986).

4. Tenants Face Off with the Gang

1. Mikhail Bakhtin, *Rabelais and His World* (Bloomington: Indiana University Press, 1984), p. 8.

2. The progressive variant to which people compare the Black Kings is the Illinois Black Panther Party. The militant referent would be the Blackstone Rangers street gang.

3. "Crime Rate up by 9 Percent," *Chicago Tribune,* June 23, 1988.

4. Martin Sanchez Jankowski, *Islands in the Street: Gangs and American Urban Society* (Berkeley: University of California Press, 1991).

5. The core-peripheral distinction is a classic one among scholars who have studied street gangs. Typically, scholars identify a much smaller core group, but a "corporate" gang managing an economic operation over a 1.5-mile stretch has tremendous labor needs; thus, it is expected that a greater number of individuals would be "core" BK members. See Steven D. Levitt and Sudhir Venkatesh, "The Financial Activities of an Urban Streeet Gang," *Quarterly Journal of Economics* (Summer 2000).

6. Prince reintroduced a BK custom that encouraged members to graduate from high school; in 1990, only members over the age of eighteen could

sell narcotics. After 1993, however, BK leaders did not strictly enforce the edict.

7. For a discussion of the gang's historic role in the black community from the perspective of an Illinois Black Panther Party member seeking to turn the gangs away from crime, see John F. Rice, *Up on Madison, Down on 75: A History of the Illinois Black Panther Party* (Evanston, Ill.: The Committee, 1982).

8. See Ruth Horowitz, *Honor and the American Dream: Culture and Identity in a Chicano Community* (New Brunswick, N.J.: Rutgers University Press, 1983); Gerald D. Suttles, *The Social Order of the Slum: Ethnicity and Territory in the Inner City* (Chicago: University of Chicago Press, 1968).

9. See Albert Cohen, *Delinquent Boys* (Glencoe, Ill.: Free Press, 1955); Lewis Yablonsky, *The Violent Gang* (New York: Macmillan Publishing Company, 1966).

10. The term "gangland" appears in Frederic Thrasher, *The Gang* (Chicago: University of Chicago Press, 1927), to refer to those spaces where gangs are prevalent in the metropolis. The link between employment and exiting out was not studied consistently before the postwar era. In William Foote Whyte's classic ethnography, *Street Corner Society: The Social Structure of an Italian Slum* (Chicago: University of Chicago Press, 1943), Depression-era gangs appeared unable to find work and so continued to remain a juvenile delinquent group well into adulthood.

11. The incorporation of life-historical data in an understanding of the development of Anthony, Prince, and the other BK leaders is motivated by the writings of the sociologist Robert J. Sampson, whose own research into criminal careers has changed the way social scientists conceive of marginal behavior. A noteworthy publication, co-authored with John H. Laub, is *Crime in the Making: Pathways and Turning Points through Life* (Cambridge, Mass.: Harvard University Press, 1993).

12. The increasing numbers of adults remaining in the gang has been documented by several researchers (see Irving A. Spergel, "Youth Gangs: Continuity and Change," in Norval Morris, ed., *Crime and Justice: A Review of Research,* 12 [1990], p. 219; and Horowitz, *Honor and the American Dream*). For data on Chicago, see Eugene Useni Perkins, *Explosion of Chicago's Black Street Gangs* (Chicago: Third World Press, 1987). John Hagedorn, in *People and Folks: Gangs, Crime, and the Underclass in a Rust-Belt City* (Chicago: Lake View Press, 1988), pp. 124–125, tracked 260 "founding" members of Milwaukee's African-American gangs and reported that "the entire group, nearly all between eighteen and twenty-five at the time of the interviews, were still hanging out on the same street corners where they began the gang five to eight years before . . . only ten percent were reported to us as employed full time, nearly three quarters were reported to us to be still involved in the gang." He notes that for the adults, gang membership is motivated not necessarily by an interest in "fighting," but rather by a need for "survival" since the gang is a means by which to locate resources and support.

13. The adaptation view has been promoted most forcefully by scholars who emphasize the link between the formation of American "underclass" communities and gang involvement (see Irving A. Spergel, *The Youth Gang Problem: A Community Approach* [New York: Oxford University Press, 1995], pp. 150–152). This account often rings too fatalistic; youth seemed destined for gangs given their objective circumstances. James Diego Vigil and S. C. Yun write, "This marginality complex, in turn, prevents many youths from attaining their version of the American dream via traditional pathways of education and hard work. Unable to adopt the dominant culture, they turn to gangs as a means of acquisition without assimilation." In slight contrast to his account, the BK leaders actually turned to the gang in order "to adopt the dominant culture" ("Vietnamese Youth Gangs in Southern California," in C. Ronald Huff, ed., *Gangs in America*, 1st ed. [Newbury Park, Calif.: Sage, 1990], p. 147).

14. For example, Spergel argues that "changes in the structure of the economy may have been largely responsible for the entry of gang members, as individuals and cliques, into drug trafficking. Changing labor market conditions in the 1960s and 1970s, especially the decrease of low-skilled manufacturing jobs, made it difficult for older gang youth to find legitimate employment and leave the teenage gang. Economic survival and the illegal drug economy created pressures to develop the youth gang as an economic base of opportunities as well as social status" (Spergel, *Youth Gang Problem*, p. 45). Others continue a psychological tradition by arguing that contemporary gangs are composed of "defiant individualists" who will leave the gang (and reenter) in a rational way pursuant to their self-interests (Jankowkski, *Islands in the Street*, p. 62). Although its emphasis is on individual cognition, the defiant-individualist thesis is not necessarily antithetical to the "underclass" hypothesis since an individual's decision to join a gang-controlled economy may be explained as a rational response to limited mainstream opportunities.

15. The refusal "to collude in their own educational suppression" is meant to introduce an idea of Marxist cultural analysis explicated by the sociologists Pierre Bourdieu and Jean Claude Passeron in their study of contemporary educational systems, namely, that "deviance"—in this case, refusing to believe in the "achievement ideology"—is, from the perspective of the excluded, a fairly accurate assessment of the impossibility of succeeding in a system in which the dominant groups "ensure the success of their own offspring and thus the reproduction of class position and privilege." See Paul Willis, *Learning to Labor: How Working Class Kids Get Working Class Jobs* (London: Saxon House, 1977).

16. Jay MacLeod, *Ain't No Making It: Aspirations and Attainment in a Low-Income Neighborhood* (Boulder, Colo.: Westview Press, 1995), p. 15.

17. Ibid.

18. Jankowski, *Islands in the Street*, p. 47.

19. See *In Search of Respect: Selling Crack in El Barrio* (Cambridge, England: Cambridge University Press, 1995).

20. For an insightful theoretical discussion of the life histories of African-American young men in poor social contexts, see Alford A. Young, Jr., "The (Non) Accumulation of Capital: Explicating the Relationship of Structure and Agency in the Lives of Poor Black Men," *Sociological Theory,* 17:2 (July 1999): 201–227.

21. Hagedorn's study of older gang members found a similar pattern among a large "core" group of drug-selling members who "aspired to settling down, getting married, and living at least a watered-down version of the American dream." See "Homeboys, Dope Fiends, Legits, and New Jacks," *Criminology,* 32(2): 197–219, quote from p. 209.

22. See William J. Wilson, *The Truly Disadvantaged: The Inner City, the Underclass, and Public Policy* (Chicago: University of Chicago Press, 1987).

23. "At-Risk Youth Learning to Earn," *Chicago Tribune,* October 19, 1986. A 1982 Housing and Urban Development report sparked national attention when it affirmed law enforcement declarations that the "underground economy seems successful in providing meaningful employment to many inner-city dwellers . . . especially in relationship to employing the so-called unemployables [such as minorities and youth]" (Op-Ed, *Washington Post,* July 28, 1982). In the report, the federal agency emphasized the need to identify why the underground economy, not its mainstream counterpart, could successfully "overcome barriers to minority teen-age employment." "Do minority and teenagers achieve any degree of upward mobility in the underground economy?" it asked, "[and] if so, what are their typical career paths?" ("Underground Entrepreneurs," *Washington Post,* July 23, 1982).

24. "Milwaukee's gang founders today thought there is little or no discrimination against blacks. They believed that experiences in the secondary labor market, for example in applying for a job at a McDonalds, had nothing to do with discrimination. The problem . . . is lack of skills needed to advance from a dead-end job to a 'good job.'" In the absence of "good jobs," the "hustling" outlook is entrenching itself among poor minority youth (Hagedorn, *People and Folks,* p. 141).

25. A lower-ranking member would not be able to accumulate substantial revenue because his earnings would be tightly controlled by the gang leader.

26. For gang leaders, the underground economy can be lucrative, but this is not the case for the majority of members, who generally make about minimum wage. See Levitt and Venkatesh, "The Financial Activities of an Urban Street Gang."

27. The gang members studied by the sociologist Ruth Horowitz *(Honor and the American Dream)* demonstrated a clear preference for work that allowed them to escape the continuous oversight or "strict supervision" of a boss or superior.

28. Irving Spergel has made a similar observation with regard to the difficulty of conducting gang intervention, when the context is ghettos that "tend to

be chaotic, with institutional arrangements highly fragmented. Offenders in such contexts are hardly connected to structured community situations other than the gang, which is ordinarily a model of stable structure and activity." *Youth Gang Problem,* p. 259.

29. "Gangs," writes the criminologist Jeff Fagan, "reflect patterns of affiliation and collective behavior *that are similar to those of other adolescent subcultures* [*and*] violence, which has historically been taken as a defining feature of gangs, and drug involvement may more accurately be conceptualized as contingent behavior among adolescents" (Fagan, "The Social Organization of Drug Use and Drug Dealing among Urban Gangs," *Criminology* 27 [1989]: 633–669, quote appears on p. 637, emphasis added). As Fagan correctly goes on to argue, "such contingencies rarely have received theoretical or empirical attention in prior research" ("Social Organization," p. 637).

30. "Beyond the unsystematic collection of anecdotal reports, there is little solid evidence to support the assertion of an increase in gang violence over the last decade or two. Our survey report of homicides in 1991 speaks to levels, not increases. It's all inferential beyond that." Malcolm W. Klein, *The American Street Gang: Its Nature, Prevalence, and Control* (New York: Oxford University Press, 1995), p. 116.

31. Malcolm Klein offers convincing evidence that the media hype surrounding "drive-by" shootings in the 1980s was not supported by evidence. "Drive-bys are certainly not new," Klein writes. He admits that they have increased, but not at levels that justify media and law enforcement attention. *American Street Gang,* pp. 117–118.

32. See ibid.

5. Street-Gang Diplomacy

1. Although the concept of "social isolation" captures the exclusion of the urban poor from mainstream institutions, it is also a useful term to explain the marginalization of segments of the urban poor within their own communities. See William J. Wilson, *The Truly Disadvantaged: The Inner City, the Underclass, and Public Policy* (Chicago: University of Chicago Press, 1987).

2. The "elite" tier of service providers in urban communities refers to established organizations that are able to consistently help select segments of the local populace by virtue of their staff size, up-to-date facilities, and political clout in wider philanthropic and funding circles. They are not without their own hardships, but they have made conscious efforts not to focus on the most troubled segments, such as gangs and public housing tenants. See Sudhir Venkatesh, "The Three-Tier Model: How Helping Occurs in Poor Communities," *Social Service Review,* 71(4) (December 1997): 574–606.

3. Useni Eugene Perkins argues that community institutions in Chicago have always been ineffective in working with gangs. See *Explosion of Chicago's Black Street Gangs* (Chicago: Third World Press, 1987).

4. Malcolm W. Klein, *The American Street Gang: Its Nature, Prevalence and Control* (New York: Oxford University Press, 1995), p. 160.

5. In BITE, teams of eighteen CHA officials and Chicago police "converge[d] secretively upon a building to root out gang activity, narcotics trafficking and weapons caches. The required police discussions with tenants were sidebars to the more intrusive searches and seizures." "Many Welcome Return of Patrols as Overdue," *Chicago Sun-Times,* April 17, 1994.

6. See Irving A. Spergel, *The Youth Gang Problem: A Community Approach* (New York: Oxford University Press, 1995), for an overview of law enforcement approaches to street gangs.

7. Harold R. Johnson, Donald R. Deskins, Jr., and Lawrence S. Root, *The Greater Grand Boulevard Area: A Review for Chicago Community Trust* (Ann Arbor: University of Michigan, 1996), p. 24.

8. "The need for therapeutic services for adolescent children and families [that target such problems as juvenile delinquency, gang and family violence, substance-abuse problems, youth unemployment, and adolescent pregnancies] is the major gap in the system of services in the Greater Grand Boulevard Area" (ibid., p. 24). The same over-reliance on police was occurring in Milwaukee (John Hagedorn, *People and Folks: Gangs, Crime, and the Underclass in a Rust-Belt City* [Chicago: Lake View Press, 1988]).

9. *The Robert Taylor Initiative* (Chicago: Chicago Department of Public Health, 1995).

10. Ibid., p. 11.

11. Sudhir Venkatesh, "Community-Based Interventions into Street Gang Activity," *Journal of Community Psychology* (September 1991): 1–18.

12. The "Beethoven Project," at the Center for Successful Child Development in Robert Taylor, was a great boon for families of young children, but it was exemplary of organizations that had only minimal desire to enter the community's "political affairs." For an evaluation of the program, see James F. Short Jr., "Personal, Gang, and Community Careers," in C. Ronald Huff, ed., *Gangs in America,* 2nd ed. (Newbury Park: Sage Publications, 1996).

13. The service providers' de-politicization of their role in urban poor communities must be tied to increasing conservatism in the service delivery of individuals in social work fields. See Stanley Wenocur and Michael Reisch, "Author's Reply," *Social Service Review* 62(3) (1987): 267–268. See also Barbara Levy Simon, *The Empowerment Tradition in American Social Work* (New York: Columbia University Press, 1994); Robert R. Roberts, *Social Work in Juvenile and Criminal Justice Settings* (Springfield, Ill.: Charles C. Thomas Publishers, 1983). See also the collection of essays in *Smith College Studies in Social Work,* March 1986.

14. For a trenchant critique of the use of "social disorganization," see Loic J. D. Wacquant, "Three Pernicious Premises in the Study of the American Ghetto," *International Journal of Urban and Regional Research* (July 1997): 341–353; quote p. 346.

15. Ibid., p. 347.

16. Martin Sanchez Jankowski, *Islands in the Street: Gangs and the American Urban Society* (Berkeley: University of California Press, 1991).

17. See Spergel, *Youth Gang Problem* (p. 251) for a historical overview of the "use of gang structure" approach in American cities.

18. "Gang programs have always been initiated in response to the inflexibility of traditional youth programs" (Hagedorn, *People and Folks,* p. 147).

19. The criminologist Jeffrey Fagan has made this general point by noting that families with other "immediate concrete issues," such as rent payments and medical care, may privilege those concerns rather than activities that involve the presence of street gangs. "Neighborhood Education, Mobilization, and Organization for Juvenile Crime Prevention," *Annals of the American Academy of Political and Social Science,* 494 (November 1987): 55–70.

20. See Spergel, *Youth Gang Problem,* for an overview of these programs.

21. Ibid., p. 252.

22. Klein, *American Street Gang,* p. 138.

23. See Hagedorn, *People and Folks,* for a brief review.

24. Frederic Thrasher, *The Gang* (Chicago: University of Chicago Press, 1927).

25. See Gerald D. Suttles, *The Social Order of the Slum: Ethnicity and Territory in the Inner City* (Chicago: University of Chicago Press, 1968).

26. See Hagedorn, *People and Folks.*

27. Klein writes that "most gangs are relatively age-graded, autonomous units" (Klein, *American Street Gang*). But Irving Spergel, challenging Klein's view, writes, "Gangs with the same name are now 'spread' or developed across many communities. Gang members and units or sections increasingly identify themselves as part of nations. Population movements of minority groups, local community structural changes, and the greater economic survival concerns of gang youths may be responsible for these changing gang organizational patterns" (*Youth Gang Problem,* p. 76).

28. Spergel, *Youth Gang Problem,* presents a thorough and critical review of the evidence for and against the thesis that street gangs are complex organizational entities that span neighborhoods and that are linked in hierarchical command structures and underground commercial webs.

29. Spergel, *Youth Gang Problem,* pp. 75–76.

30. See J. Michael Olivero, *Honor, Violence and Upward Mobility: A Case Study of Chicago Gangs during the 1970s and 1980s* (Edinburg, Tex.: University of Texas-Pan American Press, 1991).

31. Hagedorn offers an interesting account of cross-neighborhood street-gang development in Milwaukee. Forced busing of schoolchildren into unfamiliar neighborhoods led to racially homogenous peer-group formation and the use of such groups for protection against intimidation and physical harassment. Gangs formed through the process of maturation. Hagedorn also writes that 80 percent of the founders of the gangs grew up in the same neighborhood, but five years after they formed the gang, the majority recruited new members elsewhere, leaving the neighborhood as a "place to hang out," as opposed to a "turf" to be defended (Hagedorn, *People and Folks,* p. 147).

32. See Camille Graham Camp and George M. Camp, *Management Strategies for Combatting Prison Gang Violence* (South Salem, N.Y.: Criminal Justice Institute, 1988).

33. Klein, *American Street Gang,* p. 134.

34. The most irresponsible and poorly researched document to incite popular unrest was the Chicago Crime Commission's report, *Public Enemy Number One: Gangs* (Chicago: Chicago Crime Commission, 1995).

35. In Milwaukee, for example, residents were less likely to conduct gang intervention because "desegregation has meant that the corner where many gangs hang out is not in their neighborhood. Instead of a corner group of the children of families on the block, we have a gang whom frightened residents do not know and so police are called when trouble erupts" (Hagedorn, *People and Folks,* p. 147). In Los Angeles' Chicano communities, gang intervention at the local level sometimes meant visits or solicited approvals from inmates, who were not necessarily gang members but who held stature and respect in the eyes of gang members.

36. George Knox has conducted the most exhaustive review of gang-intervention programs. See *An Introduction to Gangs* (Bristol, Ind.: Wyndham Hall Press, 1994), p. 447.

37. Wacquant, "Three Pernicious Assumptions," pp. 345–346.

38. The CHA received numerous reminders that its buildings were becoming uninhabitable and that the focus on security vis-à-vis sweeps might not be the most optimal use of resources in Robert Taylor. HUD "unannounced inspections" had been occurring several times a year, and notifications were sent out to the CHA regarding its delinquency in maintenance and upkeep. One such report is exemplary: "Your 1 to 45 ratio of maintenance employees to units is low. However, the work output of the maintenance staff appears to be more than adequate. An increase in staff would accelerate improvements at this development." Gertrude W. Jordan to Vincent Lane, October 2, 1992, CHA Archives: HUD 2–37 Files.

6. The Beginning of the End of a Modern Ghetto

1. Steven Gregory, *Black Corona: Race and Politics of Place in an Urban Community* (Princeton: Princeton University Press, 1998), p. 174.

2. Jeffrey K. Olick and Daniel Levy, "Collective Memory and Cultural Constraint: Holocaust Myth and Rationality in German Politics," *American Sociological Review* 62 (December 1997): 921–936; quote from p. 922.

3. The use of memory and past experience by political actors has been well documented by scholars of social movements, but only recently has this been a topic of concern for those examining African-American urban communities. The most forceful explication is Steven Gregory's ethnographic study of politics and everyday life in *Black Corona.*

4. Seventy percent reported receipt of AFDC and only 17 percent were on the General Assistance or Social Security Insurance.

5. The term is used by street-gang researchers. For a history of the BSU gang, see Sudhir Venkatesh, "Gender and Outlaw Capitalism: An Historical Account of the Black Sisters United Girl Gang," *Signs: A Journal of Women in Culture and Society* 23(3) (1998): 683–709.

6. See August Meier and Elliot Rudwick, *From Plantation to Ghetto* (New York: Hill and Wang, 1976), pp. 271–272.

7. The signs of rising CHA vacancy rates could be seen in the early 1980s. By the end of that decade, nearly one-sixth of the 40,840 CHA units were vacated and not being rehabbed, despite 10,000 applicants waiting for available space. "The agency was losing more than four apartments a day because they became uninhabitable." "CHA Flat Vacancies Soaring," *Chicago Tribune,* June 26, 1988.

8. The limited resources that LAC members possessed made mailings, flyers, and large-scale advertising drives impossible to conduct. Thus, having to advertise by word of mouth, the officers should have found it difficult to gather very many tenants for any activity. However, in poor communities, information dissemination and advertisement nearly always proceed through social networks, and at times in Robert Taylor, thousands of people might turn out for an event as a result of advertisement conducted in these informal ways.

9. *Chicago Tribune,* August 19, 1993.

10. Tempo, *Chicago Tribune,* December 11, 1988.

11. For recent evaluations, see Irving A. Spergel, *The Youth Gang Problem: A Community Approach* (New York: Oxford University Press, 1995); Malcolm W. Klein, *The American Street Gang: Its Nature, Prevalence, and Control* (New York: Oxford University Press, 1995); and Klein, *Gang Suppression and Intervention: Community Models* (Washington D.C.: Office of Juvenile Justice and Delinquency Prevention, U.S. Department of Justice, 1994).

12. In the Chicago newspaper coverage of the proposed redevelopment of Robert Taylor, few editorials and articles defended high-rise public housing.

The most vituperative attacks came in the *Chicago Tribune* (see "Rethinking Public Housing," July 7, 1996, and "Editorial," October 11, 1995), which has always had the reputation of being pro-development and anti–public housing. Although metro reporters at the *Chicago Sun-Times* offered more balanced coverage, its editorial staff also fully supported high-rise demolition ("Editorial," September 12, 1996). The most informative coverage on the politics of redevelopment was David Peterson, "A Great Chicago Land Grab," *Z Magazine,* April 1997, pp. 34–37.

13. "CHA May Demolish Most of Its Units," *Chicago Tribune,* October 23, 1997.

14. A lawsuit was filed in 1966 in the U.S. District Court by the American Civil Liberties Union against the CHA, on behalf of seven black tenants, including Dorothy Gautreaux. The "Gautreaux" ruling found that the CHA "deliberately and with intent" discriminated against public housing tenants by not placing them in available apartments in white neighborhoods. As a result of the ruling and subsequent negotiations between the federal government and the CHA, the Housing Authority has had to seek housing for black applicants in non "racially impacted" areas, that is, predominantly African American, poor communities. The consequence has been an inability to build housing in existing African-American communities.

15. "The Education of Miss Kelly," *Chicago Tribune Magazine,* September 18, 1999.

16. "U.S. Lends Hand on Plan to Raze, Rebuild Taylor," *Chicago Tribune,* October 9, 1996.

17. This was the opinion of the *Chicago Tribune* editorial staff ("Plan for a City sans CHA Rises," *Chicago Tribune,* September 12, 1996).

18. Gerald D. Suttles, *The Man-Made City: The Land-Use Confidence Game in Chicago* (Chicago: University of Chicago Press, 1990), p. 83.

19. D. Bradford Hunt, "What Went Wrong with Public Housing?" paper delivered at the Newberry Urban History Group, Chicago, May 16, 1998, p. 1.

20. This could occur in different ways, including direct preference for whites, such as hiring by municipal departments or acceptance to union-controlled training and vocational apprenticeship programs, the creative redirection of government financing for areas of "severe economic distress" into projects benefiting largely white middle-class constituents, and subsidization of redevelopment outside of inner-city areas. (For an extended discussion, see Joel Rast, *Remaking Chicago: The Political Origins of Urban Industrial Change* [DeKalb, Ill.: Northern Illinois University Press, 1999]). A white constituency not faring well during these moments of economic decline is based on the city's North Side, in areas where rural Appalachian migrants once settled.

21. "Industrial investor choices in the period 1970–1983 are progressively oriented away from the region's black community which is concentrated on Chicago's West and South Sides and in the northern portion of Lake County, Indiana" (Suttles, *Man-Made City,* p. 42).

Author's Note

1. Important exceptions are Steven Gregory, *Black Corona: Race and the Politics of Place in an Urban Community* (Princeton: Princeton University Press, 1999).

2. John L. Comaroff, "Dialectical Systems, History and Anthropology: Units of Study and Questions of Theory," *Journal of Southern African Tribes,* 8 (1982): 146.

3. For a general discussion, see George E. Marcus and Michael M. J. Fischer, *Anthropology as Cultural Critique: An Experimental Moment in the Human Sciences* (Chicago: University of Chicago Press, 1986).

4. "In general, then, the worldly circumstances of human action are under no inevitable obligation to conform to the categories by which certain people perceive them. In the event they do not, the received categories are potentially revalued in practice, functionally redefined." Marshall Sahlins, *Historical Metaphors and Mythical Realities: Structure in the Early History of the Sandwich Islands Kingdom* (Ann Arbor: University of Michigan Press, 1981), p. 67.

5. "We shall have to examine how indigenous peoples struggle to integrate their experience of the world system in something that is logically and ontologically more inclusive: their own system of the world." Marshall Sahlins, "Cosmologies of Capitalism: The Trans-Pacific Sector of the World System," *Proceedings of the British Academy,* 74 (1988): 1–51; quote p. 4.

6. Sahlins, *Historical Metaphors.*

7. The anthropologist Sherry Ortner makes the following recommendation to researchers discerning the actions of those who are actively "resisting" and coping with their predicament: "If we are to recognize that resistors are doing more than simply opposing domination, more than simply producing a virtually mechanical re-action, then we must go the whole way. They have their own politics . . . all the local categories of friction and tension: men and women, parents and children, seniors and juniors." "Resistance and the Problem of Ethnographic Refusal," in *The Historic Turn in the Human Sciences,* Terrence J. McDonald, ed. (Ann Arbor: University of Michigan Press, 1996), p. 285.

8. The term "collective memory" is not new, but it has been receiving much attention in recent years from academic researchers. Jeffrey Olick is largely responsible for making this overused and underspecified concept into something more rigorous and consistent. Jeffrey K. Olick and Daniel Levy, "Collective Memory and Cultural Constraint: Holocaust Myth and Rationality in German Politics," *American Sociological Review,* 62 (December 1997): 921–936.

Acknowledgments

I wrote this book in 1998–1999 during my tenure at the Society of Fellows, Harvard University. The Junior Fellowship provided me with an unencumbered space for reflection and the constant company of gifted scholars who taught me that the mindful life begins at the borders of one's discipline. Professors Daniel Aaron and Bernard Bailyn were especially encouraging, as were my colleagues Gavin Jones, Kristin Ardlie, and Jeffrey Dolven.

Dissertation research funding was provided by the National Science Foundation, the Johann Jacobs Foundation, and Chapin Hall Center for Children at the University of Chicago. Subsequent fieldwork grants were awarded by the John D. and Catherine T. MacArthur Foundation, the Milton Fund at Harvard University, and the Graham Foundation for the Advanced Studies in the Fine Arts. A Five College Fellowship from Amherst College, and the friendship of the faculty in its Department of Anthropology and Sociology, gave me the opportunity to translate fieldnotes into narratives. The support of my colleagues at Columbia University, in the Department of Sociology and the Institute for Research in African-American Studies, enabled me to revise the manuscript. Working with Joyce Seltzer at Harvard University Press to complete the book was a truly rewarding experience.

To Aaron Cicourel and Bud Mehan, sociologists at the University of California, San Diego, I offer my heartfelt gratitude for teaching me the sociological imagination. At the University of Chicago, I am indebted to Professors Edward Laumann, Harold Richman, and John Comaroff, all of whom continue to be a fount of knowledge and inspiration. I owe a particular debt to my colleagues Rizwan Ahmad, Raphael Cohen, Dan Cook, Nathaniel Deutsch, Baron Pineda, Vijay Prashad, Alford Young Jr., and James Quane. Matthew McGuire gave generously of his time, reading drafts and providing counsel along the way. Autry Harrison, my friend and collaborator, taught me to marry research and practice. His wisdom runs through these pages.

The members of my dissertation committee were tireless in their motivation and demonstrated unending patience as I muddled through my doctoral studies. I was fortunate to have learned sociology from Moishe Postone, a gifted thinker and a thoughtful and passionate teacher. Jean Comaroff provided encouragement throughout the project and granted intellectual clarity when I could not see the forest for the trees. William Julius Wilson was my mentor, providing counsel and wisdom with his characteristic generosity and grace. I am indebted to his stewardship, and he continues to teach me the value of making sociology engage with the larger public.

At each stage of the journey, Katchen Locke stood beside me, tolerating the self-indulgence of graduate student life. As my wife and friend, she offered insight and a critical, compassionate eye. While the shortcomings of the project are mine alone, the achievements are ours together.

Index

Crack cocaine, 135, 194, 217
Crime: petty, 29; press reports on, 44–45; violent, in ghetto communities, 113–114; in Robert Taylor, 118

Daley, Richard J., 13, 19, 20, 50, 61, 271
Dan Ryan Expressway, 19–20, 23
Davenport, Kenny, 22, 208, 246; on gangs, 30, 139, 154, 174, 178, 184; on police-tenant relationships, 73–74; on hustling, 83; on drugs, 98; on crime, 128; Grace Center and, 206, 222, 229, 232, 233, 267; on Edith Huddle, 264
Davis, Kelly, 110, 129, 144, 184, 222, 224, 227
Davis, Momo, 73, 92, 135
Davis, Ottie, 22, 24, 29, 72–73, 135, 146, 154, 158, 206, 209, 232, 267
Deacon, Charles, 81–82, 94–95
Double consciousness, 10–11
Dowell, Bobby, 22, 26, 29
Drug trafficking: hustling and, 87, 98; Black Kings gang and, 134, 135, 136, 147, 150, 157–158, 195–196, 266–267; effect on ghetto communities, 149–150; tenant-gang conflicts over public space, 176–177, 179–180; LAC-gang collusion and, 184, 186; gang-structure interventions and, 207, 210, 211, 213, 214, 224, 237; supergangs and, 217; volume, 266–267
Du Bois, W. E. B., 10–11
Dunne, George, 61

Elevator(s), 26–27; committees, 33
Ethnography: of communities, 281; notions of historical process and structure, 282–285; of Robert Taylor project, 285–287
Eviction notices, 50–51
Executive Boards, 58
Executive Council, 58, 59
Extortion, from local entrepreneurs by gangs, 110–111, 144, 177–178, 180, 181

Federal government: neighborhood initiatives and, 56–57; assistance to police, 76–77; New Federalism policy, 114–116; public housing budget cuts, 116, 148. See also Housing and Urban Development; Reagan administration
Federal Housing Authority, 16
Floor captains, 35; tenant patrols and, 80; hustling payoffs and, 94
Fort, Jeff, 84
Fourth Amendment, 254
Fraternal Order of Police, 130

Gang, The (Thrasher), 216
Gang control/intervention: community court and, 1–2, 226–227; CHA policies and strategies, 129–130, 141–142, 221–222, 254–257; "Operation Clean Sweep," 130, 198, 254–257; gang-structure strategies and, 191–192, 205–214, 236; LACs and, 191–192, 193, 203; Will Jackson and, 191–192, 193; social isolation of Robert Taylor and, 194; social service providers and, 194, 200, 201–203, 236; police and, 197–200, 235; churches and, 202–203; tenant-based informal support networks and, 203; gang drug trafficking and, 207, 210, 211, 213, 214, 224, 237; conflict resolution and, 209–210, 219–220, 222–224, 226, 236–237; Black Kings leadership and, 214–215, 232–233; citywide gang leaders in, 215; gang identities and, 218; cross-neighborhood intercourse and, 224–226; youth rallies, 227; tenant responses to, 230–231, 232; public space and, 231–232; issues in, 233–237; gang abuse of women and, 238–239; LAC leadership and, 248–